DATE DUE

GAYLORD			PRINTED IN U.S.A

STRATEGIC ISSUES MANAGEMENT

A Comprehensive Guide to
Environmental Scanning

Other books of interest:

BLOOR Reference Guide to Management Techniques and Activities
BOYLE Strategic Service Management
BRYSON Strategic Planning for Public Service and Non-Profit Organizations
DAEMS & THOMAS Strategic Groups, Strategic Moves and Performance
DOZ Strategic Management in Multinational Companies
FREEDMAN Strategic Management in Major Multinational Companies
IRONS Turning Strategy into Action
KONO Strategic Management in Japanese Companies
McNAMEE Tools and Techniques in Strategic Management
McNAMEE Developing Strategies for Competitive Advantage
ROTHWELL Strategic Planning for Human Resources

THE TECHNOLOGY AND STRATEGY SERIES

Recent and forthcoming titles include:

BOGNER The World Pharmaceutical Industry
BULL & THOMAS Perspectives on Theory Building in Entrepreneurship
STEFFENS Newgames: Strategic Competition in the PC Revolution
THOMAS & McGEE Creating Strategic Advantage

Related Pergamon Journals — Free specimen copy available on request

Accounting, Management & Information Technologies
European Management Journal
International Business Review
Long Range Planning
Socio-Economic Planning Sciences
Technology in Society
Telematics and Informatics

STRATEGIC ISSUES MANAGEMENT

A Comprehensive Guide to Environmental Scanning

by

John D. Stoffels

Marquette University
Milwaukee, WI, U.S.A.

Published in association with
The Planning Forum

Pergamon

U.K. Elsevier Science Ltd., The Boulevard, Langford Lane, Kidlington, Oxford OX5 1GB, U.K.

U.S.A. Elsevier Science Inc., 660 White Plains Road, Tarrytown, New York 10591-5153, U.S.A.

JAPAN Elsevier Science Japan, Tsunashima Building Annex, 3-20-12 Yushima, Bunkyo-ku, Tokyo 113, Japan

First edition 1994

Library of Congress Cataloging in Publication Data

Stoffels, John D.
    Strategic issues management: a comprehensive guide to environmental scanning/John D. Stoffels
    p. cm.
    1. Business forecasting. 2. Strategic planning. I. Title.
    HD30.27.S86 1993
    658.4'012--dc20. 93-39469.

British Library Cataloging in Publication Data

A catalogue record for this book is available from the British Library

ISBN 0 08 042394 9

Table 3.1 (page 20) reproduced by permission of Administrative Science Quarterly
© 1972 by Cornell University.
All rights reserved worldwide.

Printed and bound in Great Britain by Butler & Tanner, Frome

TABLE OF CONTENTS

Geographic — Format of Collection of Environmental Information: Continuity of Scanning; Methods of Scanning; Formality of Scanning Effort: Modes of Scanning — Other Elements of the Scanning System: Sources Monitored; Methods of Processing Scanning Inputs — Managing and Communicating Within the Scanning System.

LIST OF SUPPORTING ELEMENTS

Tables cont.

FIGURES

FOREWORD

Once again it is my pleasure to introduce the latest addition to our Planning Forum Monograph series: *Strategic Issues Management: A Comprehensive Guide to Environmental Scanning,* by John D. Stoffels. Carefully prepared and thoroughly researched over a period of years, this book comes as a new resource for all of those interested in this critical strategic management intelligence function.

For effective strategic management, it is essential to have the best possible picture of the arena in which survival, market share, success in negotiating the gauntlet of new regulations, and profits will be determined. Market research and corporate news sources provide a current picture, but one that often changes so rapidly it is difficult to keep up to date. Worse, it is not enough to know when new requirements are established; compliance requires action — to obey, to change direction, or to challenge the rules — and this action can take time to plan and put into motion. The real need is for management to gain a foreknowledge of what is going to happen, in order properly to prepare for it.

Exact foreknowledge of specific future events is still out of reach, but *Strategic Issues Management* tells us that the pattern of *most likely* future events is not difficult to find and interpret, and that specific high-probability events usually announce their coming clearly and well in advance. For anyone who cares, therefore, these events need not come as a surprise; all that is required is careful consideration of the messages they send ahead of them.

Environmental scanning has become a key means for obtaining the intelligence about the present and developing environment around the organization. An environmental scanning system is not difficult to set up, as this book makes clear. Well documented, with summaries of good and bad experience elsewhere, case histories, and copious references to studies and information sources, *Strategic Issues Management* provides the basic information required for designing and installing a scanning system to keep strategic management abreast of the flow of coming events — to allow strategy to be reshaped to meet new strategic issues as they arise — thus establishing effective environmental scanning as a key route to effective management of strategic issues as they arise.

May *Strategic Issues Management* make it easier for you and your organization to grow and prosper in the uncertain future!

George Sawyer
Monograph and
Book Editor

PREFACE

This is a strategic management book — a book about how to scan the business environment to learn about emerging changes early enough to gain advantage from them. The world is experiencing a pace of change unprecedented in modern times. Commercial survival has become a key business concern. Understanding the forces of change is an imperative. Environmental scanning is a key route to this understanding.

Any organization attempting to succeed in the face of an uncertain future must adjust its strategy as its environment changes, whether that organization is a business, a not-for-profit, a union, or a public agency. To manage competently and plan effectively, that organization needs environmental scanning to give its management warning in time to change course as success or even survival requires.

This book provides a framework for designing and managing an environmental scanning system to capture strategically valuable signals of change, whether social, technological, competitive, political, or financial; that is, to discover change early enough to gain advantage. The book provides framework, method and technique for designing, creating, and managing an environmental scanning system, as a key element in strategic management of the organization.

Success-oriented leaders will want to study this book for ideas and insights, and structure their organizations to recognize and respond to emerging issues. Individual managers will learn how involvement with the scanning process can enhance business unit success. Those engaged in the environmental scanning itself, or in learning about it, will find a comprehensive presentation of useful methods and techniques, together with an extensive analysis of available literature.

The intent of this book is to provide a basis for *learning leading to action.*

Plan of the Book

Chapter 1 provides an overview of the book chapter by chapter and of the subject of environmental scanning, the concept and definition of scanning, the linkage of scanning to strategy, and the purpose and need for scanning. The ideas in this chapter provide the foundations for the *what,* the *why* and the *where* of scanning in the strategic management of organizations.

Chapter 2 develops a role for environmental scanning out of the unknowns that exist between any organization and its environment. The risks and tensions related to these unknowns create a set of reasons for expending resources in scanning efforts, reasons that have motivated many organizations to scan the environment. The chapter also presents evidence for the effectiveness of environmental scanning, and the responses of its critics.

Chapter 3 focuses on models of the environment, exploring environmental complexity and how environmental turbulence influences the organization, its structure, its information gathering needs, and its subsequent strategy. Chapter 4 contains a framework for thinking about the environment in five dimensions, to specialize the information search and simplify the overall view. Collectively these two chapters define the important challenge for scanning: finding meaningful strategic signals in a turbulent, multi-dimensional environment. Chapter 5 confronts that challenge. It describes a multi-element scanning system to enable the firm to determine a productive strategy for its scanning, unique to its own circumstances and effective in aiding it in selecting appropriate business strategy.

Processes for organizing, conducting and managing scanning efforts are described in Chapters 6 and 7, together with several operating scanning systems — how they are structured, the methods and resources they use, and how scanning results are communicated to the organization. Chapter 7 concludes with a discussion of the effective use of information gathered through scanning, together with potential pitfalls from its misuse, and Chapter 8 describes environmental information available to the firm and how it may be obtained. Sources vary from personal contact to publications and documents of varying accessibility and value. The chapter explains information futurity, and gives examples of the way issues and events can be predicted.

The monitoring of personal and documentary information sources is the principal methodology of scanning. Yet, the information obtained usually needs to be refined, correlated and synthesized before a meaningful strategic signal emerges. Chapter 9 explores a variety of analysis and forecasting techniques that can supplement this search for vision through signal monitoring. Techniques of mapping, modeling and subjective analysis are described and rated for usefulness in environments with varying complexity, uncertainty, and stability. These techniques are also rated according to the resources, skill, and environmental knowledge required for an organization to use them.

The central aim of this book is to collect, to integrate, to refine, and to synthesize the existing thinking on the subject of environmental scanning. The reader will encounter frequent references to other authors whose works provide additional reading on topics of special individual interest. The bibliography is an extensive compilation of the existing literature on environmental scanning and the related subjects of issues management and competitive intelligence — from Aguilar's [5] touchstone work in 1967, to 1990. Selected references in related areas such as modeling, forecasting, futurism, organizational behavior, and the social sciences generally are included as well. Use this bibliography as a comprehensive reference guide to the subject of environmental scanning, and the Appendix will assist in the choice of publications to scan, from a classified listing of periodicals and databases drawn in part from lists used by existing scanning organizations.

Acknowledgements

Many have contributed to this book. Henry C. Doofe, emeritus Director of Research at The Planning Forum, advised, encouraged, and nurtured the expansion of my research in this area into book form. This nurturing mantle was then acquired by George Sawyer, Planning Forum Monograph Editor. Practicing environmental scanners have contributed importantly to formulating my thoughts and writings. My family deserves special credit for believing the project was worthwhile and supporting my work.

ABOUT THE AUTHOR

John Stoffels is Associate Professor in the College of Business at Marquette University. He has expertise in valuation, strategy, planning, environmental scanning and computer based-modeling, and both consults and writes in those fields. Dr. Stoffels has board, consulting and line management experience spanning manufacturing and service industries, including automotive, machinery, banking, publishing, insurance, medical, computer technology, agriculture and government.

Active in professional organizations, executive education and seminar presentations, in 1992 Dr. Stoffels became chairman of the international board of directors and CEO of The Planning Forum, the world's largest organization of professionals and executives dedicated to advancing the practice of strategic management. A former president of the Milwaukee Chapter of the Planning Forum, Dr. Stoffels has also received the organization's outstanding publication award. He is a member of the Financial Management Association and the Financial Executives Institute and holds bachelor's and master's degrees from Northwestern University and a Ph.D. from Michigan State University.

PUBLISHER'S NOTE

Since the completion of his editing and review of this manuscript, George Sawyer's kindly wit and insightful talent have been lost to The Planning Forum and its authors, through his sudden illness and death. We are saddened by this loss of of a warmly engaging person whose intellect and practical experience so often merged to bring about truly original contributions to the field of strategic management. We offer our sympathy to George's family, friends and colleagues.

CHAPTER 1

ENVIRONMENTAL SCANNING: AN OVERVIEW

It seems to me that planning has two major purposes today. The first is not so much to control as to enhance resilience and a sense of responsibility, both to the immediate and the indirect stakeholders. In order to see the possibilities as well as the problems in our uncertain world, we've got to be as clear as we can about what we don't know. The irony is that now we need planning and future studies precisely because we cannot do what we thought planning and future studies were for — gaining and maintaining control. Therefore, the second purpose of planning is to help an organization learn how to move into an uncertain future by asking itself again and again where it wants to go, how and if it's getting there, and is that still where it wants to go.

> Donald N. Michael
> Emeritus Professor of Planning and Public Policy
> University of Michigan

Not to control, but to enlarge our sense of the possibilities; not to predict, but to enhance, through learning what the external environment is and might become, our resilience and responsiveness as the future unfolds into the present — these are the roles Michael assigns to environmental scanning in the strategic management process [6,7]. This book is about the reasons for, and the methodology of environmental scanning, presenting a system for managing strategic issues that can help us "be as clear as we can about what we don't know."

What Is Environmental Scanning?

Environmental scanning: a methodology for coping with external competitive, social, economic and technical issues that may be difficult to observe or diagnose but that cannot be ignored and will not go away.

Environmental scanning seeks to identify emerging situations, hazards and opportunities in society, particularly those that may be difficult for the manager or the organization to absorb or turn to advantage. Scanning deals with issues that do not lend themselves to unilateral definition or solution, even though they may critically influence the organization's growth, performance, success and survival; this is its value. It identifies the segment of a firm's strategic management activities requiring a view outside the firm's boundaries. In one corporate futurist's opinion, the essence of the futurist's orientation is strategic thinking, beginning with a study of the external environment [106].

1

Scanning invokes a process of externalization, causing the firm to expand the focus of decision-making to include the perspectives of outsiders — for example, present and prospective competitors, customers, regulators or community members. The lowest level of environmental scanning is observation, by which the firm seeks to learn "what is." The highest level of scanning is prediction or synthesis, as the firm seeks to integrate signals of future events or conditions into a meaningful model upon which to build strategy. The key conditions inviting environmental scanning are external turbulence with observable signals yielding distinguishable consequences, as summarized in Table 1.1. These signals can provide the basis for plausible anticipation of changes with relevance to strategy, and meaningful adaptation to the change can follow.

Table 1.1: Conditions for Fruitful Environmental Scanning

- **External Turbulence**
- **Observable Signals**
- **Distinguishable Consequences**
- **Plausible Anticipation**
- **Relevance to Strategy**
- **Commitment to Adaptation**

Because the firm can exercise little control over external events, it must seek to anticipate and understand them. If scanning can enhance the predictability of the event itself or the opportunity for strategic responses to it, then the firm has an incentive to spend resources on scanning. To the extent that scanning exposes events and circumstances that hold promise (an opportunity) or could inflict pain (a threat), value is created through the firm's strategic adaptation, and the anticipated benefits of environmental scanning exceed its costs in present value terms.

Sometimes events appear both uncontrollable and unpredictable. Such a case occurs where the firm can *imagine* a future possibility, is perhaps convinced of the eventual likelihood of it, but is unable to bring the timing, the form or the shape of the possibility into meaningful focus. Manufacturing in outer space may now represent just such an unpredictable possibility. One can imagine that breakthrough changes will be made to support this possibility in communications, transportation, materials, methods, systems and services. Despite the desire to link a given company to some aspect of that future supply and production chain, one cannot *today* make a meaningful strategic investment to assure that linkage. But that company can invoke *today* a low-level environmental scanning effort to alert itself to events that will reduce the remoteness and increase the predictability of the future possibility. At some future time, that scanning effort might signal the need for a much more active search for signals from that environment.

Environmental Scanning and Business Strategy

The dynamics of markets and economies create the links between managerial strategy and the environment. In the traditional planning methodology goals, strategies and tactics are responsive to opportunities, threats and planning assumptions developed from external environmental assessment. The environmental scan follows the objectives set by the planning process.

Strategy evolves from unique strengths possessed by the firm, from identifying weaknesses in competitors and from finding new markets, new customers, new technologies, and other new forces in the environment. Among these, only unique strengths may be environmentally independent, and even that independence is ephemeral since such strengths rely on a competitive advantage in technology, design, delivery or operations that could be eroded under a plausible set of future conditions.

As environmental scanning enriches and expands the set of opportunities for developing basic and core business strategies, it becomes the very essence of hedge strategies. Environmental scanning methodologies support the identification of high-impact scenarios and the assessment of probabilities of those scenarios. In short, scanning permits the identification of key contingencies for which hedge strategies are needed.

Advocates of an open-systems view of strategic planning methodology suggest that the nucleus of strategic direction should emerge from the mission statement of the organization, in the form of a strategic vision [91;341]. Using this methodology, external environmental issues are generated, explored, prioritized and analyzed as antecedents to the expression of corporate values, strategic orientation and strategic choice. In the words of Brown and Weiner:

> Institutional vision must grow out of a disciplined and participatory process set up within the organization for the purpose of continuously scanning the external and internal environments and identifying reasons for change, opportunities to master change, and people best suited to understand and implement new processes and procedures. [57,285]

The Purpose of Environmental Scanning

Scanning can provide early warning signals for the organization from emerging environmental issues, threats and opportunities. Scanning helps companies develop and modify strategy to meet changing external circumstances, thereby helping the organization succeed and survive. It can help shape the internal structure of the organization and sensitize managers down to the project level to the needs and benefits of adaptive strategies [305]. There is evidence that the personal success of managers is enhanced as a result of their environmental scanning efforts [56]. In short, environmental scanning helps the organization adapt its behavior to the changing reality of the external world.

The purpose of scanning the environment is to learn, to increase responsiveness and to enhance the adaptability of decision-making systems. Surveillance systems put in place for the purpose of scanning provide signals. The signals are analyzed by information systems to determine whether an event has occurred or has a changed probability of occurring. Diagnostic systems then determine threats and opportunities [4].

The scanning practices of nine large corporations were catalogued by Thomas [472]. Scanning added value in four principal areas:

- Fostering education and mind-stretching experiences for management.
- Assisting in formulation of policy and strategy.
- Promoting the development of operational programs and action plans.
- Providing a frame of reference for budgets.

How Does Environmental Scanning Fit into the Organization?

The collected experience of scanners and researchers provides us with a set of questions that will help assess the effectiveness and potential success of scanning programs. Considering them before and during the implementation of scanning programs will help you ensure positive results:

1. Does the company accept new ideas, concepts and processes?
2. Are there open communication channels in the company that the scanning function can utilize?
3. Is the company capturing the environmental information that is readily available to it through current activities and interactions?
4. Are the linkages of environmental change to the company's operations properly assessed?
5. Are environmental signals, inputs and analyses documented to permit benefits and productivity enhancements to be measured?
6. Is environmental intelligence integrated into strategic planning? Into operations?
7. Are scanning analyses, reports and outputs tailored to the needs of differing audiences within the firm (focus, detail, frequency, time horizon, delivery)?
8. Is the level of investment in environmental scanning an element of strategy for the organization?

The following chapters develop models and processes for environmental scanning complying with, and depending upon, the standards suggested by these eight questions.

Why Is Environmental Scanning More Necessary Today?

Today's greater environmental uncertainties may be the result of previously unforeseen long-run consequences of the planning models and beliefs business and society have traditionally embraced by viewing companies as isolated from the environment (see Fig. 1.1). In the typical strategic planning process, the environment has been a given from which management has taken factor inputs such as interest and wage rates, taxes, and available technology. The environment seemed inapproachable, delivering at random "events" such as grain embargoes, oil cartels, nuclear accidents, anti-trust suits, terrorism and hostile take-overs. Except for a few obvious cases, such as lead smelting in Kellogg, Idaho, or the oil company pressure to reduce royalties that motivated the formation of OPEC, the environment has appeared uncontrollable and unaffected by any one company's actions.

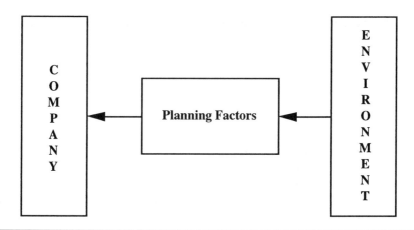

Figure 1.1: The Firm Separate from Its Environment

By applying this environmental model, businesses have permitted themselves the luxury of planning for short-range outcomes — planning mainly based on the assumption that rapid growth permanently delivers the prosperity observed in rising output measures such as earnings per share and per-capita GNP (see Figure 1.2).

This focus on short-range output measurements breaks down because it oversimplifies the long-run, indirect and less measurable consequences of rapid economic growth, and because it underestimates the social and economic readjustment rapid growth demands. Failing to detect the consequences of radical technological innovation and change, managers had no grasp of the complexity involved in matching the production system with the consumption system in a world marketplace. If this mismatch was observed, it appeared as an uncontrollable environmental "event" and therefore did not cause anyone to hesitate.

Figure 1.2: The Impacts of Growth

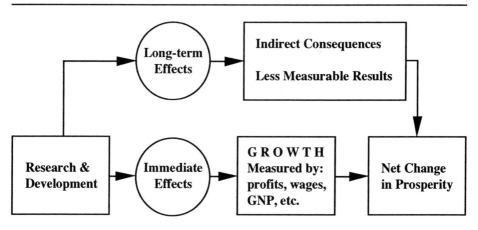

The fuel for the simple growth model over the past 39 years has been research and development expenditures. Expenditures nationwide for all forms of research and development grew from $5 billion in 1953 to almost $158 billion in 1992, at a compound rate of over 9.2 percent, one-fourth above the 7.4 percent growth rate in GNP. Over half of those funds were expended by private industry.

There is no reason to believe future environments will be any more forgiving than the current one. At the end of the 20th century there is a potential for a common Europe — perhaps including Eastern Europe — and newly independent Russian republics scrambling for private sector development. Consider the impact these events could have on global competitive intensity! For planners and managers, the turbulence of recent years and likely future changes reinforce the need for intelligent environmental scanning, beginning with the recognition that the firm is a part of its environment as depicted in Figure 1.3, and requires changes in the planning processes and techniques developed when the environment appeared more stable.

Can companies that have out-performed the economy and avoided the indirect costs mentioned in the preceding paragraphs escape the need for environmental scanning? NO! If the future is like the present, how else will any firm be able to respond to new product introductions — dramatically increasing worldwide — except by following me-too strategies? Waiting to act until "fuzzy" environmental signals become clearer, rather than investing in learning more about them now, means losing competitive leadership to other, perhaps non-domestic, producers.

Figure 1.3: The Firm Interacting with its Environment

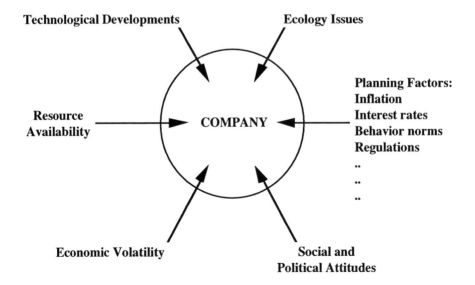

　　Business-as-usual approaches seem very difficult to justify in the post-industrial era [12,5]. Leading, aggressive firms are no longer in a sufficient power position to establish the style and pace of progress or to control their own destinies. For management, garnering meaningful signals from the environment *replaces* gaining experience as a principal guide to the future. Effective environmental scanning becomes more and more a competitive and strategic necessity.

CHAPTER 2

WHY SCAN THE ENVIRONMENT?

For many years one of the qualities that distinguished successful businesses, and their executives and managers, was a demonstrated ability to think fast and stay on top of — or even to influence the course of — the economic, social, political and technological conditions of the environment in which they operated. But in the past decade the task of a manager has changed. The environment no longer supports unlimited commercial and technological expansion. Society has become increasingly critical of business initiatives and increasingly adept at measuring and assessing the social costs of business decisions. Contests for market and ownership control have intensified to the point where the competitive environment of business is changing more rapidly and less predictably than at any time since the Industrial Revolution began. It is difficult to follow, much less anticipate, that change.

In this setting, even the best of managers and planners have found it more and more difficult to move fast enough to maintain an aggressive stance in strategy without allowing risks to run out-of-bounds. They have found the cost of misdirected or non-directed business efforts both high and rapidly rising. The growing difficulty in devising timely responses to issues from the business environment, plus the rising cost and risk of improper responses, are the fundamental reasons why environmental scanning is vital to today's CEO.

This chapter develops a rationale for environmental scanning by exploring the "why scan the environment?" question from three different perspectives: (1) four case examples of environments hostile to industries, companies and products; (2) implications of trends in the economy, evolution in planning and management methodologies, and evidence of environmental impacts; and (3) surveys of the benefits of scanning balanced by criticisms of its use.

Environmental Impact Case Examples

Following are four cases describing environmental impact on business and industry. Examples like these illustrate the rationale for environmental scanning.

Environmental Impact Case 1. General Motors' share of the domestic car market declined from 52.5 percent to 41 percent between 1973 and 1986. The cost of operating a car increased by 11 percent during the 1973 oil crisis and by *another* 11 percent as a result of the 1979 oil crisis. Consumers started shifting buying patterns to smaller, more fuel-efficient cars, and the sales of small cars rose from about 36 percent to about 55 percent of the U.S. market.

8

From 1973 to 1986, the share of mostly smaller imported cars sold in the U.S. nearly doubled, from 14.9 to 28.3 percent. In 1973, 80 percent of GM's market share came from large car sales (see Figure 2.1). General Motors increased its production of small cars after the first oil shock, but by 1979 the company still earned 69 percent of its market share by selling larger cars, a condition that continued up to 1986. By contrast, other U.S. manufacturers reversed their market concentrations between 1973 and 1979, with their combined percentage of share obtained from compact and subcompact cars rising from 35 to 63 percent during that period. Throughout the period imports were about 90 percent concentrated in small cars. In 1973, General Motors earned 5.1 percent on sales, as against Ford's 3.9 percent. In 1986, Ford earned 5.25 percent on sales, while General Motors' net margin had slipped to 2.9 percent. [Sources: 491;507]

Figure 2.1: Auto Industry Market Share by Car Size

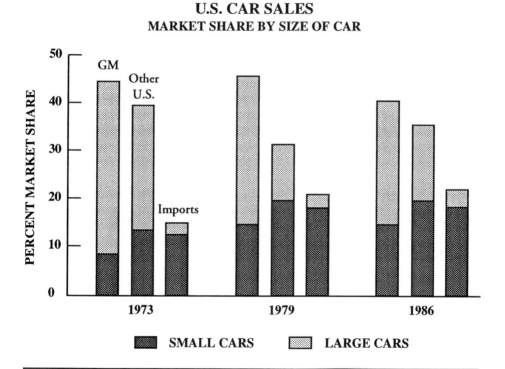

U.S. CAR SALES
MARKET SHARE BY SIZE OF CAR

Environmental Impact Case 2. Numerous independent events converged to cause a crisis in the textile industry that continued for several years. Cotton price supports were reduced in 1974 on the heels of a 13 percent decrease in allowable support acreage in 1973. Discouraged from planting, farmers had reduced cotton acreage by 30 percent by 1975 from its 1972 peak.

Trade barriers were lowered with China and Russia in 1972, increasing cotton exports and shifting exports from Korea and Taiwan to China and Russia. Because of the shift, more cotton was consumed by foreign economies and less cotton was returned to the U.S. in the form of finished fabrics. The dollar was devalued in 1972, further encouraging cotton exports, while making textile imports more expensive and thereby increasing the demand for domestically produced textiles, including cotton.

Bad weather and floods greatly reduced the 1973 cotton crop from an expected high yield. Acreage yields declined even more drastically in 1974 and remained down in 1975.

These combined demand and supply pressures depleted cotton inventories: raw cotton carry-over inventories during 1973, 1974 and 1975 fell to their lowest levels in 20 years. Cotton prices were pushed up to record levels, with the 1973-5 average price nearly double that of 1970-72. Cotton mill cotton consumption decreased nearly one-fourth between 1972 and 1975.

Alternative fibers to cotton were synthetics, such as dacron, produced through a process that requires benzene as a raw material. The sharp increase in oil prices in 1973 plus reduced supplies of crude oil, caused refiners to adjust their product mix. Benzene production was curtailed, and benzene prices rose sharply.

The combined impact of these five seemingly independent influences on textile production was severe. Total mill fiber consumption declined from 12.5 billion pounds in 1973 to 10.3 billion pounds in 1975, or by 18 percent. Based on a sample of firms included in the Compustat database, profit margins in the textile industry declined 65 percent. Suppliers to the large mills were especially badly hurt if they did not have long-term contracts that gave them access to supplies of raw cotton and fabric to sell to the mills. The cotton shortage did not begin to abate until 1976, through a combination of increased acreage and yield. Even then, cotton carry-over inventories remained low and cotton prices surged to 64 cents a pound, nearly 40 percent above the already high levels of 1972-75. [Sources: 97;352;467;491]

Environmental Impact Case 3. In 1965 DuPont introduced a synthetic substitute for shoe leather called Corfam®. Two years later, direct competition emerged from new materials developed in Japan (*Clarino*) and Britain (*Ortix*), before DuPont had even begun to promote its product outside of U.S. markets. Corfam® required nine years and $60 million to develop; chances are its investment was never recovered. By contrast, DuPont developed nylon in only four years at a cost of $27 million, and remained the sole supplier of the product for 15 years, until a competing nylon was introduced in 1954. [Sources: 52;129]

Environmental Impact Case 4. Annual growth in ordinary life insurance policies fell from 46 percent in 1965 to 11 percent in 1980. During that period, the percentage of families with two incomes — more financially independent, requiring less life insurance and qualifying for greater amounts of cheaper term insurance — rose from 47 to 65 percent. The average age of marriage increased from 20.6 to 23.3 years. The percentage of persons who have never married in the 30-34 age group more than doubled from 1970 to 1987. Birth rates declined from 2.9 (long-term growth in population) to 1.8 (long-term decline in population). Single people — especially never-marrieds — have lower life insurance needs because they have fewer dependents. Single person households rose from 15 percent to 22.7 percent of all households. The life insurance industry felt the need for a better understanding of these trends, and formed an environmental scanning task force through its industry association in 1970. [Sources: 470;491]

Four Reasons for Scanning

Each of these four cases illustrates the costly impacts of an imperfect reading of the environment: lost profits, lost market share, lost jobs, lost wealth and the destruction of share value in the marketplace. None of these examples illustrates demonstrably bad management. Judgments simply turned out to be faulty because the environment evolved into a different state of nature than strategies anticipated. There are several reasons why increased scanning intensity in today's environment could reduce the incidence of similar strategy failures in the future.

Industrial Evolution. Many authors, including Toffler (*The Third Wave*) [479], Kahn (*The Coming Boom*) [221], Galbraith (*The New Industrial State*) [168], Naisbitt (*Megatrends*) [344], and Drucker (*The Age of Discontinuity*) [126], argue that a new order is emerging, that the nation is moving from an industrial to a post-industrial society. Old rules do not apply in this new order, and a strategy based on extrapolation of experience gained using old rules is likely to be wrong. The proper inputs into the strategy evaluation process come from signals about the future environment in which the strategy would be implemented, and not from the past environment that reflects the old order. The future environment holds more surprises because of the new order. The purpose of environmental scanning is to help reduce, through intercepting and interpreting signals, the frequency and impact intensity of those surprises. Environmental scanning is at the very heart of anticipatory management and provides the richer database that analytically trained managers can use to supplement their lack of experience-based perception and intuition.

Speed of Change and Increasing Complexity. "Our environment expands faster than our perception of it," says Christopher [83,12], "because the major institutions and systems (family, work, politics, religion, community, commerce, transportation) have become interrelated as a result of population growth and industrialization." Early industrial era efforts to create standardization and production efficiency gave way to the pursuit of differentiation in product, technology or market and to the rapid rate of design, development and invention such differentiation requires. Continued growth in domestic R&D expenditures, at rates in excess of GNP growth for the past 30 years, shows society's investment in creating complexity and rapid change. Six to seven thousand scientific articles are written each day, and the number is growing at more than 13 percent per year.

Characterizing the business situation as turbulent, Ansoff [12] suggested that the shift from a product society to a market society to a post-industrial society creates the need for environmental scanning. Scanning creates inputs to a flexible and opportunistic management system. Such a system permits organizations to become responsive to their emerging circumstances, to become adaptive, and, in various ways, to "learn to dance." Companies with high degrees of strategic momentum have been shown to scan the environment much more broadly than their more reactive counterparts [214].

Evolution in Planning Methodology. In the wake of substantial criticism of the timeliness and effectiveness of the results of planning efforts, in the past decade strategic planning as a profession has undergone significant changes. A principal criticism has been that the profession has been too preoccupied with process and definition — questions such as how to organize the planning process and how to identify a good strategic decision.

Freed from preoccupation with process or form, planners can focus on more fundamental issues, such as, "What information do I need to make a good strategic decision?" In a complex, rapidly changing environment, that necessary information is mainly about the future, to some degree about the present, and little about the extrapolated past. The information environmental scanning seeks to provide fits this need.

Asymmetry of Environmental Impacts. A company with an abundance of resources might argue that it is sufficient to know about what is happening *now*. Yet, the perceived *now* may already be a step behind the real present environment and is certainly behind the environment that will exist over the period during which current decisions are implemented. "Not to worry," one might say, if threats and opportunities are evenly distributed across time and if payoffs and penalties are reasonably symmetrical. That is, a firm with enough resources to weather storms would come out about even in a zero-sum game.

However, evidence suggests that the environment can be unforgiving. Favorable and unfavorable environmental changes of a non-controllable nature have been studied to determine if the unfavorable changes related to a business downturn would be balanced by favorable changes related to an upturn. The study found unfavorable changes caused significant deterioration in firm performance in downturns, but that positive changes did not lead to significant countervailing benefits in upturns. Schendel and Patton [416] conclude that environmental monitoring is required to help avoid unfavorable impacts. As to the evenness with which threats and opportunities are spread over time, it might be worth recalling the four environmental impact cases at the beginning of this chapter.

Survey Evidence

The formal research that has tested the use and value of environmental scanning has been both empirical and impressionistic. Several research questions have been explored in recent surveys: (1) Which companies scan actively and what needs assessments for environmental scanning have been done? (2) What value do companies place on scanning activities that they actually conduct? (3) What impact has scanning had on behavior and performance?

Benefits of Scanning. Survey results can be summarized as follows:

- From a survey of opinions of 20 firms in 17 industries about environmental scanning and strategic planning:

  Of 11 firms with sales in excess of one billion dollars, 65 percent reported in-place formal scanning systems that tracked at least one external environmental area. Less than half of those firms tracked five or more of the seven environmental areas the study defined as important. Most respondents agreed that the increasing complexity of the external environment has heightened the need for systematic long-range strategic planning and formal environmental scanning practices [Franklin, *etal.*: 159].

- From a survey of the Fortune 250 largest companies:

  Fifty-two had at least an informal early warning system in place, and all of the respondents cited valid signals that had come from their scanning systems. Somewhat less than half reported that the signals generated action. About one-third believed that problems would have gone undetected without the benefit of an early warning system [Roy and Cheung: 408].

- From a survey of 90 firms responding from the Fortune 500:

  Seventy-three percent of the companies had organized environmental analysis activities. Firms with less than one billion dollars in sales were least likely to scan (44-57 percent), while larger firms were most likely to scan (85-88 percent). The smaller firms were twice as likely as large ones to consider environmental analysis to be of "crucial" usefulness to the company. Respondents cited numerous successes or payoffs from environmental analysis:

  - a noticeable tendency for managers to ask themselves if approaches used in the past will work in the future;
  - lengthened planning/decision horizon;
  - avoidance of crises;
  - anticipation of government restrictions on medical equipment led to extra effort to develop foreign markets;
  - early detection of developing shifts in trends from either excess capacity or insufficient capacity in an industry;
  - shifts in product portfolio related to vulnerability to social and government pressures;
  - identification of potential impact of the energy shortage in 1971 motivated action that led to strengthened market position [Diffenbach: 116].

- From survey responses from 47 CEOs:

Environmental factors require increasing amounts of their time, and have broadened the qualifications required of a person to be effective as a CEO [Steiner, *etal.*: 449].

- From 89 respondents in a six-company, two-industry study, where one industry was in a dynamic environment and the other in a stable environment:

    Hours spent scanning per day were higher by respondents in the dynamic industry than in the stable one. Upper-level respondents spent substantially more time per day than lower-level respondents in scanning activities [Kefalas and Schoderbeck: 238].

- From a survey of 98 hospital boards of directors, analyzing the recognition of impacts of birth rate changes on obstetrical and maternity services:

    The success in recognizing problems at an early stage was associated with the use of environmental data by a board. Early problem recognition was also associated with the ratio of externally to internally focused committees of the board [Ritvo, etal.: 399].

- Three studies have assessed scanning against performance measures:

    One of these studies focused on the financial impacts of scanning among 86 firms in six industries. For each firm, the intensity of scanning in seven sectors of the environment was measured, and three financial performance measures were obtained. Statistically significant relationships between scanning intensity and performance were found in the sectors relating to competition, suppliers and society, but were not found in the customer, government, technology or economic sectors [Snyder: 438].

    Another study used industry growth rate as a success measure, rather than financial performance. Survey data on 162 firms showed that as technological scanning increased, the growth rate of the industry did as well [Gerstenfeld: 170].

    A third study found strong statistical support for the hypothesis that the greater the match between true environmental volatility and managers' perceived environmental uncertainty, the higher the level of economic performance. Data came from 20 non-diversified public corporations in 17 different three digit SIC codes. Volatility was measured using sales, profits, and the rate of R&D plus capital investment. Profitability was measured in terms of measures of both return and earnings. Additional analysis suggested that *disagreement* among managers as to the level of uncertainty was also associated with favorable economic performance [Bourgeois: 47].

- One study investigated the hypothesis that investments in firms which actively *plan* (but may or may not *scan*) become less risky than comparable firms who do not plan. That study sought to measure the change in the market-determined risk factor *beta* that resulted after a firm undertook strategic planning methodologies. The study found no significant change when compared with a randomly selected set of surrogate firms [Kudla: 253].

- Surveys and other sources have identified these organizations as having formal environmental scanning systems [152;175;184;404;446;448;472]:

Atlantic Richfield	Ciba-Geigy
Citicorp	CPC International
Dow USA	DuPont
General Electric	General Motors
General Mills	IBM
Johnson & Johnson	McDonald's
Monsanto	Nynex
J.C. Penney	Royal Dutch Shell
Sears Roebuck	Texas Instruments
United Airlines	Union Carbide
American Council of Life Insurance	United Way
American Medical Association	American Institute of CPAs
Credit Union National Association	
American Society of Personnel Administrators	
Sunday School Board of the Southern Baptist Convention	

There are several reasons why the incidence of active environmental scanning appears to be concentrated in large companies. First, significant resources may be required to conduct thorough, systematic scanning — resources more easily provided by large organizations. Second, there may be a selection bias; many studies are aimed at Fortune-list companies because of their visibility and accessibility. Finally, more large companies may be sensitized to the need for environmental scanning or the risks of failing to conduct it.

One recent study of 88 small (30 or fewer employees) owner-dominated service or retail firms accents the differences between large and small firms. The firms were distinctive in terms of the availability of staff support resources and of the tendency of small business CEO's to operate at the strategic and operational levels simultaneously [Smeltzer, *etal.*: 430]. Among the respondents, more than half indicated that they scanned continuously, and similarly more than half indicated that they considered their environments stable. These results are at least suggestive of the ability of small firms to pare and tailor their scanning efforts to conform to small organization resources, and perhaps more importantly, personalities. Small firms can reduce the detail of scanning efforts, focus techniques used on the personalities of the key people in the organization, and modify the scanning strategy to respect the shorter response cycles of smaller organizations [Pearce, *etal.*: 362].

It should be noted that what is reported here are statistically demonstrated relationships, not the specific causation of one event or outcome by another. In social science research, no conclusive proof of the value of any activity (or other hypothesis) is possible. Research on the success of environmental scanning comes from a wide range of sources over an extended period of time. Overall, scanners seem to believe that studying the environment for signals about future conditions has value, and empirical research tends to support that belief.

Criticisms of Environmental Scanning. Environmental scanning is not without its skeptics and critics. According to the results of one survey the single greatest deterrent to effective scanning among experienced scanners may be *interpretation*:

> The problem is that of interpreting the results of environmental analysis into specific impacts on the company's businesses and into specific responses to be made by the businesses. Included is the problem of the results not being in sufficiently precise form [116,112].

There is some evidence that excessive scanning can hurt performance. Snyder's study [438] showed that firms which scanned the competitor environment intensely *underperformed* others in the same industry which scanned moderately. Although this result is counter-intuitive, several behaviors related to intensive scanning could cause the process to backfire:

1. *Intensive scanning* of competitor behavior could lead to a preoccupation with reactive *response* to that behavior, that is, to a preponderance of reactive, defensive, follower strategies. To the extent that competitors sent false signals accepted by the scanner as real, strategies would have been even more unstable.

2. Intense environmental scanning is likely to generate a greater volume of inputs or signals than casual scanning. If these inputs are not synthesized properly, the firm may develop a set of strategies that is disproportionately large compared with the "real" set of competitive threats and opportunities. The resultant lack of focus from pursuing too many strategies could impact performance negatively in the way research has indicated.

3. A company that performs an intense environmental scan may allow the "completeness" of its efforts to build false confidence in a single-scenario future. If such a company based strategy on that scenario, a bet-the-company situation would emerge because the purpose of the scanning had been misunderstood. The main benefit of environmental scanning is in providing the basis for developing or modifying strategic direction and a set of contingent strategies to buttress that direction.

One common line of reasoning critical of environmental scanning similarly misunderstands the purpose of scanning: it is impossible to predict the future with any accuracy; if the world is more complex now than before, then poor predictions can only be more expensive to develop; why spend a lot of money on bad predictions? Developing contingent strategies for quick response *in the circumstance that unlikely events occur* involves choice and judgment. Out of the infinite range of possible futures, the firm must choose events and circumstances for which to prepare contingent strategies. Choice involves assessments of the probability and impact of occurrence on short notice, and it is the job of environmental scanning to provide knowledge that supports those assessments. This is different from predicting or forecasting the occurrence of the events themselves.

Indeed, the question should not be, "was the prediction accurate," but instead, "did the scanning and assessment process help us to become both *better-sensitized to* and *better-prepared for* the uncertain future?"

Synthesis of the Evidence: Standards for Environmental Scanning

The preceding sections describe the major evidence in support and criticism of environmental scanning. Of the impressionistic studies, the balance of attitudes and beliefs assigns positive benefits to scanning. The main criticisms are associated with the failure of some existing systems to devote sufficient resources to interpretation and synthesis efforts. Empirical studies also suggest scanning has value associated with higher growth rates, faster reaction times and better financial performance. Evidence also suggests that scanning can enhance the knowledge base of the firm and its effective planning horizon.

What can we conclude about the justification of environmental scanning expenditures in support of strategic planning? In 1981, Fahey, King and Narayanan suggested that scanning was an accepted but as yet unsophisticated field [151]. At that time, the methodologies that had evolved were *adaptive* rather than *innovative*; the impact had been on broadening the perspective of corporate thinking and policy making; and the field had not yet attracted major corporate resources. In 1985, Engledow and Lenz [144;270] concluded, from observing nine "leading-edge" firms that had been engaged in environmental scanning for at least three years, that considerable shifting of resources, focus, function and organization of environmental scanning efforts was still occurring. Evolution in organizational methodologies continues because the fundamental experience with environmental scanning has been positive.

Why scan the environment? Through knowledge-seeking interaction with its environment (competitors, regulators, customers, the public), an organization not only learns how to adapt and to what; it also influences to some extent the conditions and expectations of the environment itself. An organization that remains ignorant of dynamic shifts in its environment because it fails to interact with it may continue to pursue, blindly and erroneously, results measured against obsolete historical standards. Meanwhile, outside observers such as portfolio managers and financial analysts must form their own ideas of the way in which the new environment they perceive should affect the organization. The justification for an organization to develop and maintain external communication with its environment is to obtain the value created by the synthesis of new ideas from that interaction. This process of gaining knowledge through the continual question-answer interaction of opposites, or dialectic, has its roots early in the nineteenth century, in the work of the German philosopher Hegel (see Dirsmith [119] and Zeitz [532]). Thus, even though the organizational application of environmental scanning is in the early stages of its evolution, the fundamental basis for its value is well established.

CHAPTER 3

THE ORGANIZATION AND ITS ENVIRONMENT: THE ISSUE IS UNCERTAINTY

Firms that scan their environments have a better chance of capturing opportunities and avoiding threats than firms that simply react to events, and the preceding chapters have defined a context and established a basis for environmental scanning. This chapter develops a model of the relationship of scanning to the firm and the environment, and explores dependencies between the environment and organization structure, behavior and strategy.

The environment is dominated by social institutions and systems. This chapter explores concepts and models from social science research that bring meaning to the environment, to the concept of uncertainty and to the environmental scanning process. Then these aspects of the environment — particularly perceived uncertainty — are related to the organization through a process model. This model illustrates how the firm sets a scanning strategy; seeks, receives and perceives information; and synthesizes the knowledge contributing to the organization's strategy and operations.

The driving force determining scanning strategy in this process model is environmental uncertainty. Two elements of uncertainty — turbulence, and strength of signal — are explored in detail, showing how uncertainty motivates the organization to develop and modify information systems, organizational attributes, structures and business strategy.

Models of the Environment

Chapter 1 presented a simple model of the firm and its environment, and suggested that management's enlightenment begins with the recognition that a firm is not isolated from its environment but interactive with it. Graphically, this intellectual step takes the firm out of an apparently well-defined box on a flow chart (see Figure 1.1), and drops it into a limitless environmental sea (Figure 1.3). The purpose here is to suggest structure for the environment and the interaction across the firm's boundary with it.

The transition from isolation to interaction is similar to that of shifting the focus from closed-system to open-system behavioral models. Closed systems are basically those in which inanimate objects interact with the other elements of the system, reach a steady state equilibrium and come to rest. In an open system, objects interact with their environments, reach a new steady state and continue dynamic activity, including interaction with the environment. Open-systems models more properly describe the behavior of organizations and the people within them, but many organizational theorists argue that such models are not sufficient. What is needed in addition is a model describing the "processes in the environment itself which are among the determining conditions of the exchanges [that] occur between organization and environment," according to Emery and Trist [142], who proposed a framework for the environment in the form of a matrix of connections (processes, influences, transactions, communications) that exist within it. The model clearly demonstrates three essential ideas:

1. The firm is a part of its environment.

2. The firm interacts with its environment both as a receptor of signals from the environment and a transmitter of signals to it.

3. The character of the environment the firm faces is importantly shaped by interdependencies and transactions that occur entirely outside the domain, or realm of influence, of the organization.

At the boundary between the firm and the environment, there exist input and output dependencies of the organization. Many of these dependencies can become well understood and perhaps to an extent controlled — at least on the surface and in the short run — because of the regularity of the transactions. This aspect of the firm's environment is referred to as the *task* environment or the *operational* environment and is the portion over which the company typically has a greater degree of control [474]. This environment encompasses many of the challenges a firm faces when attempting to attract or acquire needed resources, or in marketing goods and services [Pearce and Robinson: 360]. The task environment comprises well-defined, long-standing, high relevance and high controllability relationships between the organization and other individuals or organizations: e.g. customers, suppliers, bankers, consultants [Kefalas: 235].

By contrast, the *remote* environment comprises forces and relationships beyond a firm's operating situation but which may impose change on its task environment. Rarely does a firm have the power to exert any meaningful influence upon its remote environment, but it can learn to understand that environment and the ranges of new influences and conditions it may impose. Elements of this less visible remote environment interact to reshape signals that the firm observes through its boundary with the more visible task environment.

This environmental model permits us to relate scanning to strategy. An organization should scan the general environment for broad trends and for possible new product and market opportunities, i.e. for input into setting or modifying *domain definition* (mission) or primary strategies. Mission and primary strategies in turn define a task environment which is scanned in greater detail for changes and discontinuities. Such scanning contributes to the development and monitoring of *domain navigation* strategies in the product, market and resource areas (see Bourgeois [48]).

Activities that relate an organization to its environment can be described as *boundary-spanning*. Certain people are boundary spanners by virtue of their jobs, e.g., product managers [292]. Boundary-spanning, say Leifer and Delbecq [266], "protects members of the system from extra-systemic influences and . . . regulates the flow of information, material and people into or out of the system." The activity, "is a relative phenomenon depending upon the actual or perceived need for information to reduce uncertainty."

Two dimensions of uncertainty emerge from our simple environmental model. *Dynamic* environments are uncertain because of a high rate of change, or a high frequency of new factors in decision making. *Complex* environments are uncertain because they depend on many environmental factors for decision making or because those factors come from a wide range of environmental sources. Duncan tested the significance of these two dimensions for the perceptions of uncertainty in 22 decision-making units of both R & D and manufacturing organizations. The study confirmed the rank-ordering of low to high uncertainty indicated in Table 3.1, which may have significance for the design of scanning systems. The dominance of the static-dynamic dimension over the simple-complex dimension in perceptions about uncertainty implies that individual decision makers are more threatened by *change* in their environments than by *complexity* in their environments.

Table 3.1: Rank Ordering of Four Types of Perceived Uncertainty (By Decision Makers in 22 Different Environments)

Rank (I = Least)	Description of Environmental Dimensions
I	**Simple Static Environment:** Few factors in the decision environment, similar to one another, and located in a small number of environmental components. Factors and components remain essentially unchanged over time.
II	**Complex Static Environment:** Number of factors and components of environment may be large and dissimilar, but factors and components remain essentially unchanged over time.
III	**Simple Dynamic Environment:** Few factors and components in environment, but both factors and components are subject to continual change.
IV	**Complex Dynamic Environment:** Number of factors and components of environment may be large and subject to continual change.

(Adapted from Robert Duncan, "Characteristics of Organizational Environments and Perceived Environmental Uncertainty," Administrative Science Quarterly, *Vol. 17, No. 3.)*

Our simple model of the environment thus expands into a process model in which the degree of perceived environmental uncertainty drives environmental scanning within the organization, as illustrated in Figure 3.1. Uncertainty arises from the actual dynamism and complexity of the external environment, that is, from the synthesis of what we learn and already know about the environment, with what we *think we should know* about it. Uncertainty also arises when new information needs are generated within the organization through consideration of new domain definition (primary) and domain navigation (secondary) strategies. For example, considering a new primary strategy might require information about an area of developing technology not presently understood — a scanning need in the remote environment. A possible change in a secondary strategy may raise questions about packaging or distribution methods — a scanning need in the task environment. Finally, uncertainty arises in the organization's operating data, such as a shortfall from market share or profits goals.

Information about the environment and even about the firm's own operations is subject to two forms of filtering. A reception filter passes only the inputs that are observed, either by chance or by search. Next is a perception filter where inputs both from outside the firm and inside the firm (operating data, trouble symptoms and information requests) are evaluated and interpreted by *people* according to their role in the hierarchy. Here, depending on individual acuity, thought processes, biases and interactions, inputs may be amplified or dampened, integrated or isolated, understood or misunderstood. These inputs may be transmitted to the knowledge base of the organization or discarded. The perceived environmental uncertainty that emerges from the synthesis of present knowledge, and from the ongoing separate strategic dialogue in the organization, determines the format of scanning efforts that the organization will undertake.

Reception, perception and synthesis are clearly on the critical path to effective scanning strategy, a strategy that matches the form and content of environmental scanning efforts to the degree of uncertainty in the task and remote environments and to the strategic resources of the organization. Key to this scanning strategy is the perceived uncertainty of the environment.

Uncertainty of the Environment

Uncertainty in a firm's environment has two aspects: (1) turbulence, or the extent and frequency of change, and (2) strength of signal, or the "visibility" of change or impact to the alert scanner.

Turbulence. The environment has already been characterized by its connectedness with the organization in the task environment and the remote environment. The organization's need to be sensitive to the environment is externally influenced by the impact, the frequency, and the predictability of change. In stable environments, where change is not frequent, the choice of an environmental scanning strategy revolves mainly around the impact of change. Stable environments can be randomized or clustered [142,24-5]. The essential difference is that in the latter, events are either bunched or chained together

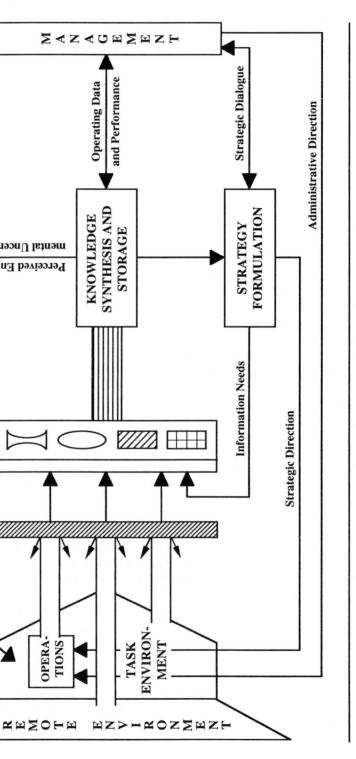

Figure 3.1: Environmental Knowledge and Scanning Strategy Determination

in such a way as to concentrate effects on the organization. In such environments, where there is otherwise plenty of room for pursuing profitable opportunities tactically, there are now potential payoffs from developing strategies for guiding the organization through the environment and for scanning the environment for information to support and execute such strategy development.

In *dynamic environments,* the major source of environmental challenge is still in the local or task environment, but the balance of the firm's input-output relationships changes. In stable circumstances the organization can act more at will, sending signals and outputs to the environment. In dynamic environments the control of the firm over its environment is lessened because competition intensifies for resources and markets; the balance shifts, and the bulk of interaction represents inputs from the environment. Also, the volume of interaction with the environment increases, making the search for signals from the environment — at least the *task* environment — more critical to strategic management.

Moreover, the *purpose* of environmental scanning shifts as stable environments change and become dynamic. In stable environments, the purpose of scanning is predicting the locus of future events to permit the organization to prepare a proper course of action. In competitively dynamic environments the *preparations* of competitors become a principal focus of the *predictions* of the organization, *and vice versa,* so that the predict-prepare process of environmental scanning itself influences the environment being scanned. Ackoff argues that in such environments prediction as an outcome of scanning is not as useful as the development of control strategies for contingency management [4,61]. That idea is explored further during analysis of the influences of environmental uncertainty on the competitive structure of the firm, and on its scanning strategy.

Intelligence about the remote environment becomes important to strategic management within *turbulent* environments (see Emery and Trist [142], Terreberry [465] and Ansoff [12]). A turbulent environment is one in which dynamic change emerges directly from the remote environment. The watch industry environment became dynamic when competition from battery-driven watches arose within the task environment. Then turbulence was created within that industry when integrated circuits emerged as a novel technology from the remote environment. Environmental change amid turbulence is characterized by uncertainty and rapidity of change in the remote environment which increasingly causes unpredictable changes in the task environment. Ansoff characterizes the turbulent environment as, "an unfamiliar world of strange technologies, strange competitors, new consumer attitudes, new dimensions of social control, and, above all, a questioning of the firm's role in society." [12,9] Twenty years earlier, Emery and Trist observed:

> For organizations, [turbulence means] a gross increase in their area of *relevant uncertainty.* The consequences which flow from [an organization's] actions lead off in ways that become increasingly unpredictable: they do not necessarily fall off with distance, but may at any point be amplified beyond all expectation; similarly, lines of action that are strongly pursued may find themselves attenuated by emergent field forces [142,26].

The transition from less to more turbulent environments is an evolutionary one; adaptive social structures inherently become more complex as they develop and interact with their environments. Change induces change. Thus, stable environments will migrate toward dynamism, and dynamic environments will evolve towards turbulence. What of turbulent environments?

Drucker [126] described an age of discontinuity. Ansoff [12] and Bell [34] wrote about a post-industrial era. Kahn [221] depicted a new class. Toffler [479] portrayed the third wave. All of these pictures of change imply a heightened uncertainty of strategic positioning, predict a shift in the centrality and structure of economic institutions, and propose emerging environmental signals, mainly from the remote environment. Three conclusions for scanning strategy emerge from turbulence in the environment:

1. Scanning the *remote* environment vis-a-vis the task environment will become increasingly important to the strategic success of the organization as the turbulence of its environment intensifies.

2. *Forecasting* from past knowledge and data will become less accurate as discontinuity gives rise to new social and industrial patterns. *Predicting* the fabric of emerging environments from concept, theory and analysis will prove more useful, not for purposes of prediction itself, but for purposes of building contingency strategies and rapid response abilities.

3. Speed of response will increasingly become an issue. Turbulent environments involve both uncertainty *and* rapidity of change. Increasing turbulence implies the prospect of conditions that emerge without our foreknowledge from the remote environment and which take shape and force quickly — perhaps more quickly than the firm can conduct a cycle of recognize-react-respond. To the extent that speed of change outstrips speed of response, increased timeliness of response systems, including environmental scanning, will be demanded.

Strength of Signal. The second dimension of uncertainty in the environment relates to the clarity of the signals. The visibility of the future diminishes with increasing turbulence, and predictability deteriorates accordingly [Ansoff: 12]. Weaker signals would be associated with the remote environment, where more scanning effort is directed as turbulence increases, and even in the task environment the subtlety of the signals becomes greater as competition for market share and resources intensifies under turbulence. And, in either task or remote environmental range, turbulence itself creates heightened noise levels as the sheer volume of transactions increases; with the noise all signals are harder to detect.

If the only signals received from an environmental scanning effort tell the organization what it already knows, that system is ineffective. Everything learned about the environment suggests that the breadth of sources of meaningful signals for the future of the organization is *wider than ever.* Thus, the issue of "no news" relates to the methodology, precision and cost of scanning systems to capture meaningful new signals. At one point scientists were confronted with the limits of visual astronomy as ambient light and atmospheric pollution (turbulence) reduced the effectiveness of existing telescopes whose mirrors and lenses already stretched the limits of known technology, and it was unclear whether any visual technology would overcome these limitations or allow exploration of the void of a black hole. The radio telescope, a new methodology accidentally discovered, enhanced signal detection against both of these limitations. (See *The Environment Speaks I.*)

Suburban audiophiles face a growing problem in receiving direct FM signals because of high-rise construction, the proliferation of broadcasters and the distances between urban FM stations and the suburbs where these audiophiles live. In this case, the receiver is searching for a signal it *knows* is there, where the radio telescope searches for a novel signal. Both cases call for a directional antenna, aiming devices, receivers with greater sensitivity and higher signal-to-noise ratios — i.e., scanning with greater precision.

Even with greater range and sensitivity, the astronomer and the audiophile face strategic choices. To monitor more than one precise channel or location simultaneously requires multiple receivers and escalating costs. The environmental scanner in the business organization faces the same problem but to an even greater extent. For a meaningful strategic input to be formulated, the scanner may need to integrate weak signals of different types from several sources, most of which are outputs from behavioral rather than physical systems. Such systems evolve at a pace, especially in turbulent environments, that makes the repeated observation of "identical" phenomena difficult. The challenge to scanners is to identify the meaning of signals *and* to measure their rate of change. For this reason, scanning *continuity* is a critical element of scanning strategy.

Impacts of Environmental Uncertainty on the Organization

The design of the organization and the format of environmental scanning should be jointly adapted to environmental uncertainty. That is, the uncertainty of the environment should influence the competitive, organizational and information management structures of the firm, as discussed below. The simultaneous influence of those structures and the uncertainty of the environment on scanning strategy is considered in Chapter 5.

Uncertainty and Organization Attributes. The less predictable a firm's environment, the worse a firm is likely to perform. One of the principal purposes of this book is to propose ways to offset that consequence. Empirical support for the predictability-performance linkage was found by Tuggle and Gerwin [482], who tested a simulation model of a firm in its environment. Their environment simulator was cyclical and could function with stable, dynamic and crisis models of reality and with changes in degree of uncertainty. Their firm could function with varying slack resources and sensitivity to environmental change by changing product, market and factor strategies. Two considerations moderated the poor performance of their simulated firm:

- Firms in less predictable environments did better if they had slack resources in reserve for protective and opportunistic purposes.

• Firms in less predictable environments did better if they were less sensitive to environmental changes.

The second of these findings could appear to contradict the earlier suggestion that a firm in uncertain, turbulent environments needs to scan its environment with *greater* sensitivity and reach out to more remote points. The resolution of this apparent contradiction lies in a better understanding of the analysis and response mechanisms that are triggered by scanning outcomes, and of how *changes* in these mechanisms occur in response to changes in environmental uncertainty.

THE ENVIRONMENT SPEAKS I
When Stars Talk, Earth Listens Up

Farther than the eye can see, the 27 giant, dish-shaped radio telescopes, each weighing 235 tons and standing 100 feet tall, stretch single-file across the New Mexico desert.

The computer-controlled antennas — parabolic dishes pointed toward distant space — listen for radio waves "broadcast" from the near and far recesses of the universe. The broadcasters are celestial objects from unseen stars to mysterious quasars, which may radiate invisible energy in the form of radio waves rather than the visible form of cosmic energy seen by ordinary telescopes.

Together, the 27 antennas, aptly named the Very Large Array (VLA), constitute the world's largest astronomical observatory. And, despite being about 50 miles from Interstate 25, near Socorro, New Mexico, this is one of the most worthwhile stops along the entire interstate highway system.

To the VLA, supported by the National Science Foundation and operated by the National Radio Astronomy Observatory, come the world's leading astronomers. Their quest: to unravel the endless mysteries of endless space.

Twenty-four hours a day, every day, the VLA's giant radio ears — aimed with unmatched precision and sensitivity at mere pinpoints in space — listen for the telltale radio signals emitted from celestial objects billions of light-years away.

The tiny dabs of celestial energy received by each of the VLA's mammoth radio dishes are fed into amazing computers in the complex's control building. There, at speeds of 100 million operations per second, computers translate the incoming radio signals into numbers and then into images. The final results often are startling pictures of unseen celestial objects in black and white or vivid color.

The VLA and smaller radio telescopes in the United States, Europe and the Soviet Union have helped to unmask quasars; discovered a whole new breed of star formations, the radio galaxies; shown that many celestial objects are far larger than indicated by even the largest of conventional telescopes; and probed space's monstrous celestial pits — the so-called black holes — believed by some to be formed from the debris of collapsing stars.

Radio astronomy, scarcely 50 years old, was born of a chance discovery. In 1932, the late Karl G. Jansky, a scientist working on a radio communications system at the Bell Telephone Laboratories, was perplexed by radio noise plaguing his project.

By deduction, Jansky came to the conclusion that the source of the noise must be in space. Until then, light and optical telescopes were the sole sources of astronomical observation.

The VLA's 27 giant radio wave antennas are positioned along a Y-shaped configuration of railway tracks, each arm of the Y extending some 13 miles and resulting in a sensitivity equivalent to a single dish 17 miles in diameter.

*(*Quick Stops © *1986. Reprinted by permission of Universal Press Syndicate.)*

Uncertainty and Information Systems. Proper design of the organization's information system is a key factor in maximizing environmental response effectiveness. Organizations in stable environments tend to develop highly structured information gathering and processing "habits" as their experience grows into a set of traditional beliefs about the structure and reality of their environments. Superior firm performance can result from complex systems that capture signals of change from stable, cue-rich environments. Those staid complex structures stand in the way of recognizing changes in the environment that render traditional beliefs obsolete.

Eventually, of course, even tradition-bound organizations accumulate enough experience with incongruous results to read the handwriting on the wall. At that point, a crisis may already have arisen and the opportunity to pre-plan a response is lost. To prevent such a crisis-cycle model from becoming the primary adaptive mechanism of the firm to its environment, Hedberg and Jonsson [192,69] suggest several steps for making an organization better able to deal with changing environments:

For the organization: Encourage experimental behavior by managers; define roles ambiguously; encourage informal communication networks that short circuit "structure;" filtering of information, filtering routines.

For the information system: Adopt dead-dates or pre-determined revision requirements for reports, processing and decision routines and models; turn off filtering routines — such as seasonal smoothing, outlier and "random signal" rejection rules — regularly, and increase that regularity as time passes from the last major system revision.

The evolution in information system design makes possible the accumulation of non-routine information and the satisfaction of non-routine database inquiries. Relational database structures and mixed text-and-data database environments make more information from the environment potentially available to managers than ever before, and available in targeted (cut and sliced) form, rather than buried in voluminous reports. Emerging executive information systems focus on gathering information exclusively on business issues. One author cites the experience of an international bank that put an executive information system in place to monitor the results of foreign operations and to keep track of data on political climates and customers' businesses in foreign countries [Friend: 166]. Specialized computer systems are increasingly becoming available to deal with specialized, unstructured problems in imaginative ways [160,289]. With some of the additional features Hedberg and Jonsson suggest, an information system should be capable of dealing with turbulent and surprise-laden environments.

The use of information technology in seeking competitive advantage in environmental knowledge and product/service marketing has been shown to increase with the extent of external transactions between organizations in their value-added chain (travel agents to airlines; car manufacturers to suppliers), with short-lived products, and with environmental pressures [217,524]. Environmental pressures act as catalysts for implementing information technology where the environmental change is event-oriented, as is the case with deregulation, entry of strong new competitors, and dramatic new technology.

Uncertainty and Organization Structure. To have information systems used as well as useful requires that an organization be capable, structurally and culturally, of recognizing change in the environment at the right time. In Emery and Trist's terms, this involves early detection of signals that remote environment transactions are accumulating to produce a direct shock to the task environment.

The proper organizational structure for the firm depends on both the predictability of key environmental factors and the degree of possible discretionary response. Where predictability and discretionary response are both high, risks are low, but many strategic adjustments may be made in response to a large amount of required environmental input. Where both are low, less environmental information is available, but the strategic importance of interpreting and responding to it correctly is high because risks are high. Ball and Lorange [25] recommend decentralized management in the former case, and centralized management in the latter, to distribute both information processing and strategic decision-making responsibilities across the organization. This organizational construct is also consistent with Tuggle and Gerwin's findings (p. 25) about the inverse relationship between success and sensitivity in less predictable environments. Low predictability is associated with less information, but each unit of information has higher strategic value upon which action is taken in a more deliberate fashion. The structural responsiveness of various organizational forms can be assessed along five dimensions:

Operating responsiveness	—	the goal is minimum cost.
Competitive responsiveness	—	the goal is optimum profit.
Innovation responsiveness	—	the goal is to exploit near-term potential.
Entrepreneurial responsiveness	—	the goal is to exploit long-term potential.
Administrative responsiveness	—	goals are related to support, coexistence, adaptation.

[Ansoff: 12,280-308]

Ansoff rates matrix forms superior to divisional and functional forms in terms of their responsiveness to near- and long-term opportunities in the external environment, and to internal administrative goals. These strengths are at the slight sacrifice of the great strengths of the functional form of organization in operating responsiveness, and of the divisional form in competitive responsiveness. The strengths of the matrix form are relevant only where the firm faces an uncertain environment demanding rapid responses, and where the inherent conflicts of shared responsibility and authority have been minimized.

All of these forms are surpassed in responsiveness by what Ansoff describes as an *integrated multi-structure,* where groups, divisions or profit centers come under the active strategic and operating guidance of a corporate management, but may themselves have differing organizations or structures. An organization may need this structure to meet the pressures of a uncertain environment. The organization may also need this structure to take advantage of the growing power of information technology. The centralized nature of top management in this structure is consistent with Ball's recommendations for low predictability, low discretionary response environments.

Uncertainty and Strategy. The attractiveness, or even necessity, of adopting one form of business strategy over another may be influenced by the degree of uncertainty of the environment. In stable environments, Duncan's *simple static environment* for example (Table 3.1), the low-risk concentration strategy of delivering existing technology to existing markets is adequate to generate success. The firm seeks to sell more to their customers, to competitors' customers and to new customers. If the competition intensifies to the point that growth targets cannot be met through current product/market offerings, riskier market development and product development strategies will be required. If the remote environment begins to deliver shocks that affect technology, product life cycles and consumer behavior, the firm might seek to reduce risk exposure through strategic diversification and integration moves.

Environmental dynamics thus influence the relative desirability of a set of possible strategies, both reactive and aggressive. Some integrating strategies have the prospect of *insulating* the organization from environmental turbulence, a few examples of which are described in Table 3.2. None of these insulation strategies actually reduces the turbulence in the firm's environment. But potentially, each provides a means for the firm to become less vulnerable to its environment by controlling against the impacts or effects of environmental trends and events. Another set of strategies has the potential effect of reducing turbulence itself, although in a limited way, through various forms of market or resource integration, as illustrated in Table 3.3.

Environmental uncertainty, turbulence and understanding are not the primary driving forces of strategy development. They are simply the part of the cognitive structure of the organization's executives that becomes the context for making strategic decisions [271]. But since the environment is a compelling determinant of market opportunities and company capabilities, *the perceptions of the environment* developed from environmental scanning influence the course of business strategy within the organization. Correspondingly, the state of business strategy within the organization influences the scope and format of scanning. Strategic sensitivity to and interest in the environment depends in part on where the organization stands and on where it seeks to go.

Table 3.2: Examples of Turbulence-Insulating Strategies

Concentric Diversification: purchase or develop synergies in the form of new markets for technology (market development) or new technologies for markets (product development). Product development is focused on generating entirely new product life cycles. An *innovation strategy* is the riskiest development strategy. Canon extended technology to new markets through its development of the PC10 personal copier. Chesebrough-Ponds exposed its markets to new technology through the acquisition of Stauffer Chemical as a research engine. The life insurance industry adopted a product/market development strategy in designing a multitude of interest-sensitive life insurance policies to meet specialized market segment needs. In any of these cases, if the environment were more stable, pursuing expansion of market size or market share would seem less risky.

Conglomerate Diversification: purchase a reduction in risk of failure in one market or one technology by acquiring a portfolio of technologies and markets whose fortunes are unrelated to one another. Textron and Beatrice are examples of firms that are or at one time were broadly diversified through the conglomerate diversification strategy. Experience has shown that portfolio diversification in the extreme may itself be risky, if the market discounts the value of the portfolio's constituent parts, because the absence of incentives to optimize overcomes the perceived value of risk reduction. The risk materializes if predators appear, anxious to profit from the arbitrage of breaking the portfolio apart. If the market were more stable, diversification involving potential synergies would be more attractive.

Coalition: purchase a reduction in risk of innovation, or a chance for improved product/market development by agreeing to share expertise, competitive advantage, rewards and risks with a partner. Joint venturing the development of computer chip technology, as is Microelectronics & Computer Technology Corp. (MCC), the joint research venture of the U.S. computer industry, is one example (see *The Environment Speaks II*). Alliances to trade markets for technology, are exemplified by AT&T's relationship with Olivetti, and by General Motors' joint venture with Toyota. If the environment were more stable, an internal innovation or development strategy might provide superior risk-adjusted return.

THE ENVIRONMENT SPEAKS II
NCR Introduces a Software System, Venture's First Commercial Product

NCR Corp. introduced a software system that uses computer-generated artificial intelligence to aid in the design of computer microcircuits.

The system, called Design Advisor, is the first commercial product to be based on technology developed by Microelectronics & Computer Technology Corp., an Austin, Texas, cooperative research venture of which NCR is a member. MCC started doing advanced computer research in January 1984.

Artificial intelligence is a branch of computer science seeking to create computers that can recognize and solve complex problems — i.e., mimic human thought.

The Dayton, Ohio-based maker of computers and business machines said the Design Advisor, which is used on engineering workstations, reviews proposed circuit designs and offers advice on how designs may be improved.

Industry analysts said the software is notable because it will reduce the time needed to design complicated, custom semiconductor chips. NCR is a market leader in the sale of widely used chips, known as application specific integrated circuits.

"The time savings is an important feature," said Bill Groves, vice president, technology, of IN-Stat Inc., a semiconductor market research concern. "ASIC designs tend to be complicated, and it can be very expensive to go back to check for errors. So this makes a good checkpoint before a manufacturer commits to processing."

For Microelectronics & Computer Technology, the public introduction of the system is another step in the group's shift from pure research to an emphasis on "transferring" that research to the 20 high-technology companies that own the group.

The clearest sign of that shift came in March when Grant Dove, a former Texas Instruments Inc. executive, was named chairman and CEO of MCC, succeeding Adm. Bobby Inman. Adm. Inman, a former director of the National Security Agency, was a high-profile figure needed to bring the group into being. Mr. Dove is more of a "hands-on" manager whose goal is to bring MCC's research to the marketplace.

While the NCR artificial intelligence system is the first product derived from MCC research that outside customers will use directly, a number of companies are using MCC research internally. Both Minnesota Mining and Manufacturing Co. and Boeing Co., for instance, are making microchips using MCC research into how those chips are linked to each other and the computers in which they operate.

NCR said the system will be available this fall as a service and will be sold in early 1988 as a software package for industry standard engineering workstations.

Table 3.3: Examples of Turbulence-Reducing Strategies

Vertical integration: a reduction in the uncertainty of resource availability/cost by purchasing or developing control over those resources. If a building material supplier acquires forest land, a sawmill, an insulation manufacturer and a trucking company, it vertically integrates *upstream*. It is also possible to integrate *downstream,* as if the material supplier were to acquire a building contractor. Wickes Co., which operates a chain of lumber and building material retail outlets, sought to integrate upstream when it made a takeover bid for Owens-Corning Fiberglass Corporation, a manufacturer of glass fiber, insulation and construction products (see *The Environment Speaks VI* in Chapter 4). When it failed in that bid, analysts suggested that other possible targets for a Wickes takeover included Jim Walter Corporation, a home construction contractor that would have represented vertical integration downstream.

Horizontal integration: reducing competitive risks by buying the competition. Internal expansion might be more desirable in markets with many competitors in relatively stable environments, since the costs of extending market boundaries could be more widely shared and the risks of government intervention from alleged anti-trust violations would be avoided. But in intensely competitive markets, where saturation is a threat or reality, horizontal integration may be the only way for a company to increase or maintain market share. Horizontal integration is also the result for survivors in intensely competitive industries facing instability and consolidation. Chrysler's purchase of American Motors is an example of buying the competition. In this case, Chrysler obtained productive capacity and the highly competitive Jeep name and products. Consolidation through horizontal integration has created survivors in the airline, trucking, brokerage and banking industries during the 1980s and early 1990s.

Summary

This chapter has explored an open-systems model of the organization in its environment and its interaction primarily with its task environment. The remote environment influences the firm through indirect consequences of its effects on the intervening task environment. The concept of environmental uncertainty helped to show how uncertainty of the environment influences the organization's structure, behavior, business strategy and environmental scanning needs.

This understanding of uncertainty is important because it influences both the structure of the organization and its approach to scanning. The following chapters show how the scanning strategy of the organization should be shaped to the uncertainty of the environment it confronts. Chapter 4 describes a framework for dimensioning the environment, and Chapter 5 proposes a set of 11 elements of scanning strategy to be adjusted to tune the organization's effort to scan the environment to fit its circumstances and needs.

products specialized to custom requirements. Similar productivity/reactivity tools have also emerged in service industries and support systems. High-level computer software languages are now being developed to automate the generation of computer programs, and data environments are being created that make computer systems capable of flexible response to new information or processing demands.

Other methodologies have focused on productivity through reductions in handling cost and investment. Just-in-time manufacturing moved from hope to reality during the 1980s. Not only have inventories been reduced drastically, but lead times throughout the supply chain have been reduced as the *mentality* of operations has shifted from measuring backlogs to measuring throughput. *The Environment Speaks IV* article illustrates the emergence of this methodology at two points in time. Just-in-time in 1985 was described mainly in terms of plans and goals. By 1987, actual success stories were confidently reported.

The benchmark for these productivity improving efforts, and the ultimate basis for judging success of them, is a measure of product cost and value. Success requires exceeding our competition in value per unit of cost, and thus the measurement of success requires knowing competitors' costs as well as their products. Environmental scanning can provide source and signal information to permit a competitor cost database and analysis program to be maintained. One such program is in place at Caterpillar, Inc. (see Jones [219]).

THE ENVIRONMENT SPEAKS III
2000: Labor Shortage Looms

Projections regarding the work force in the year 2000 have been prepared under the direction of the Dept. of Labor, as have analyses of the potential impact of the projections. Some interesting findings have surfaced.

Work Force 2000. A comparison of the 1985 work force with that projected for the year 2000 produces significant differences: Almost all jobs will be in the service sector rather than in the goods-producing sector. And there will be many more high-tech jobs in the information and communications industry; the occupational mix will change, with greater increases in professional and managerial jobs; many new and existing jobs will require higher-level skills, including analytical and communications skills; over the next 15 years the job growth in the economy will strongly favor the most educated segments of the labor force; it will be a work force that will be older, with more women, more minorities and more immigrants.

Services vs. Goods. Most analysts are projecting an increase in employment in services, as opposed to employment in goods production, by the year 2000. The Hudson Institute forecasts that all net new jobs between 1985 and 2000 will be in services, with net declines in manufacturing, mining and agricultural employment. U.S. Bureau of Labor Statistics (BLS) data covering industry employment over a longer period of time — between 1960 and 1995 — shows a fairly steady increase in service-producing industry employment while goods production is almost flat.

White Collar vs. Blue Collar. The post-war trend of more white collar and fewer blue collar jobs will not change. The Hudson Institute projects that between 1984 and 2000, more than 3.8 million new managerial positions; 5.8 million professional and technical positions; and 3.6 million marketing and sales positions will be created.

At the same time there will be a decrease by 400,000 of skilled and unskilled production jobs. Estimates of percentage changes in selected occupations during that period show, for example, that while there will be a 38 percent increase in managerial and management-related occupations and a 95 percent boost in lawyers and judges, there will be only a seven percent increase in helpers, laborers and material movers and a five percent decrease in machine setters, setup operators and tenders.

Workplace Literacy. The Business Council for Effective Literacy reported in 1984 that 15 percent of the work force was functionally illiterate. Employers in the year 2000 will not tolerate such a high percentage of illiterates. In fact, there will be no meaningful job opportunities for the functionally illiterate — the person whose basic reading, writing and math skills are nonexistent.

Beyond that, by 1990 some 75 percent of all jobs will require some post-secondary education. Studies of potential job requirements for the year 2000 indicate that jobs will require the equivalent of two years of college education. Therefore, at least two years of college education will be the generally agreed-upon standard for workplace literacy. Today, at least a ninth-grade education is the standard for workplace literacy.

Work Force Profile. Even if nothing else changes, shifting demographics will definitely affect the work force profile in the year 2000. The population will be older. The median age will be 36, six years older than at any time in the history of the nation. The median age of the labor force will closely track the age of the population, rising from 35 years in 1984, to 39 in the year 2000 — the oldest in our history.

Women will continue to join the work force in substantial numbers. The BLS projects that by the year 2000, women will represent 47 percent of the work force, up from 42 percent in 1980. Between 1985 and 2000, women will constitute about 63 percent of the new entrants into the labor force. The projected increase of women in the work force is primarily a result of increased participation by women with children who are in two-career families or are single heads of households.

Blacks, Hispanics, and other minorities will make up approximately 29 percent of the net additions to the work force between 1985 and 2000; between 1970 and 1985 the percentage net additions of minorities to the work force was 18.4.

(Reprinted, with permission, from "2000: Labor Shortage Looms," Industry Week, Feb. 9, 1987, pp.38–40.)

Factory automation, communications hardware development, health care delivery systems and microcomputer spreadsheets are impacting the operational dimension today. What threats and potential opportunities are to be seen on tomorrow's horizon?

The Financial Dimension

Events in the financial dimension of the environment affect the cost of capital and the revenues of the organization; the balance of those effects depends on the markets that an organization serves. In financial businesses the fabric of the financial dimension is intertwined with the competitive dimension in a product/market sense. In any business the financial dimension affects the profitability, form and risk of temporary investments. Moreover, all businesses face a cost of funds in financing their operations.

Ultimately, the value of the enterprise — the net present value of its expected future cash flows — is determined by the cost and composition of its financial structure. The 1980s evidenced an unparalleled volatility in interest rates, an unusual precariousness in the availability of long-term financing and radical growth in the number and flexibility of financial instruments. Breakthrough-like events include the invention of securitization and the bundling of financial assets such as mortgages, auto loans and leases for resale as representative securities, thus creating a new financing opportunity for many organizations.

Financial markets themselves have undergone change. Options and futures markets have expanded explosively. Competition for customers has put pressure on profits and led to consolidation, until there is an apparent emergence, beyond advertising hype, of a financial services industry combining the wide range of money, capital and risk-management services into one integrated industry including banking, thrift, investment banking, brokerage, insurance, market making, consumer finance and commercial finance. What changes will occur in the market for funds as a result? Banks, investment banks and insurance companies now compete as fund sources for intermediate-term corporate needs. Will this consolidation of financial services lessen competition and affect accessibility and cost of funds?

The auction markets for shares of corporate common stock have become an auction block for entire corporations as the corporate takeover achieved legitimacy. Such takeovers represent a rational act for achieving integration and diversification goals wherever the risk-adjusted net present value of such a takeover is greater than that of the alternative of *de novo* entry into the same markets. In many cases, the price has been right to justify bidding for firms that are cash-rich and under-leveraged. Not uncommonly, takeover bids have arrived as surprises to firms who are in the early or intermediate stages of their own restructuring, reinvesting the proceeds harvested from mature businesses. Ex-Cell-O Corporation (see *The Environment Speaks V*) was well along with its re-direction efforts, seeking greater growth and higher profitability, when Textron announced a takeover offer for the company. The initial offer was not high enough to win acceptance, and the buyout ultimately took place at a price of $77.50 per share, compared with the $54 per share market price that had prevailed for Ex-Cell-O Stock before the offer was announced.

The principal defenses against such takeovers have been massive borrowings or preferred stock issues — either directly or through leveraged buyout by groups including the present management, effectively removing companies from the marketplace by taking them private. Many takeover targets react by selling attractive divisions and distributing the proceeds to shareholders as cash dividends. The principal source of funds to complete takeovers has been the unused debt capacity of the target company, and if need be, the borrowing capacity of the aggressor company. In either case, much higher leverage and financial risk are the common outcomes of a takeover attempt, whether or not it succeeds.

To illustrate the significance of the financial risk effects of takeovers, consider Moody's planned debt rating review and possible downgrading of Owens-Corning's debt issues, even before its response to the takeover attempt by Wickes. To rebuff Wickes successfully, Owens-Corning recapitalized and paid out to shareholders over $1 billion in cash, gave shareholders $300 million in new debt securities, borrowed $1.5 billion from banks, and sold its recently acquired aerospace and strategic materials group (see *The Environment Speaks VI*). After the takeover attempt, Owens-Corning was a drastically different company — less diversified and heavily in debt. And Wickes left far richer, despite its failure to obtain the company, having made $10 million on Owens-Corning stock acquired before its takeover offer and then sold after the market run-up.

Early indications of this wave of corporate takeovers were apparent in the late 1960s, when the first trickle of successful and profitable unfriendly takeovers occurred and the threats to corporate strategy were visible. Orderly, long-term harvest-and-reinvest strategies place the firm at the risk of being bought out because of the over-capitalization, depressed return on equity and decreased market valuations that are common during strategic transition periods. Yet debt-laden, cash-poor companies relatively safe from takeover attempts lack staying power in cyclical downturns.

There is no reason to believe that the next decade will be any more tranquil than its predecessor. No firm is immune from the effects of trends and events in the financial dimension. The signals of emerging issues are around us now, and among those signals may be financial market consolidation, strategy-limiting corporate takeover defenses, and a "new moralism" in the market for takeover and junk bond financing. This new moralism has already restricted sources of funds for cash flow financing by smaller businesses. Will it stunt entrepreneurial growth?

The Technological Dimension

The closest functional counterpart to the technological dimension within a firm is research and development, where the firm may seek to apply technology already in use. Or, the R&D group might search for new uses of already-developed technology. The products and uses that emerge from such efforts can have significant consequences for the organization, as, for example, Post-it Notes had for the 3M Corporation. This accident from experimentation with existing adhesives technology became a commercial success because of a scientist's alertness and the nurturing entrepreneurial technology of the organization.

THE ENVIRONMENT SPEAKS IV

The Hope:
From Job Shop to Fortune 1000, Just-in-Time's Part of the Plan

All the hoopla about just-in-time is not just talk, according to *Purchasing*'s latest lead-time survey. In fact, one-third of the 1,700 leading-edge panelists say their firms are actually implementing just-in-time materials management strategies.

A similar *Purchasing* survey of purchasing execs recently found that 60 percent of the respondents report a strong interest in JIT, with half of that group noting that their interest has moved beyond the discussion stages to actual implementation of JIT.

Strategic goals are varied. With JIT, buyers hope to gain: reduced obsolescence, a better-quality product, an expanded production area (resulting from more floor space), improved cash flow, a higher customer service level and a larger market share. In addition, buyers want suppliers to shoulder more responsibility for inspection.

(Reprinted, by permission, from Purchasing, *October 24, 1985, p. 25.)*

*   *   *   *   *

The Reality:
Controls Maker Trims Inventory by 60 Percent in 18 Months with JIT

The harsh truth came to Cincinnati Milacron's Electronic Systems Division in the early '80s, that technology alone wasn't going to be enough to overcome the substantial price advantage enjoyed by the Japanese. The U.S. controls maker also had to find an edge in manufacturing. And that's why, in the fall of '84, ESD turned to just-in-time.

Up until that time, ESD was doing business the old-fashioned way. And the long lead-times, and storerooms crammed with inventory, were the biggest tell-tale signs. Indeed, shortly before the company crossed over into the JIT camp, it spent a bundle for a huge carousel to hold all the inventory. Every year the plant was closed for two weeks to count inventory. One might call it MRP gone amok.

That's all changed now under JIT. Storerooms were ripped out; even the brand-new carousel was pulled down. There would be no place for inventory to hide. Operating in a JIT mode, inventory was trimmed by more than 60 percent in just 18 months, reports Thomas Simmerman, director of manufacturing.

Equally impressive has been the reduction in lead-times (which, more than reducing inventory, is the heart and soul of JIT). After 18 months of JIT, manufacturing lead-times were cut from 12 weeks to four weeks. Between November of '84 and April of '85, gross MRP requirements were cut by 40 percent, says Jerry Braunstein, materials manager.

Because of the shorter lead-times, ESD could pursue its new *modus operandi* of build-to-order, buy-to-forecast.

Manufacturing costs have dropped by 24 percent since the JIT program was instituted; and the cost of quality, which Simmerman believes will ultimately provide the biggest savings, has declined from 19 percent to 14.5 percent in the 18 months JIT has been in effect at ESD. Although the ESD hasn't yet reached the point of doing away with incoming inspection, it has progressed from 100 percent inspection to sample auditing of purchased parts.

JIT has brought a great change to purchasing. From buying three to four months' worth of supplies, purchasing now buys three to four weeks' worth. "It was a big shock to our vendors," says Braunstein.

When the JIT program got under way at ESD, purchasing was one of the few departments to get more bodies. The purchasing staff was increased from five to eight buyers, says Larry Wheatley, PM. At ESD purchasers had the added responsibility of being analysts as well as buyers.

Purchasing is in the process of qualifying and reducing its vendor base. The number of distributors ESD deals with has already been trimmed from 17 to five. Wheatley sees long-term contracts/vendor partnering as essential to making JIT work.

(Reprinted, by permission, from Purchasing, *April 9, 1987, p. 28.)*

Relatively few firms have the resources for research to develop new technology from existing scientific theory. Fewer still are capable of making original contributions to scientific theory. Yet within these two areas lie the greatest payoffs to technology: true breakthroughs that may revolutionize products, processes and markets, bringing the potential for exclusivity — or at least a sustainable early lead — to the successful developer. Examples of commercial development breakthroughs include DuPont's nylon, the Univac computer, and Polaroid's instant land camera. Commercial financial success has been substantial, irrespective of the development source.

By the nature of management and of the funding, the failure rate of research in nonprofit environments is likely to be higher, even as knowledge about ongoing developments is more readily accessible. However, original contributions to science and technology often emanate from non-profit university and foundation research laboratories. This has been especially true in the physical sciences, with many recent discoveries in biotechnology.

Many new developments are the result of "product pull" rather than "scientific push." The space program brought the development of heat-absorbing and friction-reducing compounds. Initially developed to meet a specific need, these compounds ultimately pushed their way into commercial extensions as a result of a technology substitution process:

> As any student of technological forecasting knows, the basis for innovation is inevitably an amalgam of new technological capability and a perceived new need. In the era of the Technological Age the igniting element for the technological substitution process has usually been (1) a technological achievement, (2) a military threat, or (3) a business strategy to increase profitability (e.g., competitive pressure, consumer conditioning to planned obsolescence) [Linstone and Sahal: 282,xiv].

The major strategic winner from novel technology may be the developing firm, but whether a given development has an adequate risk-adjusted profit return depends on the hit rate of R&D efforts, the product/market potential of the technology and the sustainability of the firm's market share. Returns can be high, as with the Polaroid camera, or low, as with Dupont's Corfam.

THE ENVIRONMENT SPEAKS V
Ex-Cell-O Corporation Meets Textron

Ex-Cell-O Corporation was founded in Detroit by former Ford Motor Company employees in 1919. The company specialized in precision parts machining. Over the years, the company prospered through internal growth and through acquisitions. It owned the patent rights to the famous Pure-Pak paper board milk carton until and beyond the patent's expiration. It made investments in bearing manufacturing, machine tools. It bought Cadillac Gauge in 1956 and entered the gauging and ordinance equipment businesses. It merged with McCord Corporation in 1978, an automotive parts manufacturer.

Also over the years, the company's growth rate slowed and its profitability shrank, along with its stock price. During the 1980s, it sought to reverse those trends by readjusting its business portfolio. It reduced its machine tool business, and redirected the remainder toward high-technology machines. It sold industrial product divisions. It increased its commitment to defense and aerospace, producing turbine engine components, fuel metering devices and parts for armored vehicles. It bought two major aerospace companies.

The restructuring had started to pay off. In 1985, the company earned $57.6 million on sales of $1.14 billion. Its aerospace/defense business accounted for 36 percent of its total business, up from 25 percent five years earlier. Analysts were projecting earnings per share of $4.20 in 1986 and $4.80 in 1987, up from $4.05 in

1985. But, the market was not yet willing to bet on a full turnaround. The stock hovered in the low $50s per share, about 12 times earnings, compared with about 16 times earnings for the average stock.

On August 5, 1986, Textron, Inc. offered to buy Ex-Cell-O for about $920 million, $68 per share, or almost 17 times earnings. During the next few days, the price of Ex-Cell-O closed up as high as $74.63 per share by the following week, apparently anticipating a rejection by Ex-Cell-O and "a better offer." Textron had 1985 sales of $5.7 billion, of which aerospace and defense business accounted for 49 percent.

The Ex-Cell-O board met August 13th to evaluate Textron's proposal and to consider its other options: seek to negotiate a higher price from Textron; initiate a leveraged buyout to take the company private; seek to merge the company with a "white knight." Separately, analysts had suggested that Rockwell International might be a possible alternative merger partner. Ex-Cell-O also might seek to poison the takeover by issuing a large amount of preferred stock to existing shareholders, thus diluting the value of present ownership.

On August 14th, the company rejected Textron's $68 per share acquisition proposal. The company's prepared statement indicated that the price was inadequate and did not recognize future earnings gains Ex-Cell-O stood to make from its ongoing restructuring effort. Later in the day on August 14th, executives of the two corporations met. Ex-Cell-O stock closed at $76.25. Officials met again several times over the next days.

On August 18th, Textron Inc. signed an agreement to acquire Ex-Cell-O Corporation for $77.50 per share, or $1.05 billion. The stock closed that day at $77 per share, down 12.5 cents. The agreed price was 44 percent above Ex-Cell-O's $53.75 stock price immediately before the announcement of the acquisition offer August 5th.

In announcing the agreement Ex-Cell-O's chairman, Paul Casey, indicated that the company had explored "all the alternatives" to the Textron proposal, including a leveraged buyout and holding discussions with other companies. Textron's Dolan said he expected "synergy" by mixing the aerospace operations of the two companies. No stranger to acquisitions, Textron had recently purchased Avco Corporation for $1.4 billion, in pursuit of a path of "balanced diversification." Said Dolan: "I do not expect Ex-Cell-O will be the last corporation that we will join forces with."

Textron, according to a report in *The Wall Street Journal,* would finance the merger initially with debt, pushing the ratio of debt to total capital from 40 percent to 57 percent. Analysts speculated that debt would be reduced by spinning off Textron's financial services business and Ex-Cell-O's machine tool business.

(Story assembled from newspaper sources, including The Wall Street Journal *and* The Detroit Free Press.*)*

THE ENVIRONMENT SPEAKS VI
Owens-Corning Thwarts Takeover Attempt by Wickes

On Wednesday, August 6th, 1986, Owens-Corning Fiberglas Corporation reported it had received a takeover proposal from Wickes Co. The offer was $70 per share for all 29.9 million outstanding shares, or a value of $2.1 billion. Owens-Corning, a Toledo-based manufacturer, has interests in glass fiber, insulation and other construction products.

Wickes indicated that it already owned between eight and 10 percent of Owens-Corning, obtained through open market purchases of the stock. Wickes previously had sought to acquire National Gypsum Company for $1.23 billion, but failed in the attempt when National Gypsum countered with a $1.64 leveraged buyout bid that took the company private. Wickes had over $400 million in tax loss credits resulting from its recent operating difficulties and was anxious to acquire profitable firms in the building products business. Other possible firms mentioned included USG Corp. and Jim Walter Corporation. Wickes operated businesses in lumber, home furnishings, apparel, manufacturing and retailing.

In response to the offer, officials of Owens-Corning would only say that they would "consider all available alternatives, including the possibility of maximizing short-term values through a fundamental change in our business structure."

On Friday, August 8th, Moody's Investors Service Inc. announced that it intended to review the ratings of Owens-Corning Fiberglas Corp.'s senior long-term debt and short-term commercial paper. The review was motivated, according to Moody's, by two possibilities. First, Owens-Corning might undertake defensive measures that would increase its financial risk. Second, if the acquisition were to occur, "the combined companies' interest coverage would be minimal, and internal cash flow might be inadequate to cover ongoing spending requirements; however, asset sales could relieve some of this pressure."

During August, Wickes' bid became hostile, after Owens-Corning announced it would fight the takeover, and Wickes countered with a lawsuit challenging Owens-Corning's takeover defenses.

On Thursday, August 28th, Owens-Corning announced a sweeping recapitalization plan. Owens-Corning would sell its recently acquired aerospace and strategic materials group and certain other assets. The company would also borrow $1.5 billion under loan agreements with banks and would incur an additional $300 million in long-term debt by distributing subordinated debentures to shareholders. In addition to receiving $35 principal amount of debentures, shareholders would receive $52 in cash for each share held.

On Friday, August 29th, Wickes terminated its offer for Owens-Corning, after selling 303,700 shares of Owens-Corning stock that it had purchased earlier for an indicated gain of at least $8.7 million. Some analysts estimated the gain at closer to $10 million. Wickes reportedly continued to hold an option to purchase 2.2 million Owens-Corning shares at $61, compared with the $79.25 closing price of the stock on Friday. In terminating its offer, Wickes also dropped litigation against Owens-Corning regarding the company's takeover defense measures.

Wickes said it "may determine to purchase shares of Owens' stock in the open market or otherwise," presumably if the stock price dropped low enough to make a renewed takeover attempt interesting.

According to *The Wall Street Journal,* an analyst at Merrill Lynch & Co. referred to Wickes' efforts to acquire a building products company as "very successful greenmail" that has "built up their war chest even more." The analyst also commented on the multiple unsuccessful attempts to acquire companies in the building products industry, saying that if the company continued to force targets to react in the same way, Wickes may "end up forcing the whole industry private."

(Compiled from reports in The Wall Street Journal.*)*

Enterprises not actively pursuing R&D at the boundaries of scientific and technological knowledge can benefit from development by others. Environmental scanning activities can help prepare the alert observer to become an early competitor, subcontractor, supplier or licensee in the commercialization of these developments [497;506]. An architect, who years ago identified computer-aided design (CAD) as an emerging *pacing technology* with explosive potential, and acted strategically to plan for its possible commercial reality, is better prepared for the cost pressures of contemporary building construction in a competitive marketplace. Today, the rate of technological substitution of CAD systems for drafting tables threatens the ability of a manual shop to compete on cost and responsiveness. The CAD threat extends to career opportunities for draftsmen and design engineers, and to market opportunities for companies such as Great American Steel Equipment Corp. of Woodside, New York, a manufacturer of drafting tables, and Dietzgen Corporation of Des Plaines, Illinois, a manufacturer of drafting equipment and supplies.

New technology has spread from designing and drawing into pattern-making and prototyping. According to a report in *The Wall Street Journal* (see *The Environment Speaks VII*), General Motors is a beta-test site for a laser-driven prototype maker developed by 3D Systems, Inc. that promises to reduce the time necessary to build a prototype from days or months to minutes or hours. This technology has proven itself only in its own prototype stage, and still could fail as a commercially viable process. Even so, few firms that rely on prototyping should ignore the potential impact of this technology.

Once a new technology is developed, it competes with existing technologies in the competitive dimension as a *product,* or in the operational dimension as a *resource* or a *process.* As the drafting illustration indicates, consequential spill-over effects occur backwards through the supply chain. Turning that process around, it becomes clear that the relevant technology scan for an organization includes the domain of its own products and processes, and that of the intermediate and end-use products to which it is related.

Technology forecasters have studied major product and process innovations over the past century, and many agree on two conclusions: 1) the process of technological substitution fits very comfortably to the well-known S-curve or logistic curve [522], and 2) there seems to be evidence that the *rate* of technological substitution, while variable across industry and type of innovation, has increased over the last century. Technologies are more quickly accepted now and mature sooner than before. Common examples of this trend are cited in Table 4.1.

Of these four examples, the first two are processes, the third a raw material and the last a product. These technological substitution examples are dispersed across environmental dimensions. Thus, while technology is strongly associated with the R&D function, it also influences the competitive dimension through product design and development, and the operating dimension through production and process engineering as well as resource innovation. Additionally, technology has its own set of stakeholders who will bear the costs or reap the benefits of its introduction. Depending on the power of those stakeholders, and the size of the "stakes," the pace of technological development and its subsequent life cycle may be accelerated or retarded. The early 1990s saw the commercialization of recordable laser discs. Primarily a Japanese technology, the major market was in the U.S. where the largest losers to this new innovation seem likely to be commercial film companies and sound recording studios.

THE ENVIRONMENT SPEAKS VII
New Machine has Possibilities as a Speedy Prototype Maker

As the machine goes to work, a dot of light moves jerkily across the surface of a vat of liquid in a series of patterns. After several minutes, the light disappears, and out pops a hollow plastic ball.

The machine is just showing off. Developed by 3D Systems Inc., a small start-up company based in Sylmar, Calif., the machine is aimed at much more serious uses. It will let companies produce in minutes or hours prototypes of products and parts designed on a computer.

Currently, that can take weeks or months. And if a first prototype turns out to have problems, it can take weeks to make another, then more weeks for a third.

"This has the potential to revolutionize the way we do business," says Al DeWitt, an advanced manufacturing engineer at the Fisher Guide Division of General

Motors Corp., which will be one of the test sites for the 3D Systems machine, starting in September.

The machine makes use of a class of plastic that solidifies when ultraviolet light strikes a liquid form of it — a process known as photopolymerization. To date, the plastics have been used for such purposes as making bathroom tiles that don't need waxing or making annual report covers glossy. But 3D Systems found it could do a sort of three-dimensional printing by using an ultraviolet laser.

Its machine uses the laser to draw on the surface of the liquid plastic the bottommost cross-section of the prototype, then it lowers that cross-section a fraction of an inch into the liquid and draws the next cross-section on top. By repeating the process thousands of times, the 3D Systems machine produces a solid copy, accurate to within five-thousandths of an inch, of whatever has been modeled in the computer. Small items take minutes; big ones take a few hours.

The machine still has limitations. At the moment, it can't produce objects bigger than one foot square. The variety of plastics that can be used needs to be expanded. And a lot of software remains to be written so the machine can be used with all the different computer-aided-design packages on the market and so it can produce more complex models.

The 3D Systems machine will cost around $250,000 and won't be generally available until early next year. Still, it seems likely to scratch a corporate itch.

Mr. DeWitt of GM says the machine has great possibilities if it's used to ensure the pieces of a car fit together. If, as a result of the prototype, someone spots a problem with a part or a tool, "it could potentially save months or even years," he says.

Ray Freed, chief executive of 3D Systems, says he hopes the machine will be used by companies making everything from telephones to turbines. He says the Pratt & Whitney division of United Technologies Corp., for instance, normally takes nine to 11 months to make the prototypes for turbine blades for a jet engine. He says his machine can produce the prototypes in a week.

Clarence Borgmeyer, manager of computational methods at Pratt & Whitney, says enough work remains to be done on the machine that "it's a long way away from a week." But, he adds, "It has that kind of potential . . . I think it has unlimited capability."

Table 4.1: Substitution Rates for Technology: Past and Present

Substitution	Time to grow from 10% to 90% acceptance
Steam for Sailing vessels	75 years
Open Hearth for Bessemer Steel	42 years
Synthetic for natural tire cord	18 years
Detergents for soaps	9 years

The Competitive Dimension

Products and markets are at the heart of the competitive dimension of the firm's environment. But product and market decisions are also at the heart of tactical decisions of the firm, taken in action against, and in reaction to, the competitive moves of others in the industry. Because much of an organization's knowledge about the competition is a part of the business of doing business, Porter [373;374] and others have described in elegant detail the process of *competitor analysis*. Porter's comprehensive approach is devised to diagnose competitors' "future *goals,* current *strategy, assumptions,* and *capabilities,*" and he suggests over 100 questions about each competitor as part of the diagnosis.

Where does competitor analysis end and environmental scanning begin? The essence of environmental scanning is in its future focus, and the future focus in the competitive dimension occurs when the question ceases to be *what is* and becomes *what will be.* The signals for what will be come from an environmental scanning effort — the interpretation of remote signals based on a thorough understanding of present competitive circumstances. Following Porter's theme, competitor analysis is vital for current strategic and tactical action. The present is also vital as the basis for understanding the possibilities/probabilities of the future, but understanding the present is not the goal of environmental scanning.

The relevant competitive future for the organization emerges with the prospects for new products, new competitors, new customers and potential customer attitudes. Changes in market growth rates, industry structures, economic conditions and government influences also affect the organization's competitive future. Broadly, the firm seeks to learn the nature, the intensity and the rules of future competition by searching for signals of what *is changing* and what *could change* based upon the goals and discretionary power of the "actors" in the competitive dimension.

Changes in industry structure and competitive balance can emerge from several sectors of the competitive dimension. The *nature of the product* is influenced by changes in the needs/requirements of customers, by new forms of distribution/delivery and by the emergence of substitutes/complements. The *nature of the market* is influenced by the motivation and ability of individual competitors to make strategic moves and by the combined effect of competitors' probable moves on competitive intensity. The *nature of the industry* is influenced by the possibility of changes in barriers to entry of new competitors. One aspect of entry barriers relates to the power of the firm to construct such barriers, as through experience, scale economies, or dominance over resources or distribution channels. Another aspect of these barriers is the prospect of changes in barriers the firm is powerless to control: changes that might make participation in the market, even by existing players, less desirable because of either higher barriers (product liability becomes uninsurable) or lower ones (product loyalty deteriorates), or changes that might benefit the firm by impacting only new entrants, such as distribution channels being fully utilized.

The industry sector is also influenced by the prospects of any new entry. The potential for a *positive growth gap,* where market potential exceeds the plans or abilities of existing competitors, will attract new competition. If a *negative growth gap* exists, because competitors' expected growth rates add up to more than market growth potential, then the future pattern of exit barriers and inertial barriers will influence the actions and abilities of existing industry participants:

What changes are likely to occur — or can be made to occur — in barriers to exit from the industry faced by all participants, or *perceived to exist* by individual competitors?

What changes are likely to occur in the barriers individual competitors face because of *inertia?*

Continental Airlines and Wilson Foods temporarily changed an exit barrier when their Chapter 11 bankruptcy filings allowed them to break existing labor contracts. Another barrier is damage to the corporate image by withdrawal from a principal market, such as a steel company withdrawing from steel manufacture. Can customers' attitudes be altered so that diversified suppliers can safely withdraw from one market without affecting relationships in another market with the same customers?

U.S. Steel, for example, already generated well in excess of half its revenues from oil, gas and other non-steel businesses in July 1986 when the company removed steel from its name to become USX Corporation. USX may have had no choice but to alter the focus of its businesses. The U.S. market for steel declined almost 60 percent from 1978 to 1986, largely as a result of the 27 percent decrease over that period in the poundage of carbon steel used in the average American car. U.S. manufacturers' share of the steel market declined from 87 percent to 77 percent during the same period. In some specialty product lines, such as steel pipe and tubing, foreign manufacturers had gained more than a 50 percent market share [33;158;491].

If markets are competitively intense because of a negative growth differential, interest in the future prospects for competitor reactions is heightened. Is there likely to be a change in the *inertia* that prevents competitors from responding to the organization's strategies? MacMillan and McCafferty [296] developed a topology of such barriers due to inertia, including:

- Response will interfere with current strategy.
- Belief that other's move is non-threatening.
- Distracted by own problems or opportunities.
- Other's move not seen.
- Market in which move made seen as inconsequential.
- Structure of competitor prevents response.
- Competitor not prepared to revise policy or practice to respond.
- Competitor confused by own bureaucracy.

There are rich implications in these barriers, and the opportunity for capitalizing through scanning on subtle changes in rich environments is significant. For other views on competitive analysis, see [21;26;55;154;182;191;251;317;379;432;457;534].

The Stakeholder Dimension

The interests and attitudes of the various stakeholders in the organization can have an important impact on the firm's success in financing, producing, distributing and selling its products or services. A stakeholder is an entity with which the firm has a mutual relationship, or interdependence. Some sectors of the stakeholder dimension consist almost exclusively of *people,* but the term also includes the social systems and agents that represent the interests of people, and the infrastructure which surrounds and supports people. Employees are individuals and groups of individuals, as are shareholders and customers. But even these groups have institutional elements that are part of the stakeholder-organization interdependence. Employees form and operate credit unions and labor unions, for example, which develop their own agendas independent from — and perhaps in conflict with — the people they represent. Shareholders as a sector encompass individuals who own shares and the institutions that own shares in their behalf, such as insurance companies, mutual funds and pension funds. The shareholder sector includes actual and potential share owners, and the advisors, analysts and agents that represent investors — the support and execution system in the financial markets. The community and society sector of the stakeholder dimension also combines infrastructure with people to include schools, roads, churches, sewers, hospitals and local businesses supporting people.

The state of being of the stakeholder entity influences the organization, and that of the organization influences the entity. The same can be said of *changes* in the state of being. It is largely these changes that are the focus of environmental scanning in the stakeholder dimension — changes possible or probable in the future that could alter the direction, latitude or effectiveness of organizational strategy and behavior — as opportunities, as threats or as planning assumptions. The organization may evaluate, or be evaluated on, its track record in the stakeholder dimension according to models of corporate social performance (see, for example, Wartick and Cochran [510], Daneke and Lemak [105]).

The stakeholder dimension reflects both trends and abrupt shifts in societal norms and values; personal preferences and life styles; community attitudes and support; customer tastes; suppliers' business practices; shareholder risk/reward expectations; and employee health, safety, morale and commitment. Stakeholder attitudes may represent the primary driving force behind major changes in the size and growth of markets and behind the pace and acceptance of new technology. For example, animal rights groups and government oversight influence the pace of new drug testing and introductions. Social values may retard the acceptability of new technology in the marketplace, such as with disposable clothing. In Sawyer's words, "While technology is the critical variable for development of new products, social factors often determine whether anyone will buy them" [415,110].

Scanning the stakeholder dimension involves seeking to detect long-run trends and hypothesize future events that could emerge from the social systems they represent. Some demographics — e.g., birth, death and disease rates — have long-run consequences that can be studied for opportunity and risk arising *from the trend itself.* Generally, these long-run trends have the lowest scanning payoffs except for those firms who have been relatively insensitive to their current environment, where many of those trend consequences have been promulgated already. Nevertheless, it is possible that such general analyses and predictions will miss outcome patterns significant to a unique organization.

Other demographics — e.g., migration and employment patterns — are more subject to shifts and reversals and can be studied for signals of those shifts and reversals as sources of opportunity and risk (see *The Environment Speaks VIII*). Because there is less standardization in belief and understanding about these issues, there is also less generic analysis, and less awareness. Thus, the potential payoffs to scanning by a single organization are higher than is generally the case with long-term trend scanning. (See Wilson [523]).

The cumulative effects of globalization and technological advancement may ignite our awareness of significant stakeholder issues in the human resource area in years to come. Issues related to employee/employer rights, education and retraining, productivity and competitiveness, quality of work life and impacts of technology are prevalent in the current literature [49]. For a synthesis of the major issues in this area, see Burack [59;60].

The stakeholder dimension also includes the *natural environment* representing the natural physical and ecological surroundings of humankind, from which life, pleasure, and wealth are drawn. Humankind, people and organizations, are charged as trustees with the protection of the natural environment, and they have tended to polarize in their attitudes and values about the environment [Ullman: 487]. Also, the natural environment includes some uncontrollable elements — Mother Nature, if you will — and encompasses floods and droughts, extremes in temperatures, storms and earthquakes, as well as depleting and renewable resources.

Much of the uncontrollable natural environment defies prediction, although recent progress in forecasting violent weather is itself a signal of a possible future breakthrough. The remainder of the natural environment is more amenable to scanning and forecasting, since it is *interactive* with humankind, and commonly manifests impacts and reaction gradually over long time spans. With the recognition of possible cumulative consequences of industrial and population density for the world about us, society has become better attuned to faint signal scanning of this environment. Measurement is more routine than ever before, and thus more environmental information is available to scanners.

Resource scarcity, particularly of hydrocarbon-based fossil fuels, and pollution impacts are extant, and as well-known trends have little intrinsic value to the organization. Both scarcity and pollution can and will continue to deliver *events* to society at large, and perhaps uniquely to individual organizations or industries. The prospect of those events invites environmental scanning.

Breakthrough potential exists for scanning in at least two areas of the natural environment: one is in the safe substitution of new energy resources for fossil fuels — a cross-dimensional issue with technology. Another possible breakthrough could come in the understanding of the environmental impact of human and plant genetic experimentation.

THE ENVIRONMENT SPEAKS VIII
Migration Predictions Aren't Error-Free

John Kasarda, chairman of the sociology department at the University of North Carolina at Chapel Hill and a leading demographic researcher, hates population and growth projections even as he is making them. One of his most recent projections sees the population of the Southern states catching and passing the North about the year 2030, but he also knows "there are too many unpredictables. Unforeseen events can disrupt the most scientifically sound projections."

They have done just that in the last five years. In 1981, George Masnick and others at the Joint Center for Housing Studies, run by Harvard University and Massachusetts Institute of Technology, published a carefully reasoned book called "Regional Diversity," attempting to anticipate economic and population growth patterns through 1990. Among their central predictions: ongoing booms in the South and West, accompanied by stagnancy in much of the industrial North and continuing flight from its major metropolitan areas.

"There were dozens of factors at work," Masnick said in a recent interview, "so people were pretty confident at that point in saying that New York would continue to lose population, that the Rust Belt would remain in decline or equilibrium.

"The metropolitan areas' housing costs were too high, the labor costs were too high, they had unmanageable bureaucracies . . . . People seemed to be jumping a sinking ship. But things just didn't work out that way."

Instead, cooling economies and the mixed blessing of fewer newcomers distinguish many of the Sunbelt's erstwhile boom cities these days — especially those that rose and fell with world oil prices. At the same time, economic activity is up and unemployment rates are below the national average in such metropolitan areas as

Boston, Hartford, Providence, Newark, Baltimore, Philadelphia, Dayton, Kalamazoo, Milwaukee and Indianapolis. Anyone predicting such a turnabout a decade ago would have seemed less involved with serious economics than dark humor.

* * * * *

Because of immigration into [Texas, Florida, Georgia, California, and Arizona], not only by Americans but also by Asians and Hispanics, 90 percent of the population growth in the entire United States since 1980 has been in the South and West, a total of 11.4 million by Kasarda's calculations, compared with just over one million in the Northern and Midwestern states combined. Are those Sunbelt growth trends likely to continue so strongly? Or might continued growth, even though slower than in the recent past, still exceed the tolerance and livability of Orlando, Atlanta, Austin, Tucson or San Diego?

Or will a new surge in oil prices, a change in the volume of imported goods or a high-technology breakthrough comparable to the semiconductor revolution change all the rules again?

It is impossible to say; the last 15 years have delivered the U.S. into a new era in social mobility, economic restructuring and inter-regional competition for employment and investment, and also in its economic relations with the rest of the world.

(Reprinted, with permission, from Gary Blonston, "A Special Report: The Changing Face of America: Migration," The Detroit Free Press, July 20, 1986, p. 1B.)

The Omnipresence of Government and Economies

Government is present everywhere across the sectors and dimensions of the organization's external environment. The government sets limits, makes rules, allocates, competes for and absorbs resources. In performing these functions, government creates opportunities for some and threats for others, and the impact of government on any single organization can be either beneficial or cost-dominant. The challenge to the organization is to identify the ways in which emerging government policies might affect it, in *any or all* of the dimensions of the environment. Examples of the pervasiveness of governments across dimensions are presented in Table 4.2.

Governments may be federal, state and local, foreign or domestic. The wider the sphere of operation of the organization, the greater and potentially less consistent is government influence. Moreover, the locus of government involvement varies with time and with issues, from administrative to executive to legislative to judicial. Governments are capable of delivering *events* that can impact heavily as opportunities or threats on individuals and groups. Rarely, however, are such events without precursor signals, such as the publicizing of abuses, issue speeches, proposed rules and introduction of legislation, prosecutions and appeals, and lastly, political threats and intimidation.

Table 4.2: Influences of Government Across Dimensions of the Environment

Competitive	product standards, merger limits, export licenses, import restrictions, anti-trust.
Financial	central banking, deficit financing, money market operations, policing and regulation of markets and institutions.
Operational	reporting rules, tax rates and incentives, surplus commodity storage, strategic material stockpiling.
Technological	research funding; research regulation, e.g., DNA, nuclear.
Stakeholders	job training, EEO, accounting and financial reporting rules, pension funding, collective bargaining, corrupt practices litigation.

Government is deliberate if not predictable, and the content of future agendas that will seek legislative and public support can be read in advance. See for example, the development of events and literature on the issue of Federal income tax simplification in Chapter 7. Significant tax simplification actually occurred in 1986, even though the issue appeared dead a year earlier. The more or less inevitable signs of this change were visible as early as 1978 to close observers of the behavior of government institutions and the written record of expert advocates' research and opinion.

Government changes over time as power shifts between and within branches, and philosophies change. These dynamics influence the speed, the predictability and even the outcomes of future government agendas. At the present moment there may be some firm- and industry-specific payoffs from devoting scanning energies to the future composition and probable postures of the U.S. Supreme Court: will a fundamental philosophical shift occur and on what large issues will it impact most heavily? Will government policy toward industry evolve away from trade protection, subsidies, bailouts and legislative incentives? What intermediate and ultimate outcomes can occur, and when?

Economies have broad effects on people and on organizations. In the dimensional scheme described in Figure 4.1 at the beginning of this chapter, economies are defined as sectors of the competitive, operational and financial dimensions. This scheme does not ignore "people effects" but instead implies that the economic effects on people will work their way through products, markets, resources, money, and credit.

More future forecasts are available about economies than about any other sector in the environment, including forecasts of national and international aggregates, industry, product and company shipments. Acquiring and interpreting such forecasts is a relevant part of intermediate-term strategy in production, pricing, product development, capital asset acquisition and financing decisions. The nature of industry and its growth potential are heavily dependent on the behavior of government revenue, its expenditures and taxation, and on the timing and amplitude of economic cycles. Long-term plant location decisions are influenced by regional domestic and country risk analyses that are economic as well as political and demographic.

Another class of economic futures studies that is relevant to the organization relates to economic structure, as distinct from economic performance. Structure studies most frequently arise in consideration of country risk, as when the prospects and effects of a shift from republican to socialist government in France was an issue in the recent past. It is also reasonable to focus scanning on the evolution of the United States' economic structure. Current issues with potentially significant future outcomes might include the independence of the Federal Reserve System from direct legislative or executive control, the viability of tax policy in fiscal management, continued public acceptance of deficit financing; also, federal-local power shifts, public tax capacity, domestic market maturity and entrepreneurship, and availability of capital.

Dimensions, Not Blinders

Dimensioning and sub-dividing the environment for scanning purposes increases the probability that signals in the environment will be accurately observed and successfully decoded. The inherent danger of this approach is that we may over-simplify, for some emerging issues may not be identified unless elements of more than one dimension are combined. Emerging issues related to robotics will be characterized differently if they arise from the combined perspectives of the stakeholder, technology and operational dimensions than if viewed from the technological perspective alone. This danger serves only to emphasize the fact that successful environmental scanning is neither a solitary nor a tactical activity. Specialists, reflecting all of the dimensions and important segments of the firm, should interactively identify key emerging issues; Chapter 6 will discuss this idea. Finally, scanning must be undertaken as a strategy to learn and capitalize on the implications of the future, the subject of the next chapter.

CHAPTER 5

GUIDELINES FOR A SCANNING STRATEGY

For an environmental scanning strategy to be successful in the long-term, it must yield benefits exceeding its cost through its contribution to maximizing the risk-adjusted net present value of the organization. Environmental scanning promotes behavior that makes a contribution in *every dimension* of the valuation model:

- by reducing the risk exposure of the firm and thereby decreasing the risk-adjusted discount rate;

- by increasing the magnitude of cash inflows (from captured opportunities) or advancing the timing of those cash flows (accessing opportunities sooner);

- by decreasing the magnitude of cash outflows (from the impact of threats) or retarding the timing of those cash flows (through actions that delay or postpone threats).

Thus, the level of investment in scanning and the choice of specific scanning activities are elements of managerial judgment which, because of their impact on firm value, have direct strategic content. The value manifestation of properly designed environmental scanning is observable mainly through qualitative actions and outputs, while the costs of scanning efforts can be more easily measured. That is, these efforts may be vital to firm success, but problematic for budgetary decisions in the short run because of measurement difficulties.

The sections and chapters that follow present a multi-element framework for the strategic determination of where to invest in environmental scanning. This framework should result in a pure benefit-cost approach as a guide to incorporating environmental scanning into the organization's culture and strategic management fabric. The elements of that framework are identified in Table 5.1, and are the subjects of the remainder of this book, with all but the last three introduced in this chapter.

Setting the Environmental Focal Zone

Operational, financial, technological, competitive and *stakeholder;* the distinct nature of the five dimensions of the environment influences the organization directly through its task environment and indirectly through the remote environment. The first strategic decisions in the design of a scanning system are to allocate scanning resources across these dimensions, and within each dimension out to an appropriate degree of remoteness. These decisions establish the *environmental focal zone.* In analog terms, one could imagine this

56

zone as an ink blot superimposed on the dimensioned environment, as in Figure 5.1. The size of the focal zone reflects the total amount of resources committed to scanning. The *shape* of the focal zone depicts the dimensional emphasis appropriate to an individual firm. The organization illustrated in the figure, for example, chose to devote more resources to technological scanning than operational scanning and to emphasize the remote environment in the technological dimension more than in some other dimensions.

Table 5.1: Elements of a Scanning System

1. Environmental focal zone.

2. Scanning range settings.
   a. Plausibility.
   b. Time.
   c. Geography.

3. Environmental information collection format.
   a. Continuity of monitoring.
   b. Methods of monitoring.
   c. Formalism of monitoring modes.
   d. Sources monitored.

4. Scanning input processing methods.

5. Managing and communicating within the scanning system.

Signal inputs should be sought across all five dimensions of the environment. Expenditures might differ across dimensions or across sectors within dimensions because of differences in the difficulty of acquiring or interpreting environmental inputs from more remote or less familiar territory. Complex environments might also cause higher relative costs in some dimensions: Culnan [102] found that complexity of environments led managers to seek less accessible information sources.

If all dimensions are important, and unfamiliar ones are more costly to scan, why do surveys show that the incidence of scanning in the product/market or competitive dimension — the most familiar territory — surpasses all others? Aguilar [5] found that 58 percent of the information executives acquired came from the competitive sector. Other studies have found the figure to range from 60 percent to 33 percent, all in excess of the effort expended in other sectors [94;233;238]. An individual firm may focus its efforts more heavily in the competitive sector for good strategic reasons. But these survey responses could also reflect the natural predisposition of most managers to deal with tactical issues. In the tactical, day-to-day task environment of organizations that sell products into markets, the greatest magnitude of external contact occurs in the task-competitive environment. Many signals arise *spontaneously* from this sector, whereas they must be *sought* from other sectors and especially from the remote environment.

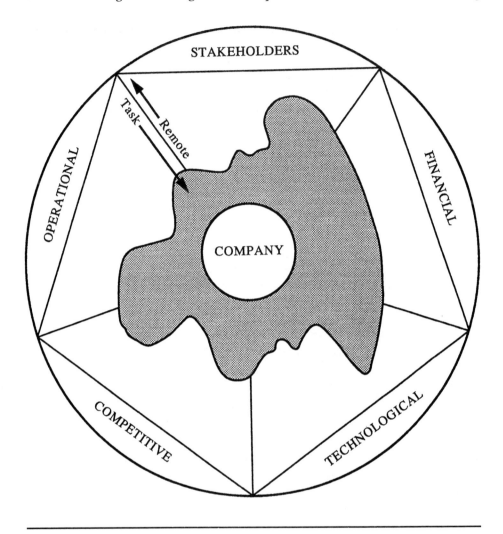

Figure 5.1: Environmental Focal Zone

Proper balance across dimensions in a scanning system relates in part to the impetus within the firm for undertaking new or expanded environmental scanning efforts. The aggressive organization is most likely to be oriented toward gaining strategic advantage, an orientation that is highly consistent with the purpose of scanning. For example, a recent study differentiated 270 S&L's according to six measures of strategic momentum. The high-momentum respondents scanned more broadly, focusing greater resources on learning about customers and about new acquisition, investment and market opportunities. Their lower-momentum counterparts were notably more defensive in their scanning approaches, and perhaps more passive as well. They concentrated most of their scanning efforts on learning about competitive and regulatory threats [214].

Passive scanners are more likely to confront problems or threats that emerge unexpectedly from the task environment and are unexplained because the firm doesn't know much about the competition, the industry or the markets for its raw materials. Such an organization has two needs. First, it needs to learn about the competition and the industry as it stands today; this is a vital precursor to environmental scanning. Second, it needs to develop a scanning system to trap signals of future events that could influence its strategies and success. The investment in scanning is separate from the investment in explaining what happened; if the two are combined into one "external information cost" total, the resource allocation across dimensions could appear to be biased.

The goal of *scanning all dimensions* assures that the firm will make at least some scanning investment in every dimension of the environment and thereby increase the chances of capturing cross-dimensional implications. As an example, consider the impact of increasing pollution in the natural environment *(stakeholder)* on cost and productivity in polluting industries *(operational)* requiring new methods of control *(technology)*. Heavy investment must be made in response, with little promised return, using funds from the capital markets *(financial)*, with an end result of greater capital intensity in production *(operational)* increasing the potential of reduced employment *(stakeholders)*.

A variety of factors can influence the way in which an organization may adjust its scanning efforts toward an environmental focal zone that closely matches its real needs. Several general approaches and some specific issues regarding the design of the environmental focal zone are presented for consideration.

Governments, Economies and Environmental Focal Zone. The broad influence of these two sectors across the environmental dimension was discussed in the previous chapter. Because no organization is immune from the future course and structural changes that emanate from these sectors, *all organizations* should devote scanning resources to assessing environmental futures in each dimension as they relate to government, economic conditions and structure. The research that the U.S. government is funding today among universities, think tanks and military contractors will become the technology of tomorrow, and the production processes and product opportunities of the days after that. The same can be said of presently observable signals from the legislative, judicial and economic policy/structures that will lead to new policies in the future.

Organizations that fail to scan in these two sectors because they "can't do anything about the state of government or the economy" have missed the point. The purpose of environmental scanning is to achieve maximum control over the *organization's* strategic future, not to achieve control over the factors or dimensions of the economy. But there is evidence that organizations *can and do* influence government through legislative and policy advocacy efforts, and the economy through group actions such as strikes and cumulative individual actions such as capital equipment purchase decisions.

Critical Success Factors and Environmental Focal Zone. At the first level of environmental analysis, the critical characteristics, events, conditions and variables that drive the success of an organization — its critical success factors — can help define the organization's information needs and scanning strategy [265]. To enlist the aid of these factors, which should be well-known as an outcome of strategic planning efforts, it is necessary to push *backwards* from them into the environment to find the key elements there that could influence each factor. For example, managers might be asked to suggest the external environmental sources of five positive and five negative impacts for each of the organization's critical success factors. For those sources identified that were too closely related to the task environment, managers could be asked in a second round to suggest a number of more remote possible sources of impact for *those* sources of impact. Frequency tallies by environmental dimension, sector within dimension and source of impact within sector could become the foundation for an estimated *importance allocation* of environmental scanning resources.

Ultimately, the environment itself will shape and reshape these critical success factors (CSFs); thus it is dangerous to cling to any *existing* set as the device for limiting the scope of environmental scanning after an initial calibration. A better subsequent approach is to validate a revised set of CSFs based on scanning outcomes, as follows:

1. What evidence does the *task environment* provide that existing CSFs are still valid and important? Do the behaviors in competitive and resource markets continue to support the assumptions upon which those CSFs were built? How rapidly are those behaviors evolving?

2. In what way has the organization itself changed so that factors critical to its success before no longer apply? For example, Chrysler Corporation was critically cash-flow dependent during its financial crisis, and that CSF drove a significant portion of its environmental scanning (especially economic conditions and interest rates) and operating strategy, *but only until debt was reduced to a manageable level,* whereupon both scanning and secondary business strategies changed.

3. What signals can be detected in the *remote environment* that support the emergence of *new or different* critical success factors at the horizon?

4. Identify five sources from deep in the environment with positive and negative impact on each new and revised CSF.

The partitioning of the environment implied by these questions essentially focuses task environment analysis on demonstrating that CSFs are the same and focuses remote environment analysis on demonstrating that CSFs are imminently changing. Because the firm's critical success factors emanate from its culture and strategy, and are fundamentally related to the environment to begin with, there is a good chance that the list of *critical environmental questions and sectors for scanning* that emerge from this approach will be comprehensive.

Market Strategy and Environmental Focal Zone. Market strategy can alter environmental sensitivity and scanning needs in the organization's task environment. For example, a concentration strategy, through which the firm seeks to grow by delivering existing technology to existing markets, implies the need for increased future focus on:

Technology	for substitute product possibilities that could affect market growth and new production methodologies that could affect cost structure;
Competitive	in the government sector for emerging policies that could affect the possibility or the risk of horizontal mergers;
Stakeholders	especially in a mature market, for the risk of takeover by an aggressor seeking harvested cash flows.

For a firm with this concentration strategy, the operational and financial segments of the environment would receive correspondingly less emphasis.

Alternatively, consider a firm following concentric diversification as one of the turbulence-insulating strategies discussed in Chapter 3. By diversifying with a market development strategy — seeking new markets for existing technology — the organization would face a similar technology challenge, and would probably have heightened financial dimension scanning needs because of an increased reliance on the markets for financing internal development or acquisitions. But the stakeholder dimension might hold less special interest if absorption of excess financial resources into new investment reduces the threat of a hostile takeover attempt.

Organizations pursuing concentric diversification through new technology or product development strategies might shift the focus of their technological scanning further out toward the boundaries of knowledge, with more or less intensity depending on their capacity or interest in innovation. For such firms, emerging and developed technology should already have been incorporated in their product development and diversification activities in the task environment.

These examples suggest ways in which environmental scanning could be adapted to other market strategies. Future-focused environmental scanning should be structured to extend beyond the knowledge base that supports the conduct of a strategy. Scanning should be adapted to incorporate new sectors and potential issues occasioned by the limits in focus of that strategy.

Market Dominance and Environmental Focal Zone. The organization that dominates its market, because of market strength or low cost, and frequently both, confronts different environmental scanning needs. Because of its dominance, the organization plays an important role in determining at least part of its own environment. While the dominant firm needs to maintain competitive surveillance, the focus of scanning shifts more to market/ industry issues and away from those of product/competition. Meanwhile, the competitors may see the dominant firm as their principal environment. In announcing a new line of accessories compatible with IBM products, a vice president of Burroughs Corp. commented: "These products will enhance our ability to co-exist in an atmosphere created by the competition. IBM is more than the competition; they're the environment we compete in."

Dominant firms focus scanning efforts more heavily in the operational dimension, where a cost advantage must be maintained in the long run. They may have a greater need to scan the stakeholder dimension because of their visibility to many publics. These firms are interested in technology from a developmental perspective; existing technology has already been factored into their task environments to allow them to achieve a cost advantage. They are less focused on the financial dimension because their recognized dominance in the industry provides a cachet that gives them access to money and capital on favorable terms.

Innovators and Environmental Focal Zone. Innovators push technology into the marketplace and must do basic market research in their competitive environments as part of their product development strategy. But their scanning focus on the competitive environment is less than others, because as long as innovation continues, their products create their own demand. Thus, competitors are less important in their task environment, and market/industry growth issues are less important in the remote environment.

Technology is vital to the success of the pure innovator, and the technology focus in the task environment must be supplemented with a strong technology focus in environmental scanning, to feed the pipeline with new engines for automation. Because of heavy reliance on external capital and debt to fund rapid growth, such firms may also need to focus added scanning resources on the financial dimension. This is a difficult task for many technology-based organizations because of their typical structure under the control of a founding genius who may be bored by discussions of economic and financial issues. Operational issues, along with most competitive issues, do not come to the forefront as long as the innovation strategy succeeds, except, perhaps, for long term critical resource inputs to the product.

Innovators need to anticipate when the need to become market- and cost-competitive will occur. For example, *The Environment Speaks IX* describes the transition experience of Lotus Development Corporation, as its superstar product, Lotus 1-2-3, began to mature. By coupling scanning in the technology area with product planning efforts, an innovator organization might detect signals of a coming slowdown in innovation. That signal should motivate the firm to focus both strategy and scanning more on competitive and operational issues than in the past, since that is where the challenge will emerge when the product no longer sells itself. The detection of this kind of signal relies on an existing and ongoing environmental scanning system.

Turbulence and Environmental Focal Zone. In Chapter 3, uncertainty in the environment was identified as a function of turbulence and signal strength. When turbulence is high and signals from the environment are weak, a complex environmental scanning problem exists; evidence shows that executives increase the frequency of their scanning [104;267]. Two measures of industry volatility have been developed and validated that can be used to judge current environmental turbulence [260;480;47;439;440]. These measures may be useful signals of the need to adjust the frequency or intensity of monitoring, discussed later in this chapter. They may also be useful in adjusting the environmental focal zone. The two measures are:

Market Volatility	the average of coefficients of variation in sales revenue changes for the firms in the industry;
Technological Volatility	the average of ratios of R&D plus capital expenditures to total assets for the firms in the industry.

High market volatility implies the need to increase the proportion of scanning resources in both the competitive and operational sectors. High market volatility may imply shortened product life cycles, frequent shifts in the composition and strategies of the competition, and increased sensitivity to economic cycles. High market volatility might also arise from resource issues — availability of raw materials and other factors of production — or capacity limitations. High market volatility may place special pressures on future operational and competitive decisions.

High technological volatility refers jointly to significant investment in new plant and equipment, either for growth or for replacement, and to high rates of investment in the development of either product or production technology. If current growth is driving the volatility measure, the future issues rest heavily in the competitive sector (future market growth, new competitive entry) and operational sector (productivity and cost-effectiveness when growth slows). If replacement of capacity is driving volatility, productivity is a *present issue* and enhanced scanning in technology and finance is needed to optimize the search for production and financing resources to assure future competitiveness.

Organizations in low-technology industries should be cautious to avoid under-investing in technology scanning. Substitute products often arise from technologies outside the present standards and thinking, and therefore outside of the perception of most managers in the industry, a category of risk that increases with market size.

Stakeholder Interdependence and Environmental Focal Zone. Scanning emphasis in the stakeholder dimension should be related to the organization's visibility, to its dependence upon, and to its interaction with the sectors of that dimension of the environment. Large organizations, especially if dominant, tend to have higher visibility. Industries or firms that have high dependencies on a stakeholder group or sector can benefit more from future-focused scanning in those sectors, and in areas that could impact on those sectors. For example:

brewers	depend on	*local water quality.*
utilities	depend on	*investors.*
contractors	depend on	*trade unions.*

THE ENVIRONMENT SPEAKS IX
Lotus Development: From Technology to Marketing

Many of the recent examples of innovation have been in computer hardware and software development, and one of the most vivid among these is Lotus Development Corporation and its premier product, Lotus 1-2-3. In 1986, four years after it emerged as a high-flying startup company with 1-2-3 in its pocket, Lotus grew to a $225 million company, with an installed base of 1.5 million users. Lotus 1-2-3, a remarkably powerful and innovative second-generation spreadsheet software product (Visi-Calc was the premier first-generation product), became the standard for the concept of spreadsheet calculator software. It spawned, but largely ignored, competition. The product sold itself. Lotus 1-2-3 has now matured as a product, and Lotus Development faces the question of how to continue to maximize shareholder value. This is an almost textbook case of "technology push," with Lotus the innovator relying almost exclusively on the technology dimension of its environment to provide the impetus for growth. When technology development slows and existing opportunities have been exploited, operational and competitive dimensions represent a source for continued growth and value creation.

For Lotus Development Corp., this refocus became evident through a variety of changes. The *operations* of the company were refocused, as the founding president (Mitchell Kapor) stepped aside from the CEO position in 1986, bringing in a new president (James Manzi) to manage growth. Manzi has said that the development of another product as innovative as 1-2-3 is a "fundamental impossibility." Ten of the 13 top positions in the company turned over. Lotus became equally as concerned with investing excess cash productively as with fundamental product development. The company undertook a stock repurchase program of up to ten percent of its outstanding shares as a means of assuring maximum shareholder value in the short run and as a takeover defense.

The firm began to invest heavily in *market development* and in *product development*. Earlier, Lotus hadn't even tried to market its products in Japan. In 1986, Lotus opened a Tokyo office to sell a Japanese version of Lotus 1-2-3. Demonstrating its new marketing sensitivity, Lotus incorporated a digital "mouse" in the Japanese version to overcome the keyboard fear of potential older-generation users. Previous U.S. versions of the product had never incorporated that facility. New products were being developed through large expenditures on fundamental R&D for the long term and through acquisition of small software companies for the short term. Most new products took the form of enhancements to the 1-2-3 operating environment, to improve data capture, provide word processing and text interfaces, and to enhance the software-to-user language interface. To penetrate a new market, Lotus developed a product for mainframe computers to ease the translation of data into microprocessor formats; this product put Lotus in touch with corporate data processing managers to a greater extent than ever before. Finally, Lotus began to promote its products more aggressively than ever — products like HAL, Manuscript and Metro — to try to get a measure of broad acceptance that might lead to multiple purchases by corporate clients, the kind of broad acceptance that Lotus 1-2-3 generated on its own innovative merits.

Lotus Development is an example of a company that migrated from a highly focused innovator to a more mature growth company requiring operating strategies, financial strategies, product strategies, market strategies and promotion strategies. To support this broader strategic thrust, the company has become sensitive to a broader range of environmental dimensions than at any time in its past.

[Sources: 515;530]

High interaction with stakeholders also implies enhanced scanning payoffs. Paper companies are influenced by the natural environment, as by forest resources and federal land logging leases, and in turn influence it, as by waste water discharge. Dominant employers in a community are interactive with it.

Stakeholder group relevance does not flow only from demographics or categories of representation. Stakeholder alliances and networks may form around issues; indeed the issue created by an organization's action or decision may coalesce these groups and alliances into important constituencies with far more than their original collective influence. Weiner and Brown [513] suggest a multi-step model for identifying and analyzing stakeholder groups based on a careful definition of issues and their elements, of stakeholder attitudes and influences, and of possible responses and outcomes. They suggest that stakeholder mobilization can occur if elements of an issue affect:

- health and safety
- values or lifestyles
- related third parties
  (in a politician's district)

- economic loss or gain
- popular myths and beliefs
- relative power positions
  (as in bargaining)

Fahey and Narayanan advocate the study of a set of judgmental questions in assessing and projecting changes in stakeholder characteristics, especially value and lifestyle changes [152,100-102]: For a value trend or pattern, what are the forces driving the change? What is the nature of the change, its compatibility with present values, and the distribution of costs and benefits that would result? Who reflects the change; who might adopt or oppose it; what are the power and resource positions of the stakeholders?

A scheme for classifying corporate social behavior, summarized in Table 5.2, describes several levels of choice with respect to its stakeholder environment. At one extreme, the organization is principally isolated and defensive (proscriptive), accommodating only its legally defined constituencies, and only to the extent that quantitative economic criteria, such as benefit-cost and net present value, might dictate. At state three, the other extreme, the organization accepts a dynamic, future-focused (anticipatory) role with respect to a broadly defined group of stakeholders. It more willingly incorporates within its economic model the value of a wider set of ethical norms and the costs of less measurable impacts (externalities), such as point-source pollution, that its actions may impose on stakeholders.

Table 5.2: Sethi's Three-State Scheme for Classifying Corporate Social Behavior

Behavior Dimension	State One: **Obligation**	State Two: **Responsibility**	State Three: **Responsiveness**
Legitimate Acts	Legal and economic criteria only	Considers and accepts broader role for measuring performance	Accepts its role as defined by the social system
Ethical Norms	Business is value neutral	Defines norms in community-related terms	Advocates social ethical norms & issues of public concern
Account-ability	Only to stockholders	Legally to stock-holders, socially to other stakeholders	To all groups, even those not directly affected by its actions
Operating Strategy	Exploitative and defensive	Adapts reactively to identifiable external costs; advocates standards	Proactive; leads in identifying & controlling exter-nal costs; antici-pates change.

(Adapted by permission from Sethi [425,67-68].)

The visible, dependent, interactive organization can accrue strategic value by emulating Sethi's State Three behavior for resource commitments in the stakeholder dimension. Sethi argues that adopting such behaviors requires action by senior management to muster the concern of line and middle management for stakeholder issues. Acceptance relies on effective communication of the rationale and on the extent of organizational commitment [427].

Managements and organizations that meet their social responsibilities through higher states of corporate social behavior may avoid costly litigation and legislation on crucial legal environment issues likely to emerge in the next century. There is a tendency to minimize such issues where the organization views the law as essentially static. The Johns-Manville product liability and bankruptcy experience serves as a case example from which to analyze the options and risks of corporate behavior choices between the extremes of pure profit maximization and pure social welfare. (See Silverstein [429] for further exploration of these issues.)

Dimensional Focus and Balance: A Summary. The choice for the environmental focal zone depends on a set of factors that can influence a firm's balance of energies in scanning the five dimensions of the environment. This choice depends on a careful assessment of the firm's circumstances and characteristics; there are no simple prescriptions. As a general rule, the dimensional focus should be narrow enough to make effective use of resources. Yet the more narrow this focus, the greater the probability of a surprise arising from a sector not adequately addressed. And the choice of dimensional focus should be changed over time, as the firm's circumstances and characteristics evolve. Finally, the setting of the environmental focal zone is but one of several elements of an organization's scanning strategy. A discussion of those remaining elements follows.

Range Settings of Scanning

When trying to forecast and prepare for the future, it is important to study *improbable events with very high impacts.*

Plausibility Range. At the very least, such a suggestion ignites debate. But it also serves to point out several aspects of reality: (1) Improbable events as well as probable ones do occur. (2) Events that occur, probable or improbable, do so with a probability of one; only events that could still occur in the future can have a probability less than one. (3) The expected value (positive or negative) of an improbable event can outweigh that of a probable one if its impact is sufficiently high; probability and impact are independent.

The organization exists within an immediate environment subject to some uncertainty because of imperfect knowledge about its state. The organization confronts a future environment, starting tomorrow, that will comprise events that emerge from the *probable* environment, the *possible* environment and the *improbable* environment. Scanning strategy should seek to characterize high payoff (probability times impact) events from all of these environments. This is the plausibility range setting for environmental scanning.

Time Range. Uncertainty and time are related, but they should not be equated in developing a scanning strategy. For example, valuation models reflect the circumstance, common to most investments, that uncertainty increases with future time; that is, the further distant the event or cash flow, the more uncertainty attached to a forecast of it. However, the time range as an element of scanning strategy is independent of plausibility or uncertainty for at least three reasons.

First, point-in-time assessment is a highly imperfect surrogate for uncertainty assessment. Many strategies have heightened risk in their initial stages, including for example, new product introductions and resource exploration. Indeed, the fundamental probability of either probable, possible or improbable events may remain stable or even increase over time. Finite resource probabilities such as depleting oil reserves increase with time and reach 1.0 at some time in the future. Phenomenon probabilities (drought, earthquake) may remain constant over time, even if their perceived uncertainty decreases as our knowledge about them grows. Strategy success probabilities may decrease with time if they relate to time-bound events whose opportunity windows can expire.

Second, the acceptance of time as an independent range setting encourages the organization to tune its scanning posture to the apparent rate of long-run fundamental change in the environmental aspect being scanned. Thomas advises focusing scanning in an area on an *environmental long wave* [473]. This avoids an overload of detailed information about short-run events and changes that defy rational interpretation. The Federal Reserve Open Market Committee, for example, has long struggled with the difficulty of interpreting short-run moves in the money supply as indicators of the underlying, long-wave demand for funds and rate of economic expansion.

Third, the time range setting is necessary so that the balance of an organization's scanning activities into future time can be tuned to that organization's adaptive reaction time. Ansoff suggests that even firms that forecast their futures and operate on the basis of planned management principles are subject to *procrastinating behavior*. This behavior can delay action beyond the *rational trigger point* when a forecast implies the need for strategic action. Such procrastination has two causes, the first of which Ansoff calls a *systems delay* in interpreting and promulgating the threat or opportunity among strategic managers. The second cause is a *behavioral delay* caused by demands for verification, political resistance, and natural preferences to deal with familiar circumstances, rather than with unfamiliar and threatening signals [12,315-19].

If a firm is unable or unwilling to respond strategically to new strategic input from its environment, its scanning may best focus on 10 to 20 years. More agile firms may focus on a three- to 10-year range. Each firm should establish a forecasting horizon so that delayed strategic response to threats or opportunities will not cause significant costs or losses in the future. It is important not to confuse the environmental scanning time range with the planning horizon. Many firms limit strategic plans to a three- to five-year horizon or less, but that planning focus should not limit the vision of the firm's strategic early warning system.

Survey results relating to the time dimension of environmental scanning have shown two interesting findings. Fahey, etal. found significant divergence of opinion as to the "ideal scanning horizon" among three groups: corporations, government and consultants. For each of these groups, the authors found that actual scanning horizons fell uniformly short of the ideal (see Table 5.3). Corporate respondents' ideal scanning horizons were considerably shorter (five to 10 years) than those of government (10 to 20 years) or consultants (greater than 20 years), perhaps in reflection of the longer-range assignments the latter two groups tend to undertake. Each group felt that their actual behaviors led to scanning in time ranges closer than their ideal; the effect was most dramatic for corporate respondents, who actually scanned in the "near present" one- to five-year range, but ideally wished to scan in the five- to ten-year range. Because of the response of consultants, it may well be that any corporate needs for truly long-range environmental information are met with purchased consulting studies.

Table 5.3: Ideal vs Actual Scanning Horizons

(Modal Responses by Type of Organization)

Respondent Group (% choosing response)	Ideal Horizon	Actual Horizon
Corporations	5-10 yrs. (70%)	1-5 yrs. (70%)
Government	10-20 yrs. (63%)	5-10 yrs. (63%)
Consultants	> 20 yrs. (72%)	10-20 yrs. (50%)

Source: Fahey, etal. [151,35]

Geographic Range. The third scanning strategy range setting is geography. Multinational firms have a natural focus beyond national borders in their task environments, as do firms whose domestic markets involve foreign competition or whose resource needs extend to foreign sources. Wholly domestic beef processors compete with foreign imports. Catalytic converter manufacturers require platinum from foreign sources. Channon and Jalland propose a set of issues which the multinational corporation faces in each of its national environments, all of which can be viewed in the context of strategic remote environment terms as well as from an operational task environment perspective. These issues are summarized in Table 5.4.

Regardless of direct multinational corporation-host country issues, a set of remote extra-territorial environment issues confronts any organization, even if that organization today is entirely insular in its operations. The first six of the issues in Table 5.4 may be relevant to the one-country organization, but in a relative sense: relative impact of balance of payments, relative labor costs and relative market sizes. These resource issues may influence the future pattern of domestic markets or the future opportunities to become a competitive or producing force in non-domestic environments. International political issues pose broad challenges for defining future environments for all organizations, including that of monitoring and assessing political and country risks to direct investment.

Banks, for example, must evaluate the creditworthiness of the countries with which they do business from a future focus that spans the time required to recover and renew their exposures [423]. In setting scanning strategy for the far distant future, no organization today should ignore the implications of space exploration and development for future world and domestic environments [240;241;272].

Table 5.4: Multi-National Environmental Scanning Issues

- Balance of Payments Effects
- Technology Transfer
- Industry Concentration/Market Size
- Cultural Customs, Government Plans, Laws
- Labor Effects and Availability
- National Resources
- Expenditures in Host Economies
- Indirect Benefits to Host Economies
- Organizational Attitude toward Host Economies
- Costs Borne by Host Economy to Support MNC

Source: Channon and Jalland [78]

Format of Collection of Environmental Information

Chapter 3 presented a model of decision-making in the firm in which scanning strategy and business strategy interact with, and mutually determine, the nature of information collection needs. Scanning strategy is adjusted to information needs by altering the intensity of the scanning or the nature of the reception mechanism for environmental information, as summarized in Table 5.5. The intensity of collecting environmental information is influenced by the *continuity* and the *method* of scanning. The reception of environmental information can also be described as a function of two strategic elements: the *sources* scanned and the *formality* of the scanning effort.

Table 5.5: Collection of Environmental Information

Elements of Collection Intensity
- Continuity of Scanning
- Method of Scanning

Elements of Information Reception
- Formality of Scanning Effort
- Sources Monitored

Continuity of Scanning. The terms irregular, regular and continuous can be applied to scanning systems as measures of the frequency or periodicity with which scanning activities are carried out. In one survey of 20 firms that scanned at least one and as many as seven environmental dimensions, 15 percent of the firms scanned regularly, and the remainder scanned irregularly or not at all [Franklin, etal.: 159]. Irregular scanning can be associated with reactive, retrospective analysis, initiated by crises and intended to support current decision making. Viewed this way, irregular scanning is in fact not environmental scanning by our definition, which supposes a proactive motivation and a future focus designed to enhance the strategic value of knowledge of emerging opportunities and threats. However, continuous scanning can be expensive and too much of it may lead to information overload about, and even imperception of, long-wave changes. That is, our senses could be dulled by frequent observations either of conditions that appear constant because they reflect the long wave, or of conditions that fluctuate too much because of random or cyclical influences and obscure the long wave.

The organization must make a cost-benefit decision with respect to the continuity of scanning within and across environmental dimensions. The costs include not only those of acquiring environmental information, but also those of processing, analyzing and disseminating it. The benefits of continuity include lower startup costs in recovering retrospective information as context for the future scan, fewer opportunities missed or threats unidentified because of scanning inactivity at critical event points, and better integration with organizational culture and systems. Some of these benefits arise from the *permanence* aspect of continuity: the long-term commitment of the firm to conducting scanning activities. Other benefits arise from the *periodicity* aspect of scanning; the firm needs to conduct scanning exercises frequently enough to capture vital signals. Still other benefits accrue as a result of the *pervasiveness* aspect of scanning, as the firm engages in more scanning activities rather than fewer. These three aspects of continuity follow the work of Thomas [473]; he describes the first two as aspects of the "time" dimension, and the last as the "space" dimension.

The benefits of scanning continuity tend to be greater in organizations that are slow to adapt to changes in structure or the flow of information. Continuity also has higher payoffs in organizations that tend to be tactics-focused in their regular planning activities; in such organizations irregular scanning could more easily be misguided, or misapplied to short-range decision making rather than to strategy formulation.

The benefits of continuity in scanning tend to be high in environments that are dynamic, and where successful anticipation of frequent changes could bring high payoffs over time. Scanning continuity is also beneficial in normally quieter environments randomly subject to shocks whose consequences are likely to be of significant magnitude for the firm. In a study of very small firms with less than 30 employees, Smeltzer found that more than half scanned continuously, using mainly informal sources in environments believed to be stable, or where some events were more likely to be related to trends or cycles. For these firms, scanning continuity may be useful as a means to track leading observable indicators, potentially triggering an effort to scan for the coming event itself.

Methods of Scanning. The other element of scanning strategy that determines the intensity of a scanning effort can be described as the *method of scanning.* For a given environmental dimension, issue or information source, a choice must be made of the degree of structure to be applied in scanning. At one extreme, the effort may be to search for specific inputs, perhaps involving specific search parameters and programmed costs. Such searches usually make sense once an issue or problem has been fairly well defined in strategic terms. At the other extreme, a scanner may simply be asked to observe the present environment without making any effort to expand or refine the focal range, and to note anything that seems interesting.

Mendell supports such unstructured observation, which he refers to as *browsing,* because: "It is impossible to predict *a priori* what information will be needed to appreciate a situation . . . isolated information will acquire value as it becomes part of emerging, insightful patterns" [321,158]. Unstructured observation occurs already in every organization; it may be conducted inexpensively by supporting a culture that encourages observation to become a conscious activity and by providing a mechanism for collecting the fragmentary "interesting" observations. Upon analysis, these fragments may integrate to yield *new or confirming signals* of emerging environmental opportunities or threats.

Formality of Scanning Effort: Modes of Scanning. The amount and character of environmental information an organization obtains is partly a result of the intensity of effort. But receiving the right information also depends on where the organization looks and how well-conditioned the organization is to observe or find it. These are issues related to the reception filter in Figure 3.1, and to the selection of sources for environmental information. This source selection involves balancing documentary vs. human or personal sources with varying characteristics of futurity and timeliness. Scanners access these sources using approaches determined by the current prescriptions of the organization's reception filter. Scanning may be *informal,* as through daily or episodic contact, or *conditioned* to be alert for certain issues, signals or data to which the organization has become sensitized through earlier environmental exposure and analysis.

Combining the method element of scanning intensity with the formality element of scanning receptivity yields a simplified classification of the modes of scanning as *informal* or *conditioned* observation, and *informal* or *formal* search, as summarized in Table 5.6. Informal observation is the most economical and common mode of environmental scanning. Properly motivated and utilized, informal observation can be an effective way to sense, if only vaguely, a new issue, opportunity or impression of change that might warrant further study. The organization should encourage communication and dialogue about environmental impressions, and document and correlate the impressions it receives, recognizing that most will be fragmentary but possibly meaningful in combination with other fragments.

If informal observation permits the company to articulate an emerging issue well enough to know the kind of additional information it seeks, the field of vision on that issue can be narrowed. Particular kinds of data and perhaps particular classes of sources can be identified. Should the firm become more certain about sources or types of inputs needed to support analysis of an emerging issue or opportunity, an informal search for information may yield data. The pursuit can be unstructured, but the purpose is to obtain enough valid input to permit the development of proactive goals and strategies. Informal search procedures also apply to the tracking of known issues and trends for the purpose of assessing the relevance of, or need for, changing existing strategies and tactics.

Table 5.6: Modes of Scanning

- Informal Observation
- Conditioned Observation
- Informal Search
- Formal Search

Some issues do not lend themselves well to informal search procedures. Data can be elusive and costly, or issues complex or interdependent, creating internal conflict in the organization, benefiting one unit at the expense of another. Issues may raise detailed analytical questions that cannot be answered in an unstructured framework. In such cases, a formal search may be required, using a pre-established methodology and a separately planned and budgeted effort to resolve a specific issue or obtain specific information.

Because formal searches involve relatively high resource demands, they should be undertaken with caution and deliberation. The basic research and development commitment an organization makes is a formal search, as in the search for acquisition opportunities. Formal search studies of key issues relating to new operating strategies may also be justified by the high stakes or potential payoffs of the incremental scanning costs.

Ironically, most ad hoc, reactive, crisis studies also become formal searches because of the tactical urgency attached to them. Thus, organizations that fail systematically to conduct environmental scanning at the more informal levels not only lose the opportunity to respond strategically to their environment, but the environmental intelligence they eventually obtain is acquired in the most expensive fashion.

Other Elements of the Scanning System

Sources Monitored. Environmental scanning inputs are collected so that inferences about the future may be drawn from them. But environmental inputs, even if they arrive unsolicited from customers or suppliers, are utilized only if the organization seeks to observe them. Moreover, the search for environmental scanning inputs should be a result of strategy and purpose, not serendipity. Thus, the organization may not wish to limit itself to, nor even fully decode, the free information it receives if better knowledge can be gained from other information investments. Chapter 8 details the sources of environmental information to the organization, and how choices can be made to shape information sources to the strategic needs and resources of the organization.

Methods of Processing Scanning Inputs. Inferences from source data emerge in the form of analyses and forecasts from the processing phase of environmental scanning, according to the *methods* the organization has chosen to process environmental inputs. A host of techniques can be applied in pursuit of an integrated and organized view of the future, ranging from quantitative to qualitative, from statistical to inferential, from data-rich to data-poor, and from models to mind games. These methods and techniques are explored in Chapter 9. Using some subset of these techniques over time, the organization develops its own methodology for identifying possible future events and conditions and assessing their probable or possible impacts on attaining the organization's goals and on the success of its strategies.

Managing and Communicating Within the Scanning System

Central to the idea of environmental scanning are two of the most difficult concepts to communicate in an operationally useful way: *risk,* and *inferences about unknown systems.* The organization must find an appropriate method for reporting on these concepts to an audience unaccustomed to dealing with ambiguity in information reports. Environmental scanning communications compete for acceptance and validity with sales, budget and market research reports, and engineering studies. Scanning is likely to be disadvantaged against these more "concrete" communications, and therefore effective scanning communication needs to be highly specialized and individualized.

The fabric of an organization's scanning system is the organization of management resources to ensure the compatible operation of a "futures business" side-by-side with a "strategies business," an "operations business," a "measurement business" and a "funding business." Environmental scanning not only needs the support of management, it also needs integration into management's thinking and into the pattern of organizational behavior. The following chapters discuss the management and communication of environmental scanning within the context of the firm.

CHAPTER 6

THE MANAGEMENT OF
ENVIRONMENTAL SCANNING

Today, most businesses see some type of turbulence in their environment, signaling an increased need to scan even its remote reaches. Signals from remote environments are weak, and people are less prepared to detect them in an objective and undistorted fashion, as well as less anxious to devote time to scanning rather than to their more immediate responsibilities. Assuring the productivity of scanning efforts requires thoughtful attention to systematizing scanning efforts and integrating those efforts into the culture of the organization. The task involves managing structure and people — the subjects of this chapter, which considers four key elements of the management of environmental scanning:

- Piloting the process with an external environmental council.
- Driving the process with an executive champion.
- Developing a scanning culture.
- Selecting and inspiring people as scanners.

Structure of Scanning Efforts

The complexity of the environment determines the design of the organization and the format of scanning efforts the organization should undertake. There is no one structure that is universally appropriate for scanning, but Figure 6.1 suggests some structural elements that should be incorporated into all scanning systems.

The External Environmental Council. Scanning should be organized around a council or task force broadly constituted from the functions, SBUs and other *constituencies* within the firm. This network hub is important because future environmental conditions and insights about them are vital intelligence for all parts of the organization. Participation of various constituencies in the organization is important because each may observe and apply environmental insights *differently* according to its distinct context, in terms of focus, objectives, tasks, and even language and thought patterns. As members of the external environmental council, representatives of these constituencies are a key link. They contribute their distinct contexts to the council's search and insight-generating activities, and they translate those activities in a meaningful form as communications from the council back to the constituencies.

It may be possible for a generic communication about fringe benefits to be communicated effectively throughout a company and successfully understood; it is much less likely

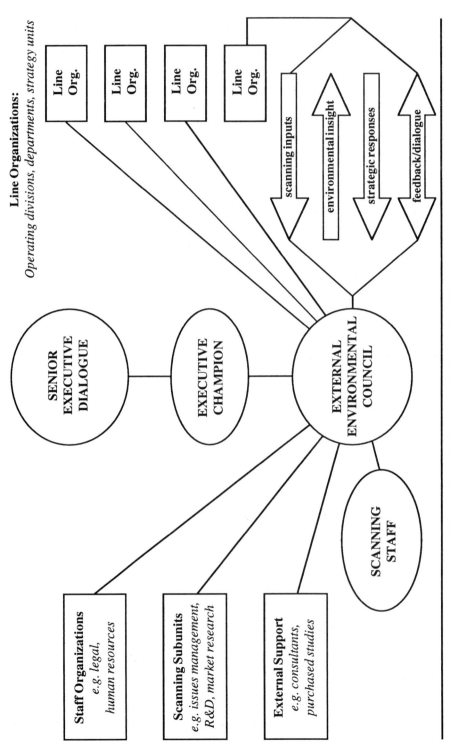

Figure 6.1: Environmental Scanning Structure

that a generic communication about future regulatory or technological environments will be successfully incorporated into strategic sub-unit behavior. At a generic level, statements about future environments are inherently general and vague in their application to specific tasks. Indeed, it is this abstract quality of future studies that caused many past efforts to be ignored. External environmental council members prevent the problems caused by generic communication by communicating environmental insights to their own constituencies in the relevant language, culture and context.

The environmental scanning council's role should be active, synthesizing its own scanning inputs and those of others into strategic environmental insights, and communicating those insights to the organization through its members. In that way, the council coordinates the corporate knowledge about the reception, reaction and adaptation of constituencies to environmental information. The members of the council are positioned to observe how scanning intelligence is received and processed within their constituency, and the response it brings. These members can also bring to the council the outputs of environmental scanning which the constituency itself may conduct as part of its operations, and which might otherwise remain outside the scanning system, perhaps undisseminated. These other environmental sources include market research, the Washington office, research and development, tax planning, treasury and the legal department.

With *people* actively linked into the broader organization, scanning activities, outcomes and impacts can be effectively documented and communicated. With *people* as links to the scanning network hub, or council, accountability can be assigned and measured. Porter suggests in describing competitor intelligence-gathering that, "whatever the mechanism chosen . . . there are benefits to be gained from one that is formal and involves some documentation. It is all too easy for bits and pieces of data to be lost, and the benefits that come only from combining these bits and pieces thereby forgone" [373,74]. The external environmental council is the unifying force that formalizes the idea of environmental scanning and integrates its functions, as summarized in Table 6.1.

Table 6.1: Functions of the External Environmental Council

- Sustains locus of scanning activities.
- Represents distinct organizational contexts.
- Provides specialized communication interfaces.
- Coordinates organization-wide environmental knowledge.
- Monitors environmental adaptation.
- Measures accountability.

Staff Infrastructure. The environmental scanning effort needs some infrastructure, although it need not be a freestanding scanning unit or department. One or more supporting staff as well as clerical resources are needed to do follow-up work and preparation for the periodic meetings of the environmental council. There are library functions, such as serials maintenance, external database manipulation, reference work and archiving. As numerous authors suggest, it may be desirable to maintain an environmental intelligence database. Internal awareness of the scanning effort, and a supportive and participating constituency for scanning, might be enhanced through the publication of an in-house scanning newsletter. The environmental issues and scenarios articulated by the external environmental council may be documented and published by the scanning support staff. The scanning staff may assist in the publication of top management's *corporate environmental vision,* the highest strategic purpose to which environmental scanning can contribute.

A minimum of one scanning professional is needed, not only to guide scanning efforts, but also to provide the impetus for creative and non-conventional outward-focused thinking within the organization. That professional is the person to call with questions requiring scanning expertise, and the person to represent and advocate the corporate scanning effort to those in the organization who may not be directly involved through contact with a scanning council member. It is this person's responsibility to see that the "futures business" scanning represents operates compatibly with the other "businesses" of the organization. These associated areas are the "strategies," "operations," "measurement" and "funding" businesses. These businesses must not simply coexist; they must contribute jointly to organizational goals.

Probably the biggest mistake that can be made in structuring an environmental scanning effort is the same biggest mistake that can be made in structuring a strategic planning effort: namely, building a separate, freestanding department to do the scanning. No matter how *intensive* the scanning effort called for by the scanning strategy, the organization should never retreat from *extensive involvement* in scanning by people in sub-units whose strategies are affected by the environment. Just as line people should *plan,* line people should *scan,* although the tasks may call for different people in each role.

The Executive Champion. The critical juncture of environmental scanning is with corporate strategy development because scanning and strategy must interact at the highest levels of the organization. Yet the scanning infrastructure is staffed at the professional — not executive — level, and the environmental council is likely made up of a mix of professionals and officers, but probably not senior officers. The scanning council has no inherent power, such as through a revenue base, and to provide it with power and visibility, there is a need for a senior executive to be informed and involved as an element of structure in the scanning system. The executive champion sponsors, funds and validates the work, and engages other senior executives in dialogue about the emerging issues identified by the scanning council. The scanning council generates grass-roots involvement with the environment, while the senior executive champion generates top-level involvement to shape the corporate strategic vision to the realities and possibilities of the environment.

The Scanning Culture. The executive champion has an even bigger role to play than legitimizing the existence and communications of the external environmental council. That executive, as leader, has the opportunity to create a culture that will turn the entire organization into "a web of eyes and ears" sensitized to react to signals from the environment and communicate them to the organization. Cultures are slow to change, and such change requires consistent, simple messages from leaders that instill new values while their actions consistently reflect and support those new values. The visible elements of a scanning system, infrastructure and external environmental council, communicate the priorities of the organization. For the people not directly involved in "priority activities," both training and performance incentives may be useful in building acceptance and support of the scanning culture. As an example, one company set aside 30 percent of sales commissions as a bonus pool related to information gathering [175].

Outside Involvement: Resource and Reality Check. With broad, open involvement and structured process, it might seem that environmental scanning becomes a largely objective enterprise, likely to lead to a clear-sighted vision of the future. Not so, according to Michael:

> There are futures that, given the values and preoccupations of an organization, seem more likely or more natural. But you want to be alert to the fact that it's their own values and preoccupations that make it seem so [6,6].

To assure that these internal values and preoccupations do not create barriers to the view of the world, or barriers to acquiring insights and intelligence the organization would otherwise overlook, it may be useful to involve "outsiders" in the environmental scan. Outside involvement can take three essential forms: domain- and cohort-based scanning, and consultative intelligence (see Table 6.2). Domain-based environmental scanning envisions a joint scanning effort by a group of key decision-maker representatives from several interdependent organizations. For a given industry, for example, these may include customers, suppliers, creditors, investors, manufacturers, related service-providers, community members and government representatives, all of whom depend upon or influence to some extent a common economic or geographic province.

Table 6.2: Three Approaches to Scanning Support from Outside the Organization

Domain-based scanning	joint scanning dialogue among interdependent organizations, e.g. customers, regulators, community leaders.
Cohort-based scanning	joint scanning dialogue among competitors.
Consultative support	process, information or scanning study support.

The value of such a joint-scanning group is that the differing attitudes of each contributor about the stage of development, consequence or power of impact of any environmental issue or interaction of issues may enhance the understanding by the group (see McCann: [306]). Notwithstanding its apparent value, such a multi-group environmental scan is very difficult to organize, manage and follow through to action. Preconditions of such a scan include supportive cultures for scanning across the group, and the willing availability of individuals from each organization with the authority and inclination to speak openly on the issues.

Cohort-based scanning implies that competitors in the same industry collaborate in their scanning efforts. In the U.S., antitrust laws may prevent such joint efforts despite constructive intent and potentially positive results. Yet, one form of such cohort-based scanning occurs when a trade association conducts scanning in its own right for the benefit of its members. The American Council of Life Insurance Companies, cited as an example below, engages in such environmental scanning for the benefit of its members. Other examples include the Credit Union National Association, the American Society for Personnel Administration, and the American Institute of Certified Public Accountants. Academic researchers who publish results of survey information on views and attitudes on the emerging future are also a source of cohort-based scanning.

FORTUNE 500 VP'S PREDICT 1995 ENVIRONMENT

   More than one hundred Fortune 500 executives participated in a survey of business and marketing conditions they expected in 1995. The study was conducted by professors Gene Laczniak and Robert Lusch and published in the *Journal of Consumer Marketing* [254].

   Respondents predicted a variety of political, social and natural environment conditions, but generally positive economic and technological developments. Competitiveness and customer focus characterized the predicted markets of 1995, with distribution rising in importance against promotion and pricing strategies.

Consultative support services can range from purchased environmental scanning studies, to information abstracting services, to scanning process facilitation, all involving single clients or pooled client groups. JCPenney and Nynex make use of a combination of such services, in addition to their own in-house scanning activity. Outside support services may be particularly useful in helping to establish the frame of reference for scanning and in helping to set scanning information priorities [64].

A large organization could obtain all environmental scanning input through studies by consultants, but it might then fail to reap the benefits of the scanning intelligence to which its own employees already have access; it might also dissipate the values of an environmental scanning culture internal to the organization. Moreover, the necessarily episodic nature of such purchased studies, unsupported by an active internal scanning network, consigns scanning to *irregular* intensity as described in Chapter 5. Such irregular scanning may fail to capture signals of change in a dependable manner and is likely not to be cost-effective.

Survey Evidence on Scanning Structure. Environmental scanning is a relatively new focus for many organizations even though the problems it addresses have been around for a long time. Experience with the structuring of scanning efforts is thus relatively limited. Because scanning in the past has been more commonly construed as part of planning rather than as a distinct activity, there is much more survey knowledge of attitudes about the process of scanning the environment than about the structure of scanning efforts. Engledow and Lenz conducted interviews with 10 firms known for their involvement in environmental scanning [144]. Nine of those firms originally structured their environmental scanning efforts as freestanding units. Only two of the units remained freestanding at the time of the study. Three efforts had been abandoned altogether and the remaining four had been merged with other corporate- or division-level activities, typically strategic planning units.

Klein and Linneman surveyed and then interviewed large firms in both the U.S. and internationally in 1981-82 [243], to compare their scanning activities with a 1977 survey. They reported an increase from 11 percent to 20 percent in the proportion of Top 1,000 domestic industrial companies with formal environmental scanning units. In 1982, nearly half of the Top 100 domestic industrials and Top 500 foreign industrials had such formal efforts in place. The authors note: "The establishment of [environmental scanning] units appears to be closely linked to a commitment to formalized strategic planning."

Klein and Linneman also identified a tendency among some companies to structure *multiple* scanning units. The typical case is one where an *environmental scanning unit* exists as part of the strategic planning effort of the organization, while an *issues management unit* is attached to the public affairs arm of the organization. Some striking differences were identified by type of firm. While almost no foreign firms had multiple units, about 60 percent of domestic non-industrial companies had them, more than double the incidence among domestic industrials.

Rationale for Separate Scanning Sub-Units. There are several elements of *issues management* that broaden its charge beyond environmental scanning. These are obligatory activities if the organization truly seeks to *manage* elements of the external political, social and regulatory dimensions of its environment (see Table 6.3). The first element relates to the formulation of a posture on sensitive public and policy issues, and to current reporting to management on issue action items. The second is to manage dialogue with a perhaps critical public, even including specialized approaches to handling crises and disasters [Reinhardt, etal.: 389]. The third relates to advocacy, attempting to shape the resolution of issues that affect or could affect the organization's operations, such as by prompting change through a catalytic strategy of political action [99].

These aspects of issues management are independent of environmental scanning. They represent the implementation of aggressive strategies and tactics that seek to shape either the immediate present or the future. The aim of these aspects of issues management is to alter the threat/opportunity matrix in a manner favorable to the firm's objectives and goals.

Table 6.3: Elements of Issues Management

- Formulate issue posture.
- Perform current issue reporting.
- Manage dialogue with public.
- Advocate policy positions.
- Scan environment for emerging issues.

The precursors to such public posturing and advocacy are the environmental scanning and strategic planning that identified the threat/opportunity matrix and need for strategy in the first place. Thus, for a firm with significant public policy dependencies or linkages, it may well be productive to establish a separate staff sub-unit to deal with both scanning and strategy in a specialized form, and to staff the unit to pursue that specialized mission. A rich literature has developed on the subject of issues management, encompassing both its scanning and advocacy functions [10;15;18;19;32;56;80;99;100;156;188;206;283; 284;332;337;350;354;392;393;426].

Comparable situations exist where technology forecasting is mainly conducted by specialists in the research and development function, and where competitive and market scanning/intelligence activities are part of the charge of the market research arm of the organization. As with issues management, these sector-based scanning efforts are closely associated with tactical decision making. Market intelligence, for example, comprises knowing about "what is" in the marketplace and among competitors, and includes developing a tactical sense of competitor response abilities and intentions. But it can also cast a wider net, deeper in time, to encompass remote and extended task environment scanning, seeking signals of possible and probable change in markets and the conditions of competition. (See Evans [148]).

The main risk of mixing environmental scanning responsibilities with operational intelligence-gathering is that too much of the latter will be conducted in the name of the former. Operational intelligence is, after all, more immediately useful and less frustrating to define and describe. An additional risk of assigning environmental scanning responsibilities to an operating unit is that both scanning inputs and intelligence can be lost to the rest of the organization if they are not shared through some orderly process. To control against these risks, *the scanners in the issues management, R&D and market research functions should be directly linked to the external environmental council and obliged to bring their scanning intelligence to that forum.* There, they join people representing all of the other strategy-linked sub-units of the organization, with the mission of integrating, synthesizing and diffusing environmental intelligence throughout the organization in a high-relevance, high-payoff manner.

The structuring of separate scanning units is a mistake if those units are isolated or introverted from the rest of the organization, or if, by their separation, unproductive duplication of resources occurs. These are avoidable mistakes likely to be repeated unless the organization consciously seeks to avoid them. To illustrate, Urban and Hauser's *Design and Marketing of New Products* [489], does not mention the concepts of gathering or sharing environmental scanning intelligence. Nor is there any mention of the subjects in Gibson's *Managing Research and Development* [174]. Thus, it appears necessary to adapt these specialized development organizations, using sub-models of the organization's overall scanning effort.

People Who Scan

A second ingredient in the management of environmental scanning is the assurance that the people doing the scanning are properly attuned to their task. People are the "environmental radar" in identifying and analyzing data related to important environmental factors [346]. Few organizations staff environmental scanning functions as a continuous full-time effort. Instead, the persons assigned to identify emerging environmental issues are almost certain to have other responsibilities and interests — their regular jobs — competing for their time. Indeed, the uncertainty and discomfort associated with the scanning process could cause scanning to receive only minimal commitment from participants. For example, Lysonski [291] found a significant relationship between scanning and role conflict among product managers. This barrier, and several others described below, suggest the need to choose carefully, and to motivate properly those chosen for the responsibility of scanning.

Divergent vs. Convergent Thinking. Environmental scanning is behaviorally threatening, as compared with better defined and circumscribed responsibilities, because it forces the individual to think broadly *from* a point of focus instead of narrowly *to* a point of focus. In our normal thought processes, most of us are problem solvers, gathering and analyzing facts and data to reach an answer or a solution. We are convergent thinkers (see Figure 6.2), seeking to convert the unknown into the known by applying accepted models. As environmental scanners however, thoughts start from a known position and use questions to develop *more questions,* rather than answers, and to seek problems, not solutions. Scanners are charged with thinking divergently. Mendell describes this problem as "the myth of rationality":

> Most people like to believe that they are working on well-structured, "under-control" problems. We can apply rational methods to well-structured problems and get well-defined, permanent answers. But non-rational thinking has to be employed to solve ill-structured problems and this scares people. So people treat futures problems as well structured and dither over how to improve our methodologies, rather than how to improve our intuition and creativity [321,150].

Accustomed thought patterns and accustomed points of view introduce the potential for distortion in human perception and interpretation of information from the amorphous

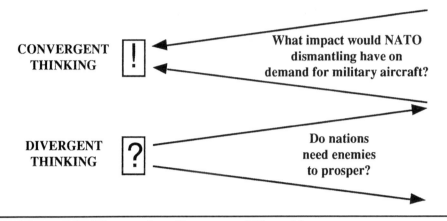

Figure 6.2: Divergent vs. Convergent Thought

external environment. Thinking patterns may be subject to "assimilation prior to input," encouraging scanners to see familiar signals and characteristics even after the data or circumstances have in fact changed [Campbell: 66]. Over time, the bulk of the environmental impact on a firm is likely to be the result of *changes* in conditions rather than *startling* or *unique* events, so that this unintentional human tendency in thinking is a significant barrier to effective environmental scanning. Scanners need to develop a sense of when and how to trigger a shift in their *frame of reference* in evaluating environments [El-Sawy, *etal.*: 141].

Simple vs. Complex Cognitive Styles. The mind, according to de Bono, functions so as to create patterns in the form of models or concepts that "condense, organize and give meaning to the incoming information" [109]. When new information is received, it is tested against accumulated knowledge or old thought patterns. If it is consistent with those patterns, it is integrated with them, perhaps causing extension, expansion or reorganization. When new information is inconsistent with accumulated knowledge, the tendency is to discard it. Thinking about the future requires one to develop the ability to discard or set aside old thought patterns. Otherwise those old patterns prevent us from creating new patterns out of new information.

One way to cultivate a new pattern bias in handling information from the environment is by reducing the volume of detailed information inputs received and processed by the scanner. This occurs naturally with a shift in focus from the immediate to the remote as the main source of environmental information. It may also be necessary to change the cognitive style of the scanner to prevent approaches that seek to force detail and resolution from the remote environment, since the real need is for the scanner to pursue intuition and synthesize insights from diverse signals. Hedberg and Jonsson [192] cite research over the past 20 years indicating that the value of complex integrative capacity in individuals depends on the task to which they are committed. Individuals with simpler cognitive structures are more able to reform their thinking and to operate efficiently in decision situations where inputs are few and diverse. Such individuals may be more capable in the capacity of remote scanners. Conversely, highly integrative individuals may be more productive working with remote scanners and focusing on the task environment, because of their abilities to adapt to a wider range of environmental contingencies. These findings suggest the need for a balanced mix of cognitive styles among scanners inclined towards the simple in dynamic environments and the complex in static environments.

Intuition vs. Truth-seeking. Mendell [321] contends that ill-structured futures problems can be treated only as open-ended processes with no solution and no "truths." He advocates putting environmental scanning under the control of intuitive information evaluators, those who look for cues and insights in the whole of a situation. Because the systematic application of analytical methodologies can uncover cues, the intuitor should have some truth seekers as direct reports. One of each of the following might be useful:

- A Lockean inquirer who seeks truth by analyzing data using existing models and finds truth in goodness-of-fit statistics;

- A Leibnizian inquirer who seeks truth in underlying models and laws for which support data can be found;

- A Kantian inquirer who seeks truth where the same conclusions can be drawn from several models;

- A Hegelian inquirer who seeks truth where models that should explain a circumstance don't.

Without the intuitor in control, the Lockean would be overwhelmed by data, the Leibnizian would discard most of the data that didn't fit preconceptions, and the Kantian and Hegelian would be in endless conflict as to what constituted truth.

Even to intuitive scanners, environmental input is subject to *interpretation* bias, a systematic distortion in receiving or communicating information because of a scanner's limited comprehension of, or familiarity with, data outside personal training or knowledge. Further, intentional distortion or bias in interpretation could result from the self-interest of the individual in considering the implications of issues for the managerial space that that individual customarily influences and manages.

Commitment and Power as Motivation. Effective scanning can be achieved in part by selecting and training participants for creative and divergent thought processes, by providing realistic support resources and by motivating participants to seek goals beyond their current responsibilities. Constant reinforcement of the corporate commitment to a scanning culture assists in crystallizing priorities. The mission of the members of the environmental council is to help senior management better understand the business environment that will shape the company in the coming years. Through their role in identifying emerging issues, scanners become experts upon whom the organization must rely for external intelligence with potentially immense strategic importance.

Scanning involves the responsibility and conveys the right to pay attention to any and all externally caused problems the company might confront. It also implies that as a member of an environmental scanning council, that person is allowed freely to look beyond the confines of his or her own customarily limited authority. This creates access into otherwise closed policy circles of the firm, and the opportunity to experience a breadth of perspective denied to all but a few peers. It is the power of this broad perspective that can motivate scanning participants away from the territorial bias of their "other jobs" and toward the future opportunities that can be captured.

CHAPTER 7

THE PROCESS OF ENVIRONMENTAL SCANNING

The preceding four chapters dealt with elements of the environmental scanning process. The ideas and approaches presented in these chapters can be applied to assess the uncertainty of an organization's environment, describe a scanning strategy to match that uncertainty and structure a scanning team to accomplish the task. The process of scanning is described by the flow chart in Figure 7.1.

The three main action elements of scanning — (1) gathering inputs and processing information; (2) synthesizing and evaluating emerging issues, and (3) communicating environmental insights — are explored in this chapter, with examples of comparative scanning systems and a discussion of organization and process for each. The chapter concludes with a discussion of the barriers to effective environmental scanning, and methods of avoiding and overcoming them.

Figure 7.1: Global View of Scanning Process

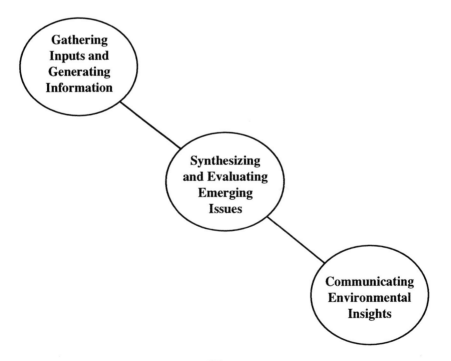

Gathering Inputs and Processing Information

Scanners must maintain limited baseline knowledge of the current state of nature in each of the sectors of the environment. Without a knowledge of what is, it is difficult to observe signals of change. Organizations new to scanning must create such a knowledge base against which to compare scanning intelligence, because an understanding of the dynamics of the organization's industry and of related actors and instructors is essential; this permits inferences to be drawn about driving forces and relationships, and about past and possible future break-points in the environment. In many enterprises, people learn what is happening in their own areas of responsibility by reading trade publications and by spanning boundaries to talk with customers and suppliers. The main need is that people obtain "what is" knowledge about areas other than their own; the presence of an active external environmental council is helpful in assuring this transfer of information.

Armed with a knowledge of the present, and a scanning strategy appropriate to its circumstances, the scanning organization uses its information sources to gather clues and cues about the future (see Figure 7.2) by using everyone's eyes and ears to extract bits and pieces of information about change, and therefore about the future (see Table 7.1). The process is formalized by writing an abstract or summary to capture the essence of each piece of information and perhaps to document the scanner's view of the implications. Who should be conducting active scanning? Ideally, everyone with something to contribute. If "everyone" contributed one abstract each day, even allowing for duplication, a scanning database could be rapidly built.

Figure 7.2: Gathering Inputs, Generating Information

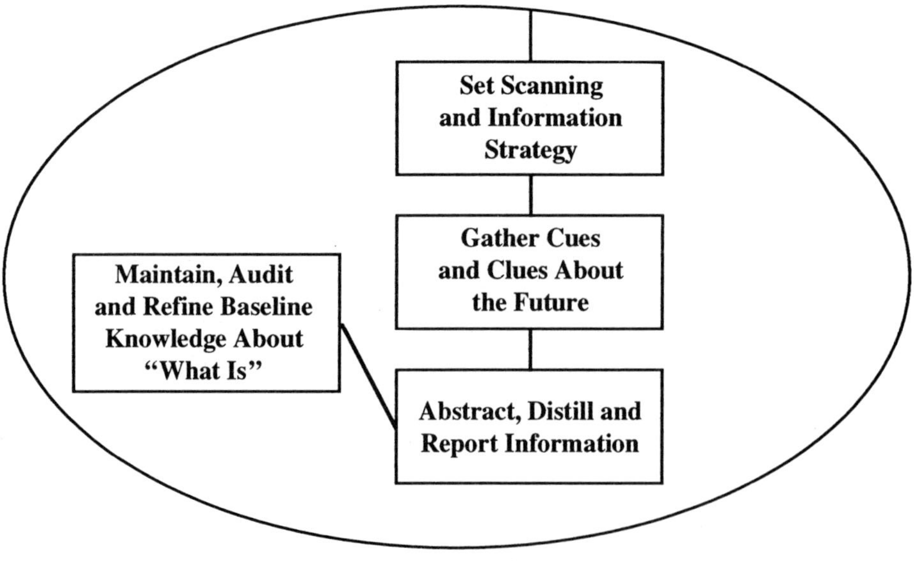

> ## Table 7.1: Types of Information Sought by Scanners
>
> | | |
> |---|---|
> | Data | Facts and Detail |
> | Analyses | Ideas |
> | Inferences of Others | Predictions |
> | Hints | Signals |
> | Evidence | |

Synthesizing and Evaluating Emerging Issues

The object of collecting and documenting scanning results is so that the bits and pieces of this information can be combined, compared, contrasted and correlated in ways that produce novel quantitative and conceptual patterns (see Figure 7.3). All information obtained should be indexed and classified as finely as possible by subject, content, time frame and relationship key words. The basic data format used by the Dairy Council of California for their scanning information base is illustrated by this sample record:

> [The record] includes the fact that the issue is dietary fat and the source is the *Los Angeles Times,* July 14 (section and page are also noted). The key point is listed next: that excess saturated fat intake — not cholesterol — is the strongest dietary link to heart disease. Finally, an inference is drawn: dietary cholesterol may be losing ground to saturated fat as the key factor in the prevention of heart disease [481,34].

Figure 7.3: Synthesizing and Evaluating Emerging Issues

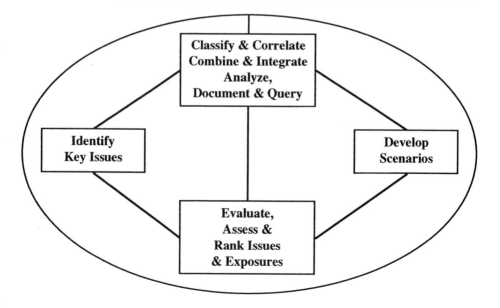

The classification of scanning information units can be implemented and managed through available computerized database technology, which supports both numeric and textual processing. *INQUIRE/Text* (Infodata Systems Inc.) is a mainframe software system designed for this task. *Folio Views* (Folio Corp.) is also a microcomputer text management system. Other software tools can support the data-inference process, such as through outlining (e.g., *PC-Outline*) and idea management (e.g., *AskSam*). These kinds of systems allow data to be manipulated and retrieved easily to support the search for new patterns and interesting ideas.

Some of the information the organization gathers may be suitable for analysis because it can be broken down into parts and the parts examined for meaning. Events with far-reaching consequences might require analysis into smaller intelligence units, out of which implications and inferences could be drawn.

ENVIRONMENTAL INFORMATION REQUIRING ANALYSIS

On Memorial Day, 1989, President Bush proposed to NATO ministers a plan for a sweeping, 20 percent reduction in conventional forces in Europe, simultaneously indicating willingness to discuss limits on aircraft and military helicopters. Shortly thereafter, a remarkable restructuring began in eastern Europe, leading to the ouster of communist governments in Poland, East Germany, Hungary, Czechoslovakia and Rumania. This occurred with the tacit approval of the Soviet government, which was engaged in its own program of economic and military reforms, with its surprising outcome in the collapse of Communist political and economic domination.

This combination of events has the potential of truly stunning impacts in every dimension of the environment. But these cannot even be cataloged much less evaluated, without more detailed analysis. Analysis might begin by recognizing that about half of U.S. military spending at the time was funneled through Europe. The potential of this aspect might be analyzed by arraying possible first and higher order ramifications in markets for labor, material, and Federal spending — the so-called "peace dividend."

Intelligence information units that have emerged from the analysis of events and signals, and other information, particularly intuitive and inferential data, may integrate into patterns that permit novel implications to be synthesized. For example, Charles J. Hess, a partner in Inferential Focus, an intelligence-gathering service organization, shared such a synthesis with the editors of *Financial World* in late 1987 as a result of the convergence of events leading to the belief by Americans that "things have gotten out of control." The events Hess listed were: the Challenger explosion, freeway shootings, the Contra scandal, AIDS hysteria, pit bull attacks, aircraft near-misses and crashes, nuclear accidents and chemical spills. This led Hess to say "Americans have reacted by seeking ways to ensure their personal safety and gain more control over their lives" [536,126]. Repercussions were observed in increased seat-belt use and in the accelerated sales of products to the public, from condoms to home security systems and protective running shoes.

To an extent determined by the level of staff support, the external environmental council becomes involved with the functions of analysis, synthesis, classification, correlation and integration of information. The conduct of these activities may generate additional information queries or documentation requests. Documentation and query may also be motivated by subsequent scanning processes via feedback. Countervailing influences are needed to prevent the scan-query-scan loop from becoming an uncontrolled cycle. Deadlines are a simple form of control; a decision analysis approach to making information-gathering decisions may provide better results (see Brown, etal.: [58, Chapter 36]).

The end purpose of the external environmental council is to prepare preliminary insights about the future environment for consideration and debate by an evaluative group (see Figure 7.3). These insights may take the form of an elaborated *list of issues* for the senior planners to consider. The description of Monsanto's scanning process, below, alludes to this issue orientation. Nynex Corporation's bi-monthly *Environmental Scan* provides background on several issues and suggests their implications. *What's Ahead,* the environmental scan of the United Way, identifies selected social, economic, regional, political and technological implications for their organizations. These implications flow from nine major trends, or change drivers, envisioned to prevail in the next 10 years.

Insights of the external environmental council may also take the form of *future scenarios,* combinations of factors and sequences of events representing possible or plausible future states of nature the organization might face. Royal Dutch Shell is known for its use of such scenarios in planning, and Atlantic Richfield Company (ARCO) builds multiple scenarios, with related product and price forecasts for a 20-year period.

Debate by senior executives over these inputs from the environmental council, whether based on issues or scenarios, may yield unanswered questions or missing links that generate additional queries and requests for information. These information needs constitute a feedback mechanism from the senior planners to the environmental council.

The principal task of the evaluative group is to assess and rank a relevant set of insights about the future environments that the organization may face. This evaluative group *could* be the external environmental council itself. Yet, while that group is undoubtedly knowledgeable enough to meet the challenge of the task, its objectivity could be questioned, as could its ability to reflect the corporate vision, given the junior-to-middle-management level of its membership. An evaluative group comprising senior executives of the organization would have both broader authority and vision with which to make choices about key environmental issues to be considered in charting the organization's future. It is in fact these senior executives who will set the strategy for the organization. Senior executive dialogue on assessing environmental issues is a valuable way to enrich, validate and update the assumptions and "cause maps" that influence their thinking and decision making [271].

Assessing and ranking issues or scenarios essentially involves five questions:

1. What is the extent of the organization's exposure to the issue, in terms of probability and overall impact?
2. How pivotal is the issue because of its *cross-impacts,* or influences on or from other issues?
3. What is the probable timing of the exposure?
4. What is the organization's level of ability to respond?
5. How long will it take for a cycle of analysis/response to occur?

Issues or scenarios containing small exposures or extremely long time delays before likely exposure may be disregarded. The presence of issues to which the organization has little ability or insufficient time to respond may compel the organization to consider tactical withdrawal or abandonment. Issues with high exposure and imminent timing within the operating flexibility of the organization represent high priorities for contingent strategic response. Kastens suggests the following:

> If you are like most managements, you will end up with one helluva laundry list. Now analyze these items, using three categories: Could they possibly (1) increase or decrease your sales or your earnings by 10 percent in the next full fiscal year, or (2) increase or decrease your sales or your earnings by 50 percent in five years, or (3) put you out of a major part of your business or triple the business potential within 10 years? Be honest, but not alarmist. Those items that do not fall into any of these classes are interesting, but so what? Forget them, at least until next year [228,45].

Two tasks are associated with issues or scenarios that contain important or imminent issues. First, critical elements must be interrelated with or expressed in terms of task environment factors and current operations, so they can effectively influence unit plans. Second, critical issues, and the scenarios that contain them, should be synthesized and expressed as insights about the future in ways that will lead to confirmation or modification of organizational vision and strategy. Both of these tasks are aspects of the communication element of the environmental scanning process.

Effective Use of Scanning Outcomes

Environmental scanning has no self-fulfilling purpose. Its benefit occurs when the plans or operations of an organization are enhanced by scanning outcomes. *Managers* become better value creators as environmental scanning trains them to anticipate, observe or respond to change. *The organization* accrues value if scanning yields a more consistent and coordinated vision of the opportunities, constraints and options possible and probable future environments may bring. The critical action step for the outcomes of environmental scanning is where strategy is adapted, or contingent strategies are developed, to reflect analysis of those possible or probable futures. Environmental scanning results have strategic purpose when they help the organization to allocate resources, evaluate plans, and identify new opportunities or threats with strategic business impact.

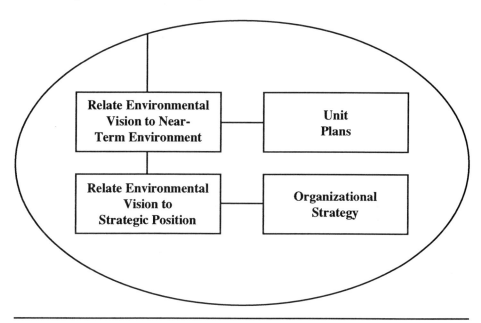

Figure 7.4: Communicating Environmental Insights

Communicating Environmental Insights. The process of executive debate and articulation of environmental issues, as illustrated in Figure 7.4 and in the Monsanto scanning example that follows, is a superior approach for implanting environmental intelligence in the corporate vision. The dialogue that emerges is in essence the primary communication device for strategically valuable environmental information. Of the two outcomes of such direct involvement by senior management, prioritizing and common understanding, only the first is possible if environmental intelligence is encoded by executives in a solitary way, such as through receiving and reading written staff analyses of environmental issues. Executive environmental dialogue incorporates the commitment to make long-range environmental assumptions flow directly into the strategic planning process at the highest levels of the organization, where the strategic corporate vision, if it is to exist at all, must be created.

Top management resolution of the environmental issues debate must be communicated to the managers responsible for planning throughout the organization. That is, managers should not only observe the changes in vision and strategy that occur at the corporate level, but should also learn about the environmental issues and assumptions — the strategic premises in Monsanto's terms — that guide the organization. This is one of the few places in the scanning process where *written documentation is clearly necessary.*

Yet these top-view environmental insights, while necessary to the manager's planning job, are not sufficient. The top view may not provide the manager with an environmental understanding that is either sufficiently specific to his or her task or sufficiently complete. For the specifics and the detail, expressed in terms and context relevant to the manager's line responsibilities, the line manager needs an environmental conduit in the form of a participant on the external environmental council. Chapter 6 developed the role of that council and the need for representation on it from the strategic sub-units of the organization. It is this linkage directly to the scanning system that will permit the line manager to receive environmental intelligence in operationally useful terms. This linkage can also transmit environmental information that would never appear in the executive, top-down channel *because it was either not an aspect, or too detailed an aspect,* of a critical corporate issue.

**ENVIRONMENTAL INTELLIGENCE FOR BUSINESS
UNITS: EXAMPLES**

A business unit would not likely learn through corporate channels about migration trends or infrastructure events that might affect the regional distribution of a product, but not the expected overall demand nor profitability of the product.

A business unit would learn through corporate channels about the emerging desirability of new investment in plant because of advances in robotics. But other communication channels, such as the external environmental council, would have to be the source of clues about enhancement in multi-axis arm repositioning speed, which might influence the unit's recommended timing of that new investment.

Environmental intelligence not critical in a corporate context could easily have strategic importance and value creation potential at the business unit level. The linkage between operating units and the external environmental council provides communication of important information about the environment. It is not self-evident that this communication should be in written form. Indeed, it may be more effective if the positive obligation of the process is for interpersonal dialogue on environmental issues at the operational level, rather than white papers, with documentary materials considered as supplementary.

Scanning and Accountability. The environmental scanning process described in this chapter involves the active participation of line management at all levels (see Figure 7.5). First of all, management influences the scanning strategy which then determines the approach to gathering and generating information. Second, management interacts through the external environmental council and with the senior evaluative group in synthesizing emerging issues. Third, management responds to the communication of environmental insights by adapting organizational strategy and unit plans.

The process thus assures line management *involvement* in environmental scanning. But for the value creation potential of environmental intelligence to be fully realized, there

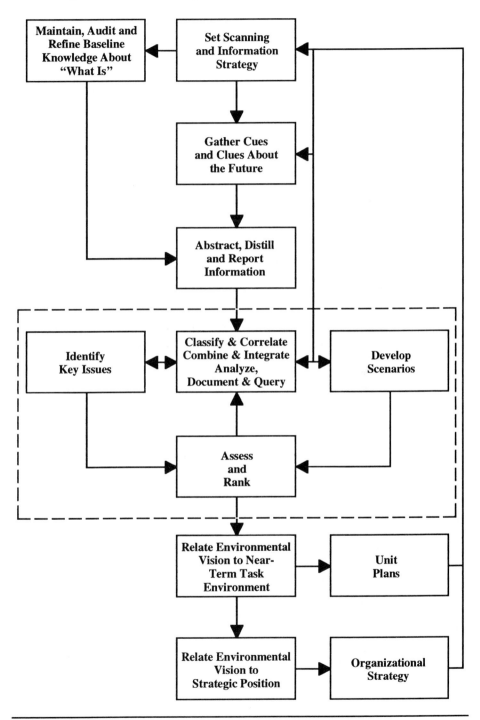

Figure 7.5: Top View of the Environmental Scanning Process

are additional requirements at the line management level. The line managers must *perceive* the value of that intelligence, must be *accountable* for its appropriate use, and must be *rewarded* according to their accountability and success.

Reward is ultimately associated with the aggressiveness of the plan and its performance. However, even if performance assessment is plan-related in time and measurement contexts, there does not presently exist any accepted methodology for defining a quantitative "environmental sensitivity" measure, such as might be used in adjusting compensation. Accountability is possible, however, as a *natural consequence* of participation in the environmental council, where, *"How is environmental intelligence being used in divisions and departments?"* can and should be an active aspect of deliberations, because knowledge about use can generate new ideas for scanning sources and methodologies. Second, knowledge about use can help balance resource commitments. Third, knowledge about use can help the scanning organization evaluate its own effectiveness in communicating environmental signals to the planners and line managers who need those signals as an input to developing operating strategies.

Scanning Process Example: American Council of Life Insurance. One of the most visible of organized environmental scanning efforts is the Trend Analysis Program of the American Council of Life Insurance. Founded in 1970, this program seeks to identify and measure trends, emerging issues and events in the world environment that are relevant to the life insurance industry. The Council has recently shifted its focus to staff scanners in the ACLI's Strategic Research Department. These professionals are responsible for scanning in their own areas of expertise: demographics, consumer attitudes and values, technology, and competitive forces in financial services. Previously, its main resource was a group of volunteer monitors from participant companies in the life insurance industry. These monitors each scanned one or two publications, reading both on and between the lines for clues of change. They sought surprising new information, ideas or contradictions of present beliefs or reality, or ideas expressed in surprising ways or from surprising sources. Attention was also given to information indicating new movements on a timeline that the monitor may have identified through earlier scanning. A monitor who found such clues wrote a brief abstract of the article and suggested implications, seeking to answer a question such as: "How will the information described in the article affect the life insurance business in particular or society in general?" Although monitors still support the scanning process, the staff centralization of scanning at ACLI has sharpened the focus of monitoring and analysis on trends of most importance to life insurance companies.

Key issues or trends are subjected to deeper study, and experts are hired to research and report on these issues. The issues are then presented and discussed at an annual Strategic Business Forum, to which member company operating executives are invited. Revised expert reports are published as TAP Reports.

The ACLI's comprehensive model for environmental scanning has been adopted by other industry/professional associations. In the fall of 1986, the American Society for Personnel Administration began the development of such a program, and since that time has developed baseline knowledge on numerous issues related to five basic areas in human resource management. They track and analyze issues using computerized information databases and a proprietary software program. (See Bower and Hallett: [49]).

Scanning Process Example: U.S. Congress. Environmental scanning is conducted by several organizations attached and related to the U.S. Congress, one of the most prominent being the Congressional Clearinghouse on the Future. The 105-member, bipartisan, bicameral Congressional Caucus funds this clearinghouse on a dues schedule basis. A current staff of 12, augmented occasionally by fellows from government agencies, seeks to identify the policy implications of long-term trends: demographic, economic, technological, political and social. The clearinghouse is oriented toward "changing issues," partly reflecting the concerns of its subscribing congressional members, and partly reflecting issues identified through the scanning of about 30 publications and through interaction with organizations such as the Council of State Planning Agencies. The focus is on issues that could influence government policy. Current issues under study by the Clearinghouse include: the aging of America; and new issues in housing, biotechnology, the information age and civil rights.

The Clearinghouse does not attempt to forecast futures on its own. Instead, it describes parameters and variables, discusses trends, reports what-if's and scenarios described by others and suggests possible policy issues with growing importance. Rob McCord, the executive director of the Clearinghouse, describes the staff as "policy entrepreneurs," seeking to develop new ways of doing public business [520,27].

Other Congressional futures groups include the Office of Technology Assessment, which has few staff members but contracts for research on issues of interest. The Congressional Research Service of the Library of Congress conducts studies on both current and future issues related to the legislative process. An emerging focus in Congressional study of emerging trends seems to be in the private-sector spinoff of previously government-sponsored efforts. Organizations have been formed such as the Environment and Energy Study Institute and the Congressional Institute for the Future, for which private-sector funding is sought to support research by a consultative staff. The Institute makes Clearinghouse publications available to the private sector.

Several Executive Branch agencies have engaged in foresight activities. These include the 21st Century Staff, U.S. Census Bureau, Department of Commerce and the Office of Strategic Planning of the Social Security Administration.

Scanning Process Example: Monsanto Corporation. The environmental scanning effort at Monsanto Corporation was created because of the enthusiasm and imagination of Margaret Stroup, and from the need she and others at Monsanto observed to probe the assumptions that were driving long-range plans across the organization. Part of this need arose from a disparity in views on conditions in the nearby task environment — interest rates, agricultural inputs and outputs, competitor tactics — that could be resolved with the promulgation of a uniform "assumption set." However, a more subtle set of disparities emerged in views of the probable future environment *beyond the immediate* that caused business units to develop "most probable" 5- to 7-year plans that were inconsistent with one another and thus *not additive* into a most probable plan at the corporate level.

Some of these disparities arose because assumptions about future conditions that were articulated and apparently consistent *had unexpressed differing meanings and implications to the managers translating those assumptions into plans.* Thus, accepted assumptions about the direction and speed of regulatory action and about the pattern of competitor product response were translated by different managers into differing implications for product demand, promotion, development and research. Other disparities arose because managers had differing beliefs and varying degrees of awareness of the implications of perceived but unarticulated future social, political, competitive and technological conditions; in effect, they were planning for different future environments.

In short, environmental scanning became necessary at Monsanto for two reasons. Erroneous but unarticulated thinking about the impacts of the future environment caused "most likely" plans at the unit level frequently to be unaccomplished. Inconsistent thinking about the impacts of the future environment, whether articulated or not, usually caused shortfalls in the corporate "most likely" plan.

The Strategic Premises program at Monsanto began in 1980 as an effort to articulate beliefs of the company, through its senior management, about the pattern of the future environment and its most significant relevant aspects, known collectively at Monsanto as "premises." It was a top-down process when the company had a centralized structure.

This process is presently taking hold at the group level as Monsanto has restructured itself into six operating companies. The process involves identifying possible issues through the interaction of a volunteer task force, constituted by invitation, of the best minds for the job, wherever they may be in the organization. With a charge to think creatively and do a limited amount of advance reading, the task force convenes for several dialogue meetings to synthesize and select a subset of issues from the environment that have operating implications for Monsanto. From these issues a set of preliminary premises is developed, each as a brief statement of potential environmental events and outcomes, their chances of occurrence, and their possible impacts on Monsanto.

As many as 11 of these premises, and as few as six, have been presented to the Executive Management Committee. With support from planning director, this executive group debates the merits of each premise with two objectives. First, an importance-imminence ranking should emerge that will permit some premises to be highlighted for importance and perhaps some that can be discarded. Second, as the beliefs of senior executives are articulated and debated, a common understanding emerges. That understanding should lead to a consensus on assumptions that should be made about the premises and about the implications such assumptions have for corporate plans. Direct involvement of senior executives in the debate over issues has also led them to sign on individually to lead monitoring and action efforts, especially on publicly sensitive issues [283;454].

To the extent that the task force or executive dialogue series develops a need for more information, staff are borrowed to undertake an information search and analysis. Otherwise, little formalized literature or media scanning is done on a regular basis. Instead, the process relies on the knowledge, creativity and intuition of the scanning task force, supported by whatever formal or informal scanning resources and activities they personally require to maintain and enhance their individual expertise.

After describing Monsanto's scanning process at a conference of The Planning Forum [453], Stroup left her audience with a list of do's and don't's for contributing to the success of scanning in motivating better planning:

DO:

- make the process active for top managers; it is not a planner's exercise;
- limit the number of issues you ask top management to consider; 11 is too many, six may be all right;
- teach; keep pushing outward management's consciousness of the external environment and its linkages with the company.

DON'T:

- expect quick results in terms of impact on the quality or consistency of plans;
- deal with issues that can't be connected to the company or unit's operations;
- be boring; lengthy white papers will be forgotten (if read) or ignored entirely.

Scanning Process Example: Motorola Corporation. In 1984, Motorola established a business intelligence department separate from the strategy and business development group as a corporate-level function reporting to its office of strategy. The department was fully functioning within two years, providing collection and reporting, analysis and information services. The focus of Motorola's intelligence alerts, internal analytical assessments and purchased consultant studies is four-fold. First, the effort supports strategic decision making, as in planning alliances, acquisitions and major capital investments in new technology, products and markets. Second, the intelligence effort seeks to provide early warning of opportunities and threats, including competitive actions and strategies. Third, business intelligence seeks to support planning and strategy development by testing and proposing key assumptions underlying plans and strategies, and by identifying changes in competitive and industry structure. Fourth, the business intelligence department tracks and assesses competitors.

The business intelligence network Motorola has developed includes both human and documentary sources. Documentary efforts encompass published literature and purchased studies, while human sources are both internal and external. The entire system is governed by a set of legal and ethical guidelines. (Legal and ethical issues of business intelligence gathering are raised in the literature [88;127;137;302].)

Experience with environmental scanning at Motorola has led to refined efforts in several areas. The scanning unit has moved to develop its own agenda: to alert the organization to opportunities, threats and decisions requiring action, and to suggest appropriate courses of action, rather than simply responding to questions. The department's efforts are also being focused on two or three issues identified jointly with the CEO as top priority because of their direct impact on major decisions or actions. Motorola also has learned that analysis of external issues must dominate and drive collection efforts to obtain environmental information, as there is a natural tendency to create big databases and promote them erroneously as information or intelligence.

The output of the department is becoming more focused on concise and timely reports, preferably verbal or electronic, directed to a few key decision makers. Reports focus on the implications of key alternatives, scenarios and decisions related to specific business and strategies, and are not focused on the basis or evidence for the issue or signal itself, and are not simply based on watching competitors. This report focus is a way to assure that environmental signals are communicated in the organization's own language. Motorola's corporate business intelligence department operates with a staff of about 10, augmented with analysis and collection efforts at the operating division level. Corporate-level positions, especially the analytical ones, are rotational in nature. The department is supported by a multi-year top management commitment of resources.

Scanning Process Example: Nynex Corporation. For a number of years prior to divestiture of its operating companies, AT&T maintained a corporate emerging issues program [92]. The staff of that program produced periodic "white papers" on issues of interest to both corporate and subsidiary companies, and encouraged company development of programs and procedures to incorporate environmental scanning into their strategic planning methodologies.

Nynex Corporation's corporate planning department maintains this environmental scanning focus through their TEAM (Trend Evaluation And Monitoring) program, supported to some degree by the consulting services of Weiner•Edrich•Brown. The consultants provide Nynex with abstracts of strategically relevant signals from scanned publications, and the Nynex corporate planning staff reviews and synthesizes these with other environmental signals.

Nynex conducts bimonthly TEAM meetings, attended by a multi-disciplinary group from business unit and staff organizations, and facilitated by Weiner•Edrich•Brown. This interdepartmental and business unit group discusses new developments and signals of change in important business trends and issues. As inputs to their discussion they have the materials developed by the staff and consultants since the previous meeting, including working papers. Their debate is summarized in a widely-distributed internal publication, intended for both officers and planners. This publication synthesizes the ideas for each of several issues, including the implications, references and abstracts as background to motivate unit-level strategic thinking.

Nynex staff also attend quarterly trend evaluation seminars conducted by WEB that include scanning staffs from other industries. At these seminars, the consultant staff presents several working papers synthesizing broad environmental trends and the evidence supporting their importance and imminence. Participants question and debate these working papers, and then present to the group for debate the issues each individual has developed relative to a special interest or concern.

Summary. The examples of scanning processes presented here emulate the larger model this book proposes; yet each process is tailored to meet the needs of specific circumstances and culture. The ACLI trend analysis program is scanning-intensive in the sense of *seeking cues and clues* from publications and other communication media. While it does some scanning on its own, the Congressional Clearinghouse on the Future is principally focused on identifying and articulating for its Congressional sponsors the key futures issues about which *constituent publics* are already concerned. The Monsanto strategic premises program is more concerned with the *internal articulation* of a consistent view of environmental issues than with the evidential aspects of developing any issue or even "just the right set" of issues. Further, the Monsanto scanning task force is based on skills and abilities, regardless of strategic sub-unit representation. Motorola's scanning efforts are more focused on intelligence gathering and information processing than the others.

Nynex, because of its dual challenges to respond to new competitive realities while reflecting a responsibility to an extremely large customer and community constituency, may take the broadest external view of any of the examples presented. In all of these models, a judgmental balance is struck between intuition and fact-finding, between breadth and depth of view, between documentation and spontaneity, and between task force representation and participant skill. Over time that balance has produced useful outcomes.

Barriers to Effective Scanning

If environmental scanning fails to enhance a manager's ability to take advantage of change or fails to bring status as a contributor to the corporate strategic vision, it may be that that effort has been handicapped by one or more of the barriers to effectiveness summarized in Table 7.2 and discussed in the sections that follow.

Table 7.2: Inherent Pitfalls in Environmental Scanning

- Forecasts are basically unsound.
- Unstructured thinking lacks credibility.
- Cost/benefit ratio indeterminate.
- Organization biased toward immediate productivity.

Inherent Pitfalls. Part of the process of drawing inferences about the future environment requires forecasts. These can be based on the past and the present but the future is unknown. Forecasting models based on past and present data relate the phenomenon we seek to forecast to other variables. But because we cannot actually know the future values of these other variables, there is an inherent weakness in the process. For example, long term forecasts of the balance of international power contain many embedded assumptions; one concerns the pricing and distribution of scarce natural resources such as oil, platinum and uranium, and another the development and possession of technology for weapons and production in space. Often in the past, careful predictions have been wrong. And in the evaluation, too often the correct prediction has been discarded by managers, along with the useful elements of the insight from which that prediction came.

Avoiding these pitfalls involves using forecasts in a way that will acknowledge their fragility and vulnerability; these are not point predictions, but possible or plausible future states of nature which, if they emerge, have a set of significant implications for our plans and strategies. The implications differ slightly with altered assumptions. The probabilities of encountering various states and circumstances can perhaps be assessed, but it is not possible to predict any significant future state with a probability of one, and the value of the environmental insight does not depend on such predictive accuracy.

Unstructured thinking is rarely the accepted culture of an organization. Thus, in most organizations unstructured thinkers are not regarded as credible or seen as fitting comfortably into teams. These are people who seem to question all the accepted truths, introduce issues from outside the time frame or responsibility domain of individual managers, and generally slow down the decision-making process. It is probably fair to say that there is a basis for mutual appreciation to develop between the archetype unstructured thinker, a "futurist crazy," and the paragon structured thinker, a "goal-driven manager." Both need some of the skills of the other to succeed in their jobs. Avoiding this cultural and interpersonal forecasting pitfall is partly a matter of skill and sensitivity training. Effective implementation of the environmental council also minimizes this pitfall by integrating scanning and managing at the level of council membership.

Even with extensive line management involvement in environmental scanning through environmental council and senior management dialogues, some staff functions are unavoidable. There is a tendency to bias against those functions because their cost must be borne by the "productive" functions of the organization. Worse yet, the benefits of scanning are much more difficult to measure than its costs. Fewer surprises, better strategic positioning, and quicker reactions are some of the positive outcomes, and while these benefits can be measured to some extent, measurement is inherently imperfect because there is no measure of the outcome that would have occurred if the scanning investment had not been made. While the inherent pitfalls cannot be eliminated, they become potentially less harmful when line and senior management are active participants in the scanning process.

Organizational Pitfalls. Scanning fails to contribute to the organization when there are barriers to it built into the organization's culture, as summarized in Table 7.3. Some organizations believe that the only solutions to problems are internal ones, because of past inabilities to understand or exploit the environment. When plans go awry, such organizations tend to seek internal solutions through reductions in cost and increases in productivity and efficiency. Where the preponderant response to adversity is "batten down the hatches," such an organization is unlikely to seek or realize value from an improved understanding of the environment. Such organizations have a built-in resistance to scanning, and this propensity is not rare. One study found statistical support for the view that managements under environmental stress, "instead of relaxing control and becoming more flexible to meet the demands of an uncertain environment . . . tended to develop more bureaucratic structures, centralize authority at upper levels, and simplify and standardize work procedures, . . . because individuals in these units are likely to interpret an otherwise uncertain environment to be controllable and even more predictable" [248].

Table 7.3: Organizational Pitfalls in Environmental Scanning

- Managers preoccupied with operations
- Management preoccupation with internal solutions
- Sluggish systems (time to learn, interpret)
- Fragmented scanning effort

Organizations with either new or tentative commitments to environmental scanning may evince other characteristics that serve as barriers to scanning success. First, scanning might be irregular or sporadic, undertaken to respond to demonstrated needs or circumstances. In such cases, the absence of an infrastructure and of accustomed scanning roles and behaviors can cause the system to be sluggish; or the time to learn, communicate and act may exceed the useful strategic reaction time to an event or trend.

Fragmentation of the scanning effort can also contribute to sluggishness, and to missed cues and clues, because the scanning intelligence obtained in one part of the organization is not integrated with that obtained elsewhere. In such cases, the learn-and-communicate aspects of scanning do not work properly. The "act" aspect of scanning can reflect failure if managers are so preoccupied with operations and contemporary issues that they don't incorporate scanning intelligence into their behavior, even where such intelligence has been effectively communicated and consciously received. "If I can just get these crises under control, I'll be able to start thinking long-run," is a typical managerial response.

These organizational pitfalls are more likely to occur when scanning is being introduced into an organization. Culture changes slowly, even where the intent to change is positive and aggressive. Alertness to these and the other pitfalls discussed above can be particularly important for the organization planning or initially implementing an environmental scanning effort; it is in these early stages that scanning is most vulnerable to the politics of resistance from operating managers, who are most greatly threatened by potential changes in the accustomed patterns of organizational thought.

Process and Interface Pitfalls. What mistakes can scanners make, even in an organization that is properly organized and acculturated for the effort? Scanners can succumb to *process pitfalls,* as summarized in Table 7.4, by inundating themselves with too much information to digest, or by becoming absorbed with the wrong kind of information, as when scanners focus on the "what is" knowledge base at the expense of seeking cues and clues of future trends or circumstances. Scanners must be dogged in their efforts to obtain signals and information, but those efforts must be driven by the *analysis* function in the scanning unit; information is simply data unless it is subjected to processes of analysis and inference.

Table 7.4: Process Pitfalls in Environmental Scanning

- Insufficient analysis.
- Information overload.
- Unreliable scanners.
- Focus on what is instead of what might be.

The scanning process can also be hindered if it is conducted by unreliable scanners. People may procrastinate because of other demands on their time, or may be overly subject to selective perception, bias or distortion because of their training or disposition. Similarly, they may be unprepared for the open-minded exploration of the environment that scanning requires. Effectively implanting an environmental scanning culture within the organization should communicate priorities and expectations in such a way that people will either adopt the culture or opt out of it. In the scanning culture, information is not for building individual power. It is a corporate asset which everyone in the organization, top-down and bottom-up, has a stake in developing and sharing.

Barriers to scanning success at the interface level, as summarized in Table 7.5, include the tendency to identify too many issues for executives and managers to deal with in their dialogues and planning. Some scanners may present these issues in arcane rather than operational terms. What is needed by the organization is a concise set of possible outcomes and action strategy proposals, targeted to a small number of key decision makers. Such presentations result when the scanning unit digests and analyzes its scanning inputs, and focuses on the context and language of the organization, its businesses and its strategies, rather than on the context and language of the environment.

When issues are presented successfully in operational terms, there is a tendency to choose for focus the one or two strategic decision areas that may be most impacted by an issue, and then to target presentations to a few key decision makers. This is a desirable approach for the presentation, but the analysis itself should seek to reconcile the impact of the issue across the organization. By forcing the diagnosis and debate of an issue broadly across the functions of an organization, it is possible to uncover subtle and unforeseen linkages that have critical impacts.

Table 7.5: Interface Pitfalls in Environmental Scanning

- Issues not integrated.
- Issue overload.
- Outputs unfocused on operations.
- Outputs not targeted to decision makers.
- Qualitative imbalance.

Finally, *managers* must avoid the temptation to expect that scanning outcomes will be entirely quantitative and specifically focused on their individual operating purviews, while *scanners* must avoid the tendency to be overly qualitative and abstract. That is, the burden of adaptation should not fall entirely upon the shoulders of the scanning unit.

Conclusions

Concluding this chapter with a description of potential barriers and pitfalls in achieving a successful environmental scanning system re-emphasizes the critical success factors for managing structure, people, process and product. Scanning must be diversified across the organization in terms of both involvement in process and accountability for encoding outcomes. Scanning intelligence must be timely and communicated effectively in operational terms, so that the organization can seek maximum benefit by tailoring its vision, strategy and plans to the threats and opportunities of the probable future.

The first seven chapters of this book present both a rationale and a methodology for making environmental scanning the fundamental underpinning of the organization's strategic information network. Searching, with a purpose, for signals of change also requires choice of information sources, discussed in Chapter 8, and analytical techniques, covered in Chapter 9.

CHAPTER 8

SOURCES OF ENVIRONMENTAL INFORMATION

Previous chapters developed models of environmental scanning, the dimensions of the environment, the elements of a strategy for scanning activities, a structure for the scanning itself and an implementation process that actively involves line management at all levels. The remaining two chapters are idea, resource and technique guides for implementing environmental scanning programs and systems. Emphasis is on pertinent information and sources in this chapter; the final chapter focuses on analytical and judgmental techniques for evaluating environmental information.

The purpose of scanning is to gain, from the environment, information that will permit the organization to identify, select and optimize strategies in pursuit of its objectives and mission. This chapter first explores where information comes from, how to obtain *early signal information* from literature and publications, and documentation of environmental information. The remaining sections of the chapter compare actual information sources, distinguishing them according to content futurity, time focus, type of publication and timeliness. A final section describes the methods of obtaining information from the teeming number of commercial, computer-readable databases.

Basis for Choosing Information Sources

The organization must decide what information it wants to aid in developing strategy. Ideally, the information the organization wants should be the same as the information it needs, but there are several reasons why *what we decide we want may be less than what the organization needs:*

1. Because perceptions of "the world" are imperfect, the organization may be unaware of information that exists or of its strategic value.

2. Less information may be sought because of limited ability to process information into meaningful form.

3. The information obtained may lack value because of limited ability to draw inferences from it.

Enhanced knowledge about environmental scanning, its methodology and its outcomes serves to bring needs and wants for strategic information inputs into closer accord, but it is probably not reasonable to expect to close the gap between want and need completely. As Mendell notes:

It is impossible to predict *a priori* what information will be needed to appreciate a situation. Information content governs the filters and patterns through which the situation can be appreciated in the first place [321,158].

Success in obtaining desired information may be constrained by its *accessibility*. The information may not exist, or may exist only in fragmentary form. The data may exist but be unavailable because it is confidential, as are competitors' costs, military weapons research or a takeover artist's financial resources.

> **Expect to work hard at building inferences about the environment that aren't obvious to everyone else too. The information we seek as direct input into our inferential judgment processes may in fact come to us as raw, unrelated data that emerges as useful information only if properly analyzed and integrated by the organization's scanning process.**

Information may be accessible but unavailable, because the scanners are unprepared or improperly organized to receive it. Further, the acquisition cost of information may be a barrier if costs relative to benefits are too high. Lastly, accessible information may be unavailable because the organization does not know it exists or where to look; it may lack skill in both the art and practice of prying out information [98].

Where Information Comes From. Most environmental input comes from people, events and documents, both within and outside the organization, as illustrated in Figure 8.1. Managers' sources of environmental information were about evenly divided between inside and outside the firm, according to Aguilar's landmark study of the scanning activities in the chemical industry [5]. Over 70 percent of the environmental information came from personal sources, about equally divided between insiders and outsiders. Inside the firm the bulk of strategic external information was communicated by subordinates (bottom up), and relatively little from superiors (top down). Outside the firm, environmental input was as likely to come from a person unrelated to the business as from a customer, lender, supplier or other person with a business relationship.

Strategic environmental information from events and documents was communicated much more frequently from outside the firm (20 percent of all information) than from within (10 percent), according to Aguilar. Publications accounted for about two-thirds of impersonal information received by the firm. Broadcast media and direct observation at trade shows, conferences and seminars accounted for only 10 percent of strategic environmental information that managers received.

The findings of a number of more recent researchers on the sources of scanning input were synthesized by Glueck [177]. Among his conclusions with respect to personal information sources were:

1. Verbal source usage increased with organizational level.
2. Strategists were more likely to favor verbal sources than managers.
3. Personal scanning sources tended to be balanced toward internal communication in large organizations and external communication in smaller organizations.
4. Among personal contacts, primary were individual/professional sources, secondary were customer/competitive, and tertiary were supplier and distribution channel sources.

Figure 8.1: Sources of Environmental Information

PEOPLE SOURCES	EVENTS, OBJECTS
External	
Business-related	Media-related Sources
Bankers, financial advisors	General
Customers	Business and Financial
Suppliers	Trade
Consultants	Technical/Academic
Regulators	
	Other Sources
Unrelated	Purchased research reports
	Technical conferences
Regular Associations	Trade shows
Friends	Educational seminars
Professional peers	Direct observation
Episodic Encounters	
Adjoining seat occupant	
Neighbor	
Internal	
Line Relationships	Reports
Superiors	Progress
Subordinates	Performance
	Projection
Staff Relationships	Activity
Peer Relationships	Meetings
	Scheduled
Counterpart Relationships	Issue-motivated
(cross-divisional)	
Other (motivated by	
personal relationships,	
mutual interest)	

The relative usage and importance of human, institutional (primarily meetings), and documentary scanning inputs to executives were studied by Kefalas and Schoderbeck [238] in farm machinery as a dynamic industry, and meat packing as a stable one. Unlike Aguilar, who found that neither meetings nor internal reports were important as a source of scanning information, these authors found that all types of meetings dominated human and documentary sources in both importance and frequency. This finding may reflect changing management styles between 1967, the date of Aguilar's study, and 1973, as "the meeting" grew in pervasiveness among management activities. Indeed, in dynamic environments, it was found that institutional meeting scanning sources dominated at the expense of individual human contact. The relative usage of documentary sources was nearly constant.

> **Human contacts are valuable sources of environmental clues, but the most productive contacts are those outside of the organization. Scanners should avoid the convenience of proximity in choosing scanning contacts. Generally, the purpose of internal human interaction is to synthesize clues into information, signals and insights, not to obtain those clues.**

Another form of interaction that has grown in recent years is the network, the popularity of which as a communication device is shown by the evolution of this noun into a popular verb. William C. Ashley, head of issues management and regulatory affairs at United Airlines, reports that UAL's scanning process includes "plugging into many organizations and establishing networks that allow us to access a wide range of information" [Stein: 446,46]. Ashley cites as examples groups such as the *Midwest Issues Network Dialogue* and *Issues Network.*

> **Encourage boundary-spanning activities by people in your organization. The purpose is to develop an ongoing dialogue with people outside your organization who like to respond to "what do you think" questions about future possibilities, and to capture elements of that dialogue as environmental data. The boundaries to be spanned are natural ones between:**
>
> | | | |
> |---|---|---|
> | salespersons | ↔ | customers |
> | purchasing agents | ↔ | suppliers |
> | professionals | ↔ | experts |

Survey data also reveals the relative frequency of use of specific sources of information by scanners. Culnan [102] studied the use of information in two large organizations, comprising 362 professionals. One was a bank, chosen for its mediating technology, which means that many line managers are placed at the boundary-spanning environmental interface. The other organization was a manufacturing firm — chosen for its long-linked technology — which, because of the sensitive and proprietary nature of its core technology, tended to limit the conduct of boundary-spanning activities related to the external environment to staff and executives. Culnan found trade subscriptions and peers to be the top-ranked sources of environmental information. The next three most important sources for information were subordinates, superiors and internal documents; databases, consultants, internal libraries and other outside sources ranked last.

Another recent survey of 37 executives and managers in 11 large corporations was supplemented by 186 questionnaire responses from Fortune 500 companies. In this questionnaire, Jain [207] elicited importance rankings for 11 classes of environmental information sources. Respondents assigned rankings to each source on the basis of one to five. These results are summarized in Table 8.1, according to the cumulative percentage of respondents that ranked each source either first or second. In a finding that supports Glueck's analysis, Jain found that the premier scanning source for these respondents was the most general one, daily newspapers such as *The New York Times* and *The Wall Street Journal*. Publications by credible trade associations, institutions and consulting organizations, along with business periodicals, captured the next three rankings. Seminars and conferences ranked sixth. Inputs from the *intelligentsia,* professional associations, universities and the elite periodical literature such as *Atlantic, Harpers,* or *The New Yorker* ranked last. Smeltzer's study of small firms [430] showed an overwhelming preference for informal sources of scanning information from family, customers, friends or colleagues. Among

Table 8.1: Sources of Environmental Information Ranked in Importance by 186 Respondents

Rank	Source	Pct. Ranking 1st or 2nd
1	Daily Newspapers	91
2	Expert Organization Publications (Conference Board, Brookings, etc.)	59
3	Business Periodicals	52
4	Futures Consultants and Forecasters	42
5	Government Publications	42
6	Seminars and Conferences	30
7	Popular Academic Journals	22
8	Proprietary Newsletters	17
9	Professional Associations	16
10	Universities	6
11	Literary Publications	3

Source: Jain [207,124]

impersonal sources — half as important to these small firm managers as were people — magazines and journals capped the list.

Most of the survey results reported here relate to U.S.-based companies. For a discussion of Japanese practices in scanning, see Engel [143]; Korean firm environmental scanning is described by Ghoshal [172].

Documenting Environmental Signals

One of the recommendations of Chapter 7 was to index and classify scanning information so that it could be accessed and manipulated through a computerized database framework. There are essentially three sources of input into such a system, each of which would require slightly different formats of documentation by the scanner.

Useful information from documentary sources should be captured in a format along the lines of Figure 8.2. Important reference data relating *to the source* includes title, publication name, date and page. The source type indicator allows the form to be used for scanning abstracts other than from print publications. Examples are sources that are heard or observed, such as media broadcasts, seminars and exhibits at trade shows.

Several items of data are important to the *scanning process,* including the primary dimension of the environment referenced, and one or more keywords relating the item to previously identified issues or topics. Word count supports the study of the cumulative literature on the subject, a methodology described in the next section of this chapter. Cross-references to other abstracts should be provided. If the scanner is able to suggest any implications or inferences from the abstract item, these should be included in brief form.

The abstract itself is a brief narrative, not necessarily of the source article, but of the underlying ideas and clues that may have relevance to the organization. Finally, identifier data on the scanner and the date of entry can be helpful in finding abstract records in the future where a partial reference forces investigative search ("I read it in January.").

A slightly different abstract form is applicable to scanning data that comes from interactions with people (see Figure 8.3). Person and place replace author and publication. The context of the contact from which the input came becomes relevant. Other abstract and reference elements are comparable to the documentary abstract.

While a scanner may suggest implications or inferences as part of any original scanning record, the true value of scanning documentation emerges when scanning data is correlated and integrated. The ideas and inferences that emerge should be made a part of the scanning knowledge database, where they can combine with other inferences to create even more ideas and inferences. The idea/inference abstract form is illustrated in Fig. 8.4.

The idea may relate to a collection of scanning database abstract entries; if so, these entries are identified by internal reference numbers. The idea may relate to a particular discussion within the organization or the scanning process; this is captured as the context of the scanning record.

Figure 8.2: Sample Documentary Source Abstract Format

ORGANIZATION NAME/LOGO

Environmental Scanning System

Documentary Source Abstract

Title: _____

Author: _____

About Author: _____

Source: _____

Source type: _____   Date: _____   Page: _____

Scanner: _____   Scan date: _____

Keywords: _____

Dimension focus: _____   Word count: _____

ABSTRACT

IMPLICATIONS/INFERENCES

Database entry: _____

As presented in figures 8.2 through 8.4, scanning abstract records exist in hard copy form. Scanners use the form to write down their observations and documentation. When transcribed into the computerized scanning database, these entries are annotated with appropriate database entry information, such as record number, date of entry or initials of entry person. However, these forms would also exist as entry templates in the database, which could be used for direct entry into the system by keyboard-oriented scanners.

Figure 8.3: Sample Personal Source Abstract Format

ORGANIZATION NAME/LOGO

Environmental Scanning System

Personal Source Abstract

Person: _____

About Person: _____

Place: _____

Context: _____

Keywords: _____

Date: _____   Dimension focus: _____

Scanner: _____   Scan date: _____

ABSTRACT

IMPLICATIONS/INFERENCES

Database entry: _____

Obtaining Early Signals from Published Literature Sources

Strategically, scanning resources that provide credible environmental signals at the longest lead times are the most valuable. These sources enable the organization to initiate strategic issue tracking and preliminary planning for strategic response. The most productive sources for environmental scanning are those that can reliably signal *what will happen.* By contrast, the executive who uses *The Wall Street Journal* or *The New York Times* as the most frequent scanning source learns more about *what has happened* and *what is happening,* categories of strategic intelligence of high immediacy but low value for learning about the future. The real value of such instantaneous sources is in confirming the resolution of strategic issues the organization should already have identified and tracked.

Figure 8.4: Sample Idea/Inference Abstract Format

ORGANIZATION NAME/LOGO

Environmental Scanning System

Idea/Inference Abstract

Idea/Inference: _____

References: _____

Context: _____

Keywords: _____

Scanner: _____ Scan Date: _____

IMPLICATIONS/INFERENCES

Database entry: _____

Sources can be evaluated according to their accuracy or credibility and cost, aspects that must be considered in the scanning strategy resource allocation decision. But since the premier purpose of environmental scanning is the early identification of *ideas whose time has not yet come,* the scanner must also evaluate sources and select them on the basis

---

MANAGE THE FUTURE FOCUS OF SCANNING SOURCES

Measure periodically the frequency of your scanning inputs by futurity of source within each dimension of the environment. Add long-futurity sources to your scanning strategy where inputs are too current.

---

of the futurity of the signals they contain. If there is a chronic imbalance in the information sources used to support scanning, it is likely to be in underemphasizing sources with long futurities. Short futurity sources, those dealing with the present, are less ambiguous. Negative futurity sources, those dealing with the past and history, are even more certain.

Enrich your fund of information about ideas that haven't yet happened. Mendell suggests these sources and activities:
  a. **Read utopian and science fiction. Writers are often sensitive to developing trends.**
  b. **Read magazines like *The Futurist* and *Futures.* "Borrow" predictions from the authors.**
  c. **Monitor long-term trends in public opinion polls; what the public wants it often gets.**
  d. **Monitor the writings of politicians and social scientists. They often create a climate of expectation or acceptance of innovations.**
  e. **Watch out for mention of precursor jurisdictions — areas or people who adopt innovation early. Then assume the innovation will find its way to other areas or people. [321,158]**

The path from isolated random data about novel behaviors or ideas to accomplished fact is analyzed by Molitor [337] as an S-curve phenomenon. His research focused on the precursors to public policy change; however, the concept of finding precursors has application in evaluating information sources throughout the environment. The essence of the idea is twofold. First, impending change appears as the cumulative sum of a series of individual events and is recognized as such at or about the onset of the acceleration phase of the S-curve. Second, the occurrence of change and of change events is foreshadowed and foretold by the actions of leading authorities and organizations and further by the documentation of those actions in leading literature sources. This cumulative information phenomenon is illustrated in Figure 8.5, which shows four transition states of knowledge about a concept: visionary, model-building, diffusion and consolidation.

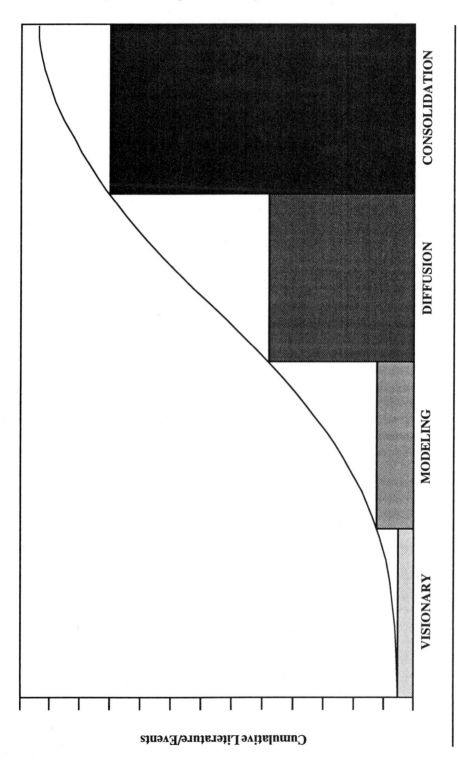

Source: Molitor [337]

Figure 8.5: Cumulative Information on an Issue

The original source of a concept may be an event, an abuse of the public conscience or the idea of a visionary. For example, Cyrano de Bergerac (see *The Environment Speaks X*), a satirist who lived from 1619-1655, may have been such a visionary. His favored satirical targets included the Church and the Bible, which in seventeenth-century France were subjects the authorities were unwilling to have criticized. To get his works published, Cyrano cast his criticism in the form of fanciful stories and imaginary voyages, and today those works appear as early science fiction. De Bergerac's book, *Voyages to the Moon and Sun,* written under the name Savinien, tells of a spring-driven voice machine and a vacuum-driven space vehicle some 300 years before anything remotely similar to these technologies actually emerged. In addition to authors such as de Bergerac, artists and poets are two other visionary sources for earliest-published signals of the future.

Naturally, the writings of these visionaries are fraught with noise, error and even whimsy. Scholars still debate whether de Bergerac's ideas about the future were his own or copied from the work of others. Visionary writings provide no basis for judging either the timing of the future implementation of a concept or its probability of occurrence. However, these early writings do provide data points regarding *possible* future changes.

The first "post-visionary" references to a concept may appear in fringe media, either editorially or as quotations from writings or speeches of lesser or unknown experts. Newton, Einstein and Jung became leading experts *because* of breakthrough work in their respective fields. Dan Lundberg, the early forecaster of the world oil shortage, became respected only *after* the crisis-related events of the 1979 decline in Mid-East oil production emerged (see *The Environment Speaks XI*). Of course, currently recognized leading authorities are innovators as well, and their seminal ideas may appear early-on in the more popular literature. Through the work of these expert people and the organizations to which they are allied, the concept of "what might be" is refined into models of how the concept might come about. Eventually these models are described in technical or professional monographs, journals, newsletters and documents.

If the literature relating to a concept reaches the acceleration phase of the S-curve, it may be because of increasing debate among experts or because advocates emerge and become more vocal. Experts and advocates are *change agents*. Acceleration in cumulative literature may also occur because interest in the concept materializes among the intelligentsia, acting as *change informants*. If this acceleration phase is reached for a given issue or idea, it will probably occur during the Modeling Phase (see Figure 8.5). Once the idea or issue reaches the Diffusion Phase, it is already becoming part of the culture, in terms of recognition, acceptance or policy response.

CAPITALIZE ON VISIONARIES

Look for forecasts of visionaries and experts. Test their ideas against your scanning knowledge base. Do you find confirming signals? If not, scan more purposefully. Have you missed these issues? Find new sources of input and signals.

THE ENVIRONMENT SPEAKS X
Cyrano de Bergerac, a Visionary?

From *Voyage to the Moon,* circa 1648:

At the opening of the box I found something in metal almost similar to our clocks, filled with an infinite number of little springs and imperceptible machines. It is a book indeed, but a miraculous book without pages or letters; in fine, it is a book to learn from which eyes are useless, only ears are needed. When someone wishes to read he winds up the machine with a large number of all sorts of keys; then he turns the pointer towards the chapter he wishes to ear [sic], and immediately, as if from a man's mouth or a musical instrument, this machine gives out all the distinct and different sounds which serve as the expression of speech between the noble Moon-dwellers. [108,136]

From *Voyage to the Sun,* circa 1650:

For eight days I hammered, I planed, I glued and at last constructed the machine I am about to describe to you. It was a large, very light box which shut very exactly. It was about six feet high and about three wide in each direction. This box had holes in the bottom, and over the roof, which was also pierced, I placed a crystal vessel with similar holes made globe-shaped but very large, whose neck terminated exactly at and fitted in the opening I made in the top. The vessel was expressly made with several angles, in the shape of an icosahedron, so that each facet was convex and concave. My globe produced the effect of a burning mirror . . . . My gaoler had gone down and the sky was overcast when I exposed this machine on the summit of the Tower, that is to say in the most open portion of my terrace; it closed so exactly that not a single grain of air could slip in except through the two openings. I had fitted inside a small, very light plank which served me as a seat. All being arranged in this way I shut myself up inside and remained there nearly an hour, waiting until it pleased Fortune to command me. When the sun emerged from the clouds and began to shine on my machine . . . I felt my entrails stirred in the same way a man feels them stir when he is lifted up by a pulley. . . I looked through the hole in the floor of my box and saw my Tower already far below me . . . the globe became a vacuum and, since Nature abhors a vacuum, she made it draw up air through the lower opening to fill itself. . . and consequently was bound to force up my machine continually. At the end of about four months' traveling, at least as nearly as can be calculated, when there is no night to distinguish one day from another, I reached one of those little Worlds that fly around the Sun, called by Mathematicians "Spots" [108,185-193].

THE ENVIRONMENT SPEAKS XI
Dan Lundberg, Oil Analyst, Dies; Forecast 1979 Gasoline Shortage

Dan Lundberg, the oil industry analyst who accurately forecast the 1979 gasoline shortage and whose biweekly survey of nationwide gasoline prices was widely quoted, died Sunday at a Torrance hospital . . . . From March 1979 when Mr. Lundberg was among the first to predict a fuel shortage after Middle East nations cut back production until his death, he was at the forefront of petroleum prophecy. It was a role he did not always relish.

"People think that I'm prescient," he said in a 1981 interview with *The Los Angeles Times*. "You can make projections, you can make forecasts and you can make predictions, but I don't do any of that. I compile data and I draw conclusions. That's it. I don't have a crystal ball."

"The Lundberg Survey was incorporated in the early 1960s, although his first gasoline survey was done in the late 1950s," Mrs. Lundberg said.

"He had been a journalist and then got into radio and television and saw an opportunity to organize segments of the oil industry, and from that he started his price surveys, starting with just the West Coast and gradually covering the nation," she said. [In 1965, he suspended publication and did not resume again until 1973, when the Arab nations imposed an oil embargo on the West. The format was completely revised, and the Lundberg Letter became a highly regarded independent source of petroleum intelligence.]

After his newsletter predicted the world petroleum shortage, major news agencies carried Mr. Lundberg's surveys of gasoline pump prices and quoted him on developments in the energy industries.

Source: The New York Times, *August 6, 1986 and July 11, 1979. Reproduced by permission of the Associated Press.*

Subsequently, the timing of the concept's implementation is resolved, and the concept emerges as a "known" rather than as a "possibility" or a "probability." During this emergence of the concept, the literature references to it may continue to accelerate but shift in source to the popular periodicals, news magazines, opinion polls and print and broadcast media. To a large extent, these sources are reporting "what is," therefore providing little in the way of strategic signals about "what will be." Finally, in the continuum of literature database formulation, a consolidation phase occurs where output lessens and its character changes to documentation and eventually historical analysis.

At or around the period of acceleration in the literature, Molitor suggests a stage of inevitability may be reached, where a watchful observer can safely predict the emergence of the idea or issue in the broader society, before others have identified it. This watchful analysis of the print, broadcast and artistic media for signals and clues for purposes of predicting a subject or issue is called *content analysis*. The function of content analysis is to gather enough *indirect evidence* about a subject to permit it to be understood, even where little or no *direct evidence* exists. The published references to the subject become documentary abstracts in the environmental scanning database, from which inferences can be drawn about future events. Inferences about the *shape* of a concept can be drawn from analysis of the literature's content and changes therein. Inferences about the *imminence* of the concept can be drawn from the rate and extent of accumulation of literature references measured, for example, by number and source of mentions, articles, pages or words. Merriam and Makower expand on this methodology in *Trend Watching* [323].

The history of content analysis is one of adventure and intrigue. Allied intelligence officers used content analysis to predict German troop movements during WWII by digesting contents of the social columns of town newspapers that indicated the presence or absence of prominent officers [68]. Naisbitt refers to a similar use in uncovering early evidence of food shortages in Germany during that period [344]. Newspaper clipping services in the past provided organized access to broad regional, national or international data that could be subjected to content analysis. Today, computerized full-text databases with sophisticated search routines can provide even more comprehensive content analysis data.

Especially with respect to social phenomena such as attitudes and behaviors, the transition from possibility to fact is gradual, and differences in adoption and adaptation are reflected in regional and national literatures. Both Molitor and Mendell refer to *precursor jurisdictions,* suggesting that Sweden leads the U.S., and that Denmark and Germany play similar roles. Within the U.S., California is a precursor innovator to other states.

The diffusion of self-service retail gasoline delivery is an interesting example of precursor jurisdictions (see *The Environment Speaks XII*). Self-service stations became well-established in both Germany and Sweden by the mid-1960s, when there were fewer than 500 stations operating in the U.S. As the illustration indicates, self-service gas did not *begin* in California; however, the U.S. conversion to self-service gasoline did not really accelerate until the movement was *accepted in California,* beginning in 1967.

THE ENVIRONMENT SPEAKS XII
Origins and Growth of Self-Service Gasoline Stations in the U.S.

In Portland, Oregon, in 1946, the Moran family opened a self-service station operated by a cashier who also instructed customers on how to use the pumps, where necessary. Four more outlets were opened before local ordinances were changed to shut them all down. Also in the mid-1940s, Vern West developed a coin acceptor unit for dispensing gasoline. By the mid-1950s West had 12 outlets. In 1959, Pat

Griffin bought West's operation and opened the first Gasamats in Greeley, Colorado and Casper, Wyoming. In a format to be copied again and again across western states, Griffin hired a retired couple to supervise the station. They lived in a house trailer disguised into the station wall and dispensed tokens for cash that customers would then feed into machines controlling the pumps.

In September, 1962, E.B. White predicted in *Advertising Age:* " . . . it is self-service for gasoline, in particular, that to me seems inevitable." In September, 1965, White proclaimed, "So today — self-service gas is here." He reported that the Tokheim Corporation, major manufacturer of gasoline pumps, after hand-building more than 200 currency-operated pumps, had scheduled them for production-line assembly in January 1966. Wayne Pump had developed both a money-operated and a remote-controlled self-service system. In February, 1966, White reported that BP already had 2,000 coin-operated pump installations in West Germany.

The first popular magazine article on the subject appeared in *Business Week*, on October 1, 1966. Entitled, "Self-service moves in on the pump," it noted that at least 500 self-service installations were operating in the U.S. By then, Griffin's Gasamats totaled 55 in number, across eight western states. A Supertron franchisee with the only known California operation at the time (in Ventura), had announced plans to build 100 self-service stations in California and Nevada. In addition to California, the article indicated that self service, "really has come into its own" in Sweden, where IC of Stockholm, a consumers' cooperative, was the major operator.

After growing modestly to 500 outlets over 15 years, the trend exploded once it was accepted in California (see graph on page 123), reaching 6,800 outlets by the end of 1971, and then growing to 13,000 by 1972 (with nine percent of the market) and 20,000 by 1977 (with 30 percent of the market). In 1982, *The Wall Street Journal* reported self-service market share at 67-69 percent of gasoline sold in the U.S. By 1991, according to Amoco Oil Company research, self-service delivery accounted for 85 percent of U.S. sales.

(Compiled from various issues of Advertising Age, National Petroleum News *and* The Wall Street Journal.*)*

Areas in New York, Massachusetts and Illinois may lead California, especially in the diffusion of new public policy. For example, laws in these states regulating the insurance industry have served for years as models for other states. The media that focus on these precursor jurisdictions may reflect valid future signals of other regions and locales.

As an example of the accumulation and interpretation of literature on an issue, consider the case of the tax simplification and reform legislation enacted in 1986. More than any tax change in recent history, this legislation substantially modified the *nature* of the federal income tax system by greatly reducing the number of special deductions, exclusions and tax brackets. Despite the unequivocal defeat of similar simplification legislation in 1985, there were signs as early as 1972 that simplification was an unsinkable issue.

Observe the sampling of events and literature contained in Table 8.2, beginning with the passage of the Revenue Act of 1969. That tax code revision incorporated some simplifying provisions, aimed primarily at low income allowances and increased standard deductions. These changes reduced the number of people who had to file returns, as well as reducing the number of taxpayers who had to itemize their deductions. But these 1969 changes were not sufficient to meet the public need and demand for tax simplification; the issue simply would not go away. During the period of 1972 to 1976, experts advocating change began to propose new methods and models for taxation. While their opinions and ideas appeared primarily in technical journals, they were precursors of change, and as such, these experts are designated as post-visionary change agents.

MEASURE THE FUTURE

Analyze the content of the literature and media for signals about emerging issues. Measure and chart the accumulation of references on high impact possibilities. Watch for signs of acceleration. Assess the imminence of change against the organization's strategic response time. Build action plans to capture the strategic advantage of future insights.

Beginning in 1976, the signs of pressure for change showed up in advocacy articles in intelligentsia publications, such as *Financial Executive* and *Money.* These articles (items 6 and 7 in Table 8.2) reflect the work of change informants, and then in 1977 a change event occurred: the passage of the Tax Reduction and Simplification Act of 1977. This might have ended the public interest in the issue, ideally leading to a rapid diffusion and consolidation of the literature. Instead, the pressure for tax simplification continued into 1978 and beyond, with increasing attention in the popular financial press, including *The Wall Street Journal* and *Fortune,* diffusing the idea into the public consciousness.

Also in 1978, Proposition 13 was passed by California's voters, who comprise one of the recognized precursor jurisdictions. Although this proposition was related as much to tax reduction as to tax simplification, it did express a level of voter irritation and activism that rapidly spread across the country. High taxes were under siege, as were inequitable tax breaks and complications.

President Carter relentlessly but unsuccessfully advocated tax simplification during his term (1977-80), and President Reagan continued the pressure during his campaign and terms of office. The Economic Recovery Act of 1981 actually worsened the situation by increasing tax preferences and complications, and therefore the pressure for simplification. Tax measures died in Congress in 1983 and 1985, but the debate continued until the sweeping changes brought by the 1986 Tax Reform Act emerged. All of the actions and events prior to the actual passage of the Act contributed to the diffusion of the idea of tax simplification until it became a national and Congressional expectation. When the 1986 Tax Reform Act became law, the idea of tax simplification was no longer novel. In the two years after the passage of the Act, there were more than 2,000 changes to the Internal Revenue Code published, nearly 75 pages of new forms and work sheets developed, and about 50 new tax regulations released by the Internal Revenue Service.

SELF-SERVICE GAS STATIONS
East and West of the Mississippi

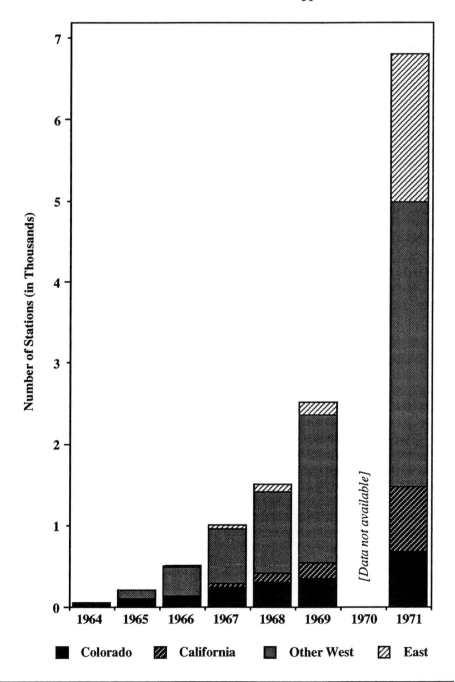

Table 8.2: Selected Events and Literature Predating 1986 Tax Simplification Legislation

1969   1.   *Early Event:* Passage of the Revenue Act of 1969.

1972   2.   *Advocate:* Wilbur D. Mills, Chairman of the House Ways and Means Committee, presented his views in: "Some Important Tax Issues That Still Need to be Solved," *Practical Accountant,* V5N3, May/ June 1972, pp. 34-36. Mills said that the 1969 Revenue Act simplified the filing of tax returns for many millions of taxpayers, but that a great deal still remains to be done.

1973   3.   *Advocate:* Edward A. Wiegner, Secretary, Dept. of Revenue, State of Wisconsin, published an article entitled: "Tax Simplification" in *National Tax Journal,* V26N3, Sept. 1973, pp. 337-339. He suggested that the rise in the use of tax preparation services increased non-filing. Public opinion and media interest all point to a considerable interest in tax simplification.

1975   4.   *Advocate:* The chairman of the AICPA's Federal Tax Division testified before the House Ways and Means Committee. Subjects included tax simplification. The institute's views and the testimony appeared in a 10-page *Journal of Accountancy* article, Sept. 1975, pp. 28-38.

1976   5.   *Model:* A new income tax plan was proposed for the U.S. which would simplify the tax while retaining its progression: Don Soule and Clyde Bates, "A Progressive Income-Tax with a Uniform Tax Rate," *Nebraska Journal of Economics and Business,* V15N2, Spring 1976, pp. 19-32.

       6.   *Intelligentsia:* William M. Horne, Jr., Senior Vice President and General Counsel of Citicorp, published "Federal Taxation — a Bicentennial Perspective," in *Financial Executive,* V44N7, July 1976, pp. 62-68. The article makes a strong case for tax simplification. It charges that Congress is making the tax laws too complex now, as it is using them to reach social and economic objectives rather than to obtain revenue. The article concludes that Congress must simplify the Federal income tax laws in the future before they become unworkable.

       7.   *Intelligentsia:* The tax simplification issue reached the popular press, in the article, "Simon Says — Simplify the Income-Tax," *Money,* V5N4, April 1976, pp. 68-69. The article reports the views of Treasury Secretary William Simon, who proposes wiping out special deductions, exclusions and preferences from the tax laws. The article included ideas on handling special problems relating to health care, banking, charitable institutions and home ownership that would be caused by the elimination of preferences.

1977   8. *Precursor Change Event:* Passage of the Tax Reduction and Simplification Act of 1977, providing a "zero bracket amount" to replace the standard deduction and make itemizing less necessary for many taxpayers.

      9. *Advocate:* Former IRS Commissioner Donald Alexander's testimony before the Joint Subcommittee on Growth and Stabilization was published as "Former Commissioner's Thought on Simplification and Tax Reform," *Tax Adviser,* V8N9, Sept. 1977, pp. 561-564. Alexander believed the code should not be cluttered with special incentives to achieve social or economic ends, and that top individual and corporate rates should be reduced.

1978 10. *Model: Tax Law Review,* V34N1, Fall 1978, pp. 27-77, published "Simplification Symposium: Federal Income Tax Simplification, The Political Process."

    11. *Intelligentsia:* "The Tortuous Road to a Modest Tax Cut — California's 'Tax Revolt' Dilemma," *Business Week,* June 5, 1978, pp. 50-51. Carter's tax simplification measures reported as having a good chance of passing. California businessmen reported as generally favoring the Jarvis-Gann tax limitation initiative, despite fears about revenue cuts at the city level.

    12. *Precursor Change Event:* Proposition 13 passes in California.

1979 13. *Advocate:* John Nolan, in "Federal Income Tax Simplification and the Political Process," *Tax Adviser,* V10N12, pp. 717-720, argues that there is widespread agreement that extraordinary new initiatives are needed to simplify the income tax.

1981 14. *Diffusion: The Wall Street Journal* (Dec.10) publishes an article, "A Proposal to Simplify our Tax System."

    15. *Precursor Change Event:* Passage of the Economic Recovery Tax Act of 1981, with new special preferences, complications.

1982 16. *Diffusion: Fortune* (July 26) publishes an article, "The Flatter-Tax Movement Picks Up Steam."

1983 17. *Diffusion:* Tax Simplification Act (HR3475) debated, but dies.

1985 18. *Diffusion:* Tax Reform Act of 1985 (HR3838) stalled in committee until December 10, 1985.

1986 19. *Change Event:* HR3838 did not die, but was renamed and enacted into law as the Tax Reform Act of 1986, incorporating sweeping simplifying changes and fewer rates.

Another view of the literature surrounding the issue of tax simplification is contained in Figure 8.6, showing the cumulative literature between the years of 1971 and 1986, based on a count of the number of articles published during each of those years. This accumulation is not complete, but does include over 400 articles from national newspapers and major technical journals, as well as popular and intelligentsia magazines. The similarity of the cumulative literature on tax simplification in Figure 8.6 to Molitor's S-curve formulation (Figure 8.5) is striking. Tax simplification literature accumulated at first slowly (visionary), then moderately (modeling), and then rapidly (diffusion) to a consolidation phase in 1986 and beyond.

The key signal in this literature can be traced to 1978, when it became clear that the literature did not cease to accumulate after the passage of the 1977 Simplification Act. Indeed, the continued accumulation of articles in the years 1978 to 1981, in about the same amounts as 1977, proved the persistence of the tax issue: the 1977 "change event" had not satisfied the public demand. By 1978, and certainly by 1979, tax simplification had reached a state of inevitability. It can be seen now; it could have been seen then.

The 1978-81 period was the time for active scanners to have encoded the opportunities and threats associated with tax reduction. Several possible simplification scenarios could have been considered, incorporating various combinations and forms of reductions in special provisions and deductions. The actual details of the final outcome could not have been predicted, but the shape of change and the imminence of change should have been predicted. Yet the earliest published hint of the inevitability of tax change was the *Fortune* article in 1982 (see item 16, Table 8.2), and most experts did not openly predict change until 1985 and 1986.

In summary, there is a continuum of futurity in the published literature around which an organization can fashion its environmental scanning source inventory. Figure 8.7 shows sources classified along this continuum, from visionary to historical. This figure introduces the subject of the next section: futurity ratings of published sources. Using these futurity concepts and the bibliography of scanning resources included in the Appendix, your organization can develop a scanning target list. That list might include other, specialized published sources allied to the technical and behavioral aspects of the environment to which it is most sensitive. While general circulation newspapers and periodicals may appear on nearly any organization's list of relevant publications, these are not generally the literature sources from which future environmental signals can be detected in time for strategic anticipation.

Such action can be triggered by the inferences drawn from analysis of a database of documented environmental signals tracked across the futurity continuum of more future-oriented literature sources. The organization that builds and maintains such a robust database stands to gain from observable signals relating many events to uncover trends and project breakthroughs. The organization which fails to learn how to read these signals confronts a future heavily laden with surprises, where tactical reaction is the only remaining strategy.

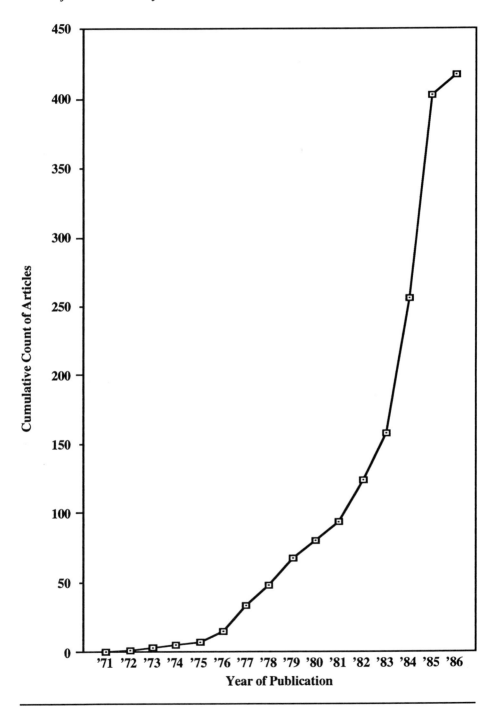

Figure 8.6: Tax Simplification Literature (1971 – 1986) Leading to the Tax Reform Act of 1986

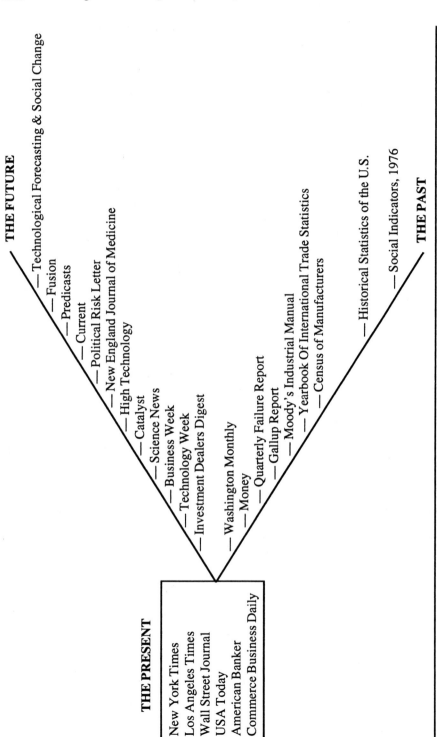

Figure 8.7: Futurity of Information Sources: An Example of Periodical Classification

Purchased Sources: The Futurity of Their Contents Varies

Sources of environmental information can be personal or documentary. Through interaction with people, individually or in groups, ideas about the future are developed. This communication permits us to discover what others have learned from their own observations and from studying documentary sources. Thus, directly or indirectly, a significant proportion of the information needed for intelligence scanning emanates from published sources.

Scanning organizations also need background materials on the methodologies of environmental scanning. They need historical base-building materials to provide a context for understanding the present, and to provide a database for model-building and forecasting. Current information is needed to assess the progression and validity of existing forecasts and scenarios. Scanners may wish to acquire the forecasts and services of other organizations to supplement internal scanning efforts.

The Appendix provides a guide to information sources for environmental scanning. Sources are broadly classified according to the time focus of their typical contents. Each source record also includes a type classification and a frequency of appearance as a surrogate for timeliness. A separate category indicates service organizations providing either data or expertise.

This source guide for scanning information is comprehensive. In addition to this author's research in available sources, these appendices incorporate guides to information sources developed by others [110;179;186;223;257;353;362;394;436;469], as well as scanning source lists from prominent scanning organizations, including the Trend Analysis Program of the American Council on Life Insurance, the Congressional Clearinghouse on the Future and consulting organizations such as Strategic Intelligence Systems.

A caveat is in order with respect to these and any other source lists of environmental scanning information; the lists are not exhaustive. They contain at least indicative sources relating to all dimensions of the environment, and spanning the four phases of the literature model developed in this chapter. Other publications exist that may have meaningful scanning content. For example, several publications incorporated in the list are from leading academic institutions (*Harvard Business Review, Business Horizons, California Management Review*). These include insightful articles by experts whose views may represent early Diffusion Phase literature and thus valid advance signals about the future. Other such publications by academic institutions exist and may reflect similar content and opportunity. In addition, the list would be different in some respects if it were focused on one or a few industries, such as from the view of one organization.

The source list reflected in the appendix should not be construed as a basic "starter kit" for environmental scanning; its length should not deter an organization from undertaking scanning activities. The sources identified here more closely resemble a selection list than a requisite inventory.

Source Types. The source listing in the Appendix inludes human and documentary, printed and computerized resources. Each of the type categories is described below.

Publications comprise a range of printed sources including newspapers, newsletters, popular magazines, specialized journals and reports. Included also are what librarians call periodicals, serials, irregulars and annuals, plus some highly specialized documents.

The listing of publications includes several generic and representative citations of industry, company and regional publications. Specialized documents include company annual reports, 10-K's, registration statements and other filings available through share ownership, request, and Disclosure, Inc. by order or by subscription. Trade and industry associations publish house organs, and will often add the general public to its mailing list on request for public relations purposes; *Scan,* for example, is a newsletter the Shell Oil Company publishes primarily for internal distribution. Cities, states and nations publish economic and demographic statistics, most of it in retrospective form. Illustrative examples include *Vermont Facts and Figures, Statistical Abstract of Illinois, Statistical Pocketbook of Sri Lanka, Metropolitan Toronto,* and *Statistical Abstract of the United States.*

Information about industries is published by others; for example, the *Lodging Industry Annual Report,* published by Laventhal & Horwath; *Comparative Financial Data of Major Department Stores,* published by Harris Bank; or "Annual Report of the Grocery Industry," published in *Progressive Grocer.* Organizations needing retrospective and contemporaneous information about specific geographic areas can readily develop sources through the use of periodical and serials directories.

Two other categories of printed sources are identified separately from publications. These are *books* and *indexes,* the former including a few selected directories, bibliographies, almanacs and compilations. Also included in this category are the works of contemporary futurists and researchers in future analysis methodologies.

The category of *indexes* includes a broad range of guides to existing published literature, typically organized by subject. Indexes provide bibliographic references to original sources and may include summaries or abstracts of the contents of those sources. Indexes are valuable guides to sources of scanning information; they cover a wide range of publications and present the contents of those sources in an organized way. There are two significant dangers in relying solely on published guides to original sources. The first is the time lag between the appearance of the original article and the availability of the index in which the article is referenced — the information may be needed immediately.

Second, the inclusiveness of the guide's subject classifications, or the contents of its abstracts, is dependent on decisions made by the editorial staff. Valuable ideas and weak signals can be lost in indexing and abstraction, because the abstract reflects only key themes according to the judgment and values of a *bibliographic specialist,* rather than a specialist in the issue under study. The reader of the original source document, or of a full-text database, gets the information more quickly and in full text format for analysis and response.

An example of differences in perceptions between abstracters is available as a result of the research done for this book. One of the important early articles in the area of issues management, authored by Charles Arrington and Richard Sawaya, appeared contemporaneously in both the *California Management Review* [18] and in *Long Range Planning (UK)* [17]. With the exception of two short paragraphs added to the second article, the text and exhibits of the two articles are identical, as the authors intended and indicated. Abstracts of both articles are available and are reproduced in their entirety in *The Environment Speaks XIII*. Note the similarities in the two abstracts in their capturing of the main themes of issues management as foresight, policy analysis, and advocacy, and the difference in the nature and tone of the other aspects of the article as captured by the two abstracts.

Publication delays for information transmission in general, and index/abstract information in particular, have been dramatically reduced with the availability of computerized databases and communication networks. The appendix references over 200 such databases; many more exist, and their availability is growing rapidly. Martha E. Williams, database expert at the University of Illinois, reported that by 1989 the number of computerized databases had grown to 5,400, up from 301 only 15 years earlier [149;521].

Some databases provide an on-line version of a printed periodical. *The Wall Street Journal* is available in print or on-line; the same is true of *Commerce Business Daily* and *Moody's Corporate News*. Other databases provide a computer accessible version of a directory, index or abstract that also appears in published, hard-copy form. The computer database may be updated more frequently: *Ulrich's International Periodical Directory* is published once each year; *Ulrich's International Periodical Database* is updated every month on Dialog Information Services. The computer database may be available more quickly, although some publishers have been reluctant to give a time advantage to network users: stock quotes and news wires are released to the public in an intentionally delayed format. Finally, some computer databases contain source information not readily available elsewhere. The FIND/SVP *Reports and Studies Index* contains references to market research studies that may not be publicly referenced. Both *Trade and Industry Index* and *Newsnet* reference publications with restricted circulation that may be unavailable to the general public.

INCREASE SCANNING PRODUCTIVITY

Use computerized databases to capture information quickly and in a timely manner. But beware of the loss of subtle implications in abstracts. And be cautious in structuring keyword searches to avoid missing valuable references. Computerized searches should enhance, not replace, full-text scanning by people.

A sampling of the service organizations that provide access to computer-readable databases, either through networks or through direct shipment of magnetic media, is included among the appendix listings of database and consulting services organizations.

Political Risk Services is an example of a source of proprietary databases dealing with foreign country data and business risk assessment; these are provided directly to users on floppy disks. Compuserve and Lockheed Information Systems are examples of online network database providers in the U.S. Datastar provides similar services in the U.K. Bibliographic database search services are provided by organizations such as SDC Orbit Search Service and Information Express.

Three source categories directly or indirectly involve a human interface. Radio and television news *broadcasts* are principally of contemporaneous content. Some broadcasts are of a length and frequency that permits in-depth reporting, and these may convey useful ideas and clues about the future. Certain *conferences* have value in conveying ideas about the future, either because of their content or because of the people attending with whom one may have contact.

Certain *organizations* provide services supporting environmental scanning, including consulting, reports, seminars and educational programs. In addition to the database service organizations these include econometric forecasters and opinion research firms. Most of these services are arranged through individual negotiation rather than subscription. Expertise and focus shift among organizations over time; therefore no consultative services guide can expect to be comprehensive. Included here are examples of those organizations well-known for their scanning support expertise, but by no means should this list be interpreted to represent the limits of available environmental scanning support.

Source Timeliness. More than once in this discussion the time lag between event and available information about it has been mentioned. Some sources publish information that is late in coming but has a long enough futurity to be valuable from a scanning perspective. Other sources may simply be chronicles of events gone by. A strategically focused scanning organization would not want to delay an action while waiting for one of the latter sources. But it might plan an action based on intuition or analysis developed from the content of one of the former sources. An organization might structure its scanning resources to include a balance of publications and guides to publications across the dimensions of futurity as well as timeliness. Timely, high-futurity information has value, especially if you are better organized to capture and interpret it than your competitors.

THE ENVIRONMENT SPEAKS XIII
The Essence is in the Eyes of the Abstracter

Below are two abstracts of an article that appears in two journals in essentially the identical form. The only difference between them is that two short paragraphs were added to the *Long Range Planning* version that set the stage for the article by summarizing some of the later conclusions. The abstracts were written by separate abstracters; while they have the same essential content, they differ remarkably in their overall tone, focus and use of language that might be captured in search keywords. Both capture the process of issues management: foresight, policy analysis, advocacy. The first abstract conveys some of the insights as to how to manage and evaluate the issues management process. The second focuses instead on the steps to implement the issues management process. Both are highly competent abstracts, and the purpose of contrasting them is not in any way to criticize the quality or content of abstract databases or the people who contribute to them. The purpose instead is to demonstrate that, because abstracting must involve judgment and choice about how to characterize many words in few, the abstract that appears in a database is not the abstract that you might write to optimize its suitability to your own environmental scanning focus and needs.

AUArrington-C-B-Jr. Sawaya-R-N.
TIIssues Management in an Uncertain Environment.
SOLong Range Planning (UK). VOL: v17n6. PAG: 17-24, 8 pages. Dec 1984.

ABIssues management is a process that employs many disciplines to handle possible discontinuities in the external environment, helping organizations to predict and respond to change. The process is made up of three linked activities: 1. foresight, 2. policy development, and 3. advocacy. A detailed description is provided of how Atlantic Richfield Co. applies issues analysis and issues management to monitor public issues and devise action programs to meet them. Assessment of the total processes should occur on a regular and qualitative basis. The need to liaise with planning is important and allows public policy issues to be integrated into company planning. Issues management corresponds and contributes to strategic planning; those involved in it must have a collective synthesizing habit of thinking. Issues management should guarantee coherent participation in external advocacy and relationships. The function should stay small and nonhierarchical and be at the core of the company's strategic thinking. Charts.

AUArrington-Charles-B-Jr. Sawaya-Richard-N.
TIManaging Public Affairs: Issues Management in an Uncertain Environment.
SOCalifornia Mgmt Review. VOL: v26n4. PAG: 148-160, 13 pages. Summer 1984.

ABIssues management should be a critical aspect of the corporate public affairs function. With issues management, a firm can anticipate and adapt to changes in its external environment. Based on the experiences of the Atlantic Richfield Co., elements of effective issues management are discussed. Issues management should involve foresight, policy development and advocacy. Issues management begins by identifying relevant issues and monitoring their impacts. Policy development for issues which present conflicting internal/external interests must be conducted: 1. objectively, questioning conventional corporate assumptions, and 2. collectively, involving all operating segments of the firm. Once corporate policy has been established, effective advocacy actions must be identified and initiated. This step may involve direct representation before legislative bodies, the formation of alliances with other firms having similar policy stances, and constituency-building within the community. Finally, issues management must be fully incorporated into the strategic planning process of the firm. Charts.

(*The above abstracts are from the ABI/INFORM Database, which is published by UMI/Data Courier, 620 South 3rd Street, Louisville, KY 40202.*)

Obtaining Information from Computer-Readable Databases

Among respondents to a recent survey of database clients by one database service, more than one-third were found to use personal computers for planning at least 11 hours per week. According to that report, General Electric uses electronic database searches to maintain up-to-date information not only on its competitors and the general environment, but on its major customers and those customers' industries [314]. The company's information center subscribes to 13 commercial database services that cover more than 1,000 separate databases. Online database use is rising fast, providing fast access to both more information and more current information [8;53;140;303;347;358;397;485;521].

Computer readable databases are of essentially four types: company, statistical, bibliographic and full-text. Some may be purchased or licensed for installation on an organization's own in-house computers, but most database searches undertaken to support environmental scanning are likely to be conducted using the facilities of a network information service.

Network information services are accessible through commercial telephone lines by dialing prescribed numbers and entering log-on commands. These commands differ considerably across vendors, but generally include at least a subset of the following sequence:

1. Dial network number.
2. Connect communicating terminal to telephone line.
3. Establish connection with network.
4. Enter a command sequence to "wake up" the network and indicate the speed of your terminal.
5. Request a network service.
6. Enter a user name or account number.
7. Provide a password to that account.
8. Request access to a database.

The terminal through which you communicate with a network computer must have at least three components: a keyboard to send commands, a display device to receive transmissions from the network, and a modem that translates commands and data for and from transmission across the telephone lines. To take full advantage of network database facilities, most users communicate with a microcomputer that also has memory, off-line storage, and intelligent communications software. The software manages the details of sending and receiving information; memory and storage allow information received from the network database to be captured and saved for future use. How the information is saved and stored depends on the software controlling the communications. General purpose programs such as *Crosstalk* save information in text files, where integrated software such as *Symphony* can capture information directly in a spreadsheet and save it as a database.

Company databases are organized to provide information about a specific company, perhaps including both financial and descriptive information. Depending on the database and the vendor's access support system, information may be obtained by specifying a company identifier, such as its name, ticker symbol, or security Cusip number and then specifying the information needed (such as balance sheets, stock prices, names of officers) for some specific time period. It may be possible to obtain the entire record for a specific company, or to search the database for companies meeting specific criteria. Selection criteria might include SIC codes, size ranges in assets or earnings, minimum or maximum levels of a ratio, keywords (concepts, products) in the description of the company or the CEO's message in the annual report. Examples of company databases include Compustat, Disclosure, and several stock price quotation databases. Industry and country databases are often organized in the same way.

Statistical databases tend to be organized around data time series and accessed under the name of the series, such as GNP or consumer prices, for the specified time period.

Bibliographic and full-text databases differ only in the amount of the text of an article, report, speech or release contained in the database record. Full-text databases contain the entire piece, where bibliographic databases have an abstract of the piece or simply the bibliographic entry itself. The basic bibliographic entry includes author, title, source, date and subject keywords. The search methodology involves specifying text strings, singly or in combination, and rules. Using the given strings and rules, the computer searches the database and selects those entries that satisfy the criteria. Initially you may be told how many entries meet the criteria; if the number is very large, the search strings and rules can be redefined. After reducing the selected records to a manageable number, these records can be transferred to a database or printed out and mailed.

If you were considering the future strategic implications of the rising cost of product liability insurance for your organization, you would select fewer entries from a database if you specified the keyword "product liability insurance" than if you specified the keyword "insurance." But by limiting your search in this way, you would fail to select a title such as, "Future Impossibility of Insuring Product Liability," unless the keyword field for the entry contained exactly the string you specified. The problem is twofold. First, "insuring" is not the same as "insurance." Fortunately search strings can be made more general, and the preceding description only gives a hint as to the power and flexibility of keyword and context database search capabilities. Training in search skills is required, and available. A trained database searcher can rapidly capture information of high value to support an environmental scanner who has a good intuitive concept of the signals he or she seeks.

One of the databases a scanning organization may wish to interrogate using keyword and context text management software is its own environmental data, information and analyses. Over time, as the volume of both inputs to and outputs from the scanning effort grows, the accessibility of data becomes at once more difficult and more vital. Rich inferences about trends and circumstances depend in part on the connection of thought and evidence fragments that may be widely disbursed across your database in time, in source and in format.

Some organizations maintain information systems as products. Examples include credit authorization and travel reservations. The value of these systems in providing reliable information about the task environment is increased if the organization has managed to be a first mover in offering a valuable information system capability spanning at least two levels of its value-added chain, or has managed to leapfrog its competition in the inherent superiority of such a system. Information systems for competitive advantage have environmental scanning value if the provider maintains long-term information access of a potentially strategic nature not available to other participants in the system [217;524].

Summary

This chapter has been primarily focused on information sources. It presents a methodology for capturing signals of future events and conditions from published information. Key indicators include the type and source of message, the nature of publication outlet and the cumulative frequency of references to that possible future. The chapter advocates a future-focused selection of information sources and provides a classification scheme of sources according to purpose, futurity, type and frequency. The Appendix contains a representative list of approximately 850 publication sources and source examples using those classifications. Processing of the information obtained from the source material is discussed in the next chapter.

CHAPTER 9

ANALYSIS AND FORECASTING TECHNIQUES

Monitoring signals from the environment is the predominant technique employed in environmental scanning. Scanning is accomplished through one or more of the observation and search modes described earlier. Management tailors these scanning approaches to the fundamental nature of a particular environment and to the degree of interaction and dependency perceived among the dimensions of that environment, and selects sources of information appropriate to its scanning strategy. Then, by managing its scanning resources and communications, an effective system for capturing environmental intelligence can be established.

Rich inferences can be drawn from environmental data in an intuitive fashion by making routine and non-routine inquiries of the environmental database. Intuition ultimately reaches its limits however, as the quantity of data increases, as the complexity of relationships grows or as environments exhibit signs of change or instability. This chapter presents a series of quantitative and qualitative analytical techniques useful as supplements to intuition in interpretation of environmental information, and in the development of inferences or forecasts of emerging conditions or events.

These environmental analysis techniques are described and classified, and available survey data on their use by scanning organizations is presented. The descriptions are brief but include references; the intention here is to describe basic outlines and provide guidance on where or when a given technique is appropriate. The chapter is organized in five sections: (1) classification scheme for analytical techniques; (2) mapping techniques; (3) modeling techniques; (4) subjective techniques of analysis, including brainstorming, role playing, scenario development, interview techniques, intuition and conjecture; and (5) advice on applicability and use. Over 22 techniques and their variations are described and classified for usefulness, with the evidence for their appeal to scanners summarized in the final section.

A Classification Scheme for Techniques

The "where or when" in choice of analytical techniques relates to a six-element classification of the 22 techniques. Each is associated with a group according to the type of technique it represents, and classified for use according to whether each of four environment parameters is rated high or low; resource and skill requirements are also evaluated. The four environmental parameters are (1) *complexity,* (2) *irreducible uncertainty,* (3) *instability,* and (4) the firm's *knowledge about* that environment.

If a firm knows little about its environment, it faces a high degree of uncertainty. That uncertainty can be reduced by gaining knowledge, since increasing knowledge is associated with decreasing *reducible* uncertainty. At some point, increased expenditures for knowledge yield decreased marginal reductions in uncertainty. The uncertainty that remains after knowledge has reached its economic limit is *irreducible* uncertainty.

Although the concepts of complexity, uncertainty and instability intersect as Figure 9.1 illustrates, they are not synonymous. The independent aspect of *complexity* has to do with the difficulty of specifying the interaction of entities and elements within the environment, or explaining the behavior of a variable; for example, difficulty in explaining fluctuations in demand for a product. The independent aspect of *uncertainty* relates to the breadth of probability distributions that are associated with values and outcomes in the environment. That is, the firm may well understand the functional determinants of demand for one of its products and be able to explain demand accurately in an *ex-post* sense, but be confounded in the prediction of future demand by the wide probability distributions (uncertainties) associated with one or more of the interacting variables in the demand equation. Finally, the independent aspect of *instability* is associated with the degree to which concepts and relationships somewhere in the environment are undergoing the processes of fundamental change. Such change might be causing the elements of the demand equation to become different, their impacts to be altered by relationships with new variables, or the probability distributions driving them to shift. The classification of techniques in the sections that follow relates to these parameters of complexity, uncertainty, instability and knowledge viewed in their independent contexts as described above.

Figure 9.1: Components of the Unknown Environment

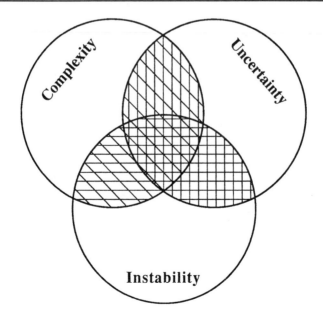

Mapping Techniques

Mapping techniques are generally for the purpose of describing the nature, extent or limits of the connection of one variable with another, or with a system of other variables. The approach may be quantitative, as with impact analysis, or descriptive, as are morphological models. The simplest form of mapping of a deterministic, sequential process, either physical or logical, is a process flow chart. Refined flow chart techniques can track influence networks and timing. Link a flow chart to a production system or to value-added concepts and it becomes an input-output analysis. Introduce uncertainty and the map becomes an impact analysis. Introduce multiple dimensions and the map becomes a morphology or a cross-impact analysis. Orient the analysis toward outcomes, or environmental trends, and the map is a trend impact analysis. Impose knowledge boundaries about your environment and about the cross-impacts of variables with one another and you may describe the range of outcomes of variables in the form of limit envelopes. These techniques are described in the sections that follow.

Flow Charts. A flow chart is a graphic map of a system of relationships. It portrays relationships in a way that may make the system easier to conceptualize — certainly easier to visualize. Perhaps more importantly, the *construction* of a flow chart forces the analyst to organize inputs, outputs, processes, linkages and decisions into a logical network. Because of the elemental nature of its building blocks, a flow chart can be used to describe highly complex processes and environments. Uncertainty can be factored into flow charts through condition test and variable response paths. Yet, the introduction of uncertain inputs or outcomes greatly magnifies the detail of a flow chart and may inhibit its usefulness as a map; tree diagrams may be a better way of portraying uncertainty. Flow charting can be a useful technique for describing unstable systems, especially as a means to find *where* in a larger system the unstable elements or relationships exist. Once found, these unstable elements may be better defined for further study, but they represent black boxes, or black holes, in the overall system that may frustrate attempts to use the flow chart for any predictive purpose. In the following paragraphs, four forms of flow charts are described: process, influence, time-process and tree diagrams, each with a distinct analytical value for environmental scanning.

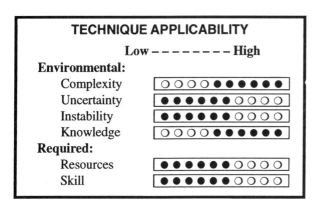

TECHNIQUE APPLICABILITY	Type:
Low – – – – – – – High	
Environmental:	**MAPPING**
Complexity ○○○○●●●●●●	
Uncertainty ●●●●●○○○○○	
Instability ●●●●●○○○○○	
Knowledge ○○○○●●●●●●	**Technique:**
Required:	
Resources ●●●●●○○○○○	**FLOW CHARTS**
Skill ●●●●●○○○○○	

Process Flow Charts. Process flow charts present in pictorial fashion the sequence of steps (shown as boxes) and decisions (shown as diamonds) that comprise the completion of a task, with connecting lines showing the direction and sequence of flows. Flow charts can be presented meaningfully at widely ranging levels of abstraction. At low levels of abstraction, elementary actions are described (such as grasp/release, add/subtract, read/skip), and elementary decisions are made (such as "is part red?", "is result zero?", "is word a verb?"). Details of this sort may be needed in the design of computer programs or production systems, but would probably be distracting to the environmental scanner.

At high levels of abstraction, the processes and decisions may themselves incorporate complex task networks. Consider the process flow chart in Figure 9.2, which depicts the steps in developing and implementing benchmark comparisons for a function or functions of a company's operations. The company first chooses a relevant function against which to benchmark itself, perhaps operating margin or market recognition. Next, a set of measurable performance variables is chosen for those functions, variables that either represent the function or derive its outcome. The third step involves selecting a set of companies to drive the comparison. Each of these three steps involves a process of selection. Those processes are embedded within the flow chart and not made explicit. The selection procedures in this example, and the measurement and management procedures that follow them may be well understood by the users of the flow chart. If they are not, this flow chart would have only descriptive, not operational, value.

Flow charting, as a mapping technique, is useful when it elicits, from the people involved, a flow diagram of their most complete joint understanding of the processes generating a set of environmental circumstances. The best result of the process occurs when participants gain enough of an understanding of some element of the environment that they begin to project, and seek to test, implications of its possible evolution. Sometimes, however, the question, "How is that step accomplished?" cannot be answered in sufficient detail to make the overall process and its implications understood. Even where the mapping effort reaches such a conclusion, it has at least served the purposes of sorting out the known from the unknown and identifying areas in which further scanning or further analysis is needed. Such an approach is illustrated in the process of Figure 9.3. Following that process, the level of detail of any step in a flow chart is expanded until the user of that flow chart understands the flow of the system it describes. Lack of understanding at any point in a flow chart may initiate a dialogue and an effort to add more detail to the description. If that detail is not known, an environmental scanning need may have been identified.

Influence Diagrams. In some complex systems, the steps from input or stimulus to outcome or response may defy detailed description. In the social sciences, researchers have dealt with these complexities by developing generalized models as a substitute for schematics. Models of supply and demand, utility-preference-choice, human behavior and interaction, organization or political and military strategy allow us to predict the direction of relationships in a system, but perhaps not the magnitude of the ultimate responses of that system to change. In describing systems that are dependent on such behavioral responses, an *influence diagram* may provide superior insight. Whereas the process flow

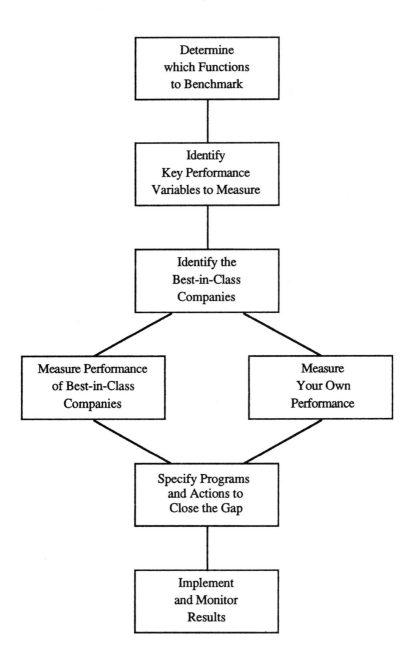

Figure 9.2: Example Flow Chart

(Courtesy of Kaiser Associates, Inc., Vienna, Virginia.)

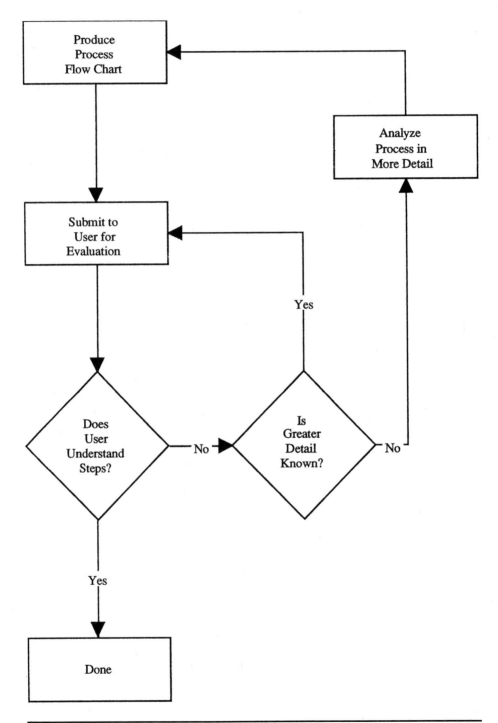

Figure 9.3: Refining Detail on a Flow Chart

chart is a sequence of steps from input to outcome, the influence diagram is a network of influences between factors in a system. Narchal [346] suggests using influence diagrams to map the relationship of environmental factors (population growth, capacity utilization) to environmental indicators (raw material price) in designing a plan for environmental scanning and in detailing scanning tasks for the people who are to serve as environmental radars. Diffenbach [117] advocates the use of influence diagrams for mapping strategic issues relating to several external dimensions of the environment simultaneously — areas where our ability to systematize behavior is limited. He suggests these examples:

- possible impacts of an emerging technology on the marketplace;
- overcapacity in an industry;
- government regulation or deregulation;
- government incentives to boost industrial productivity;
- changes in the prime rate on various product markets;
- mortgage rate influences on the housing market.

An influence diagram is a network of factors connected by links, each having a direction and a sign. The factors are not steps or processes, but measures of the outcome of steps or processes; i.e., the system may involve interaction with consumers of the organization's products and depend on their attitude toward the organization and on the pattern of their purchase decisions. Factors in the influence diagram relating to consumers might be satisfaction with service, tendency to take prompt payment discounts and tendency to place smaller orders. The strategic factor driving the consumer factors might be the balance of discount policy between quantity and prompt payment. External environmental connections might be interest rates, competitor responses and industry capacity levels. Outcome measures might be return on assets and level of accounts receivable.

An influence diagram of this highly simplified system is presented in Figure 9.4, which shows the factors described above, and both the direction and the sign (positive or negative) of the relationships between them. The effect the firm hopes to achieve by substituting prompt payment discounts for quantity discounts is shown by the *chain* [Q + C − K − L]. This is a positive chain (containing no, or an even number of, negative linkages), indicating that the net outcome of an increase in the strategic option measure is an increase in the target factor. In this case, an increase in the percentage of average customer prompt payment discounts to average overall customer discounts (Factor Q) results in an increase in return on assets (Factor L). However, the diagram shows that there are six other chains that influence the return on assets target factor. Each of these chains is described in Table 9.1. Four of the chains have positive outcomes; three have negative outcomes.

Influence chains also permit the identification of *loops* that may have interesting consequences in the system. Figure 9.5 includes a potentially vicious cycle, triggered by the implementation of a shift in the policy at [Q]. Decreased customer satisfaction [Q − A] leads to lost customers [A − D] to the competition. The competition then becomes less motivated to match the discount policy of the company [D − O] and that reduced matching by the competition heightens customer dissatisfaction further [O + A]. The overall

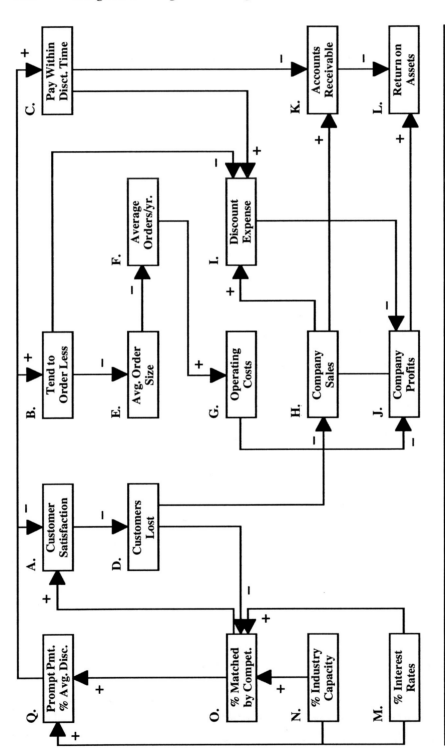

Figure 9.4: Influence Diagram for a Discount Strategy

Table 9.1: Discount Strategy Issue:
        Influence Chains Affecting Return on Assets (ROA)

[Q + C – K – L] Net positive result

> Increasing prompt payment discounts relative to quantity discounts (the strategy) increases the tendency of customers to pay within the discount period, decreasing receivables, increasing the ratio of profits to assets.

[Q + C + I – J + L] Net negative result

> But that increase in discounts taken increases total discounts, reducing profits and ROA.

[Q – A – D – H . . .]

> Decreased customer satisfaction causes a loss in sales, with three results.

[Q – A – D – H + K – L] Net positive result

> First, reduced sales cause receivables to decrease, increasing ROA.

[Q – A – D – H + I – J + L] Net positive result

> Second, total discounts decrease, increasing profits and ROA.

[Q – A – D – H + J + L] Net negative result

> Third, the fundamental impact of reduced sales on profits reduces ROA.

[Q + B – I – J + L] Net positive result

> The strategy influences customers to place more small orders; fewer quantity discounts are offered and profits and ROA increase.

[Q + B – E – F + G – J + L] Net negative result

> But more small orders means small average order size, more orders per year, greater operating costs and reduced profits and ROA.

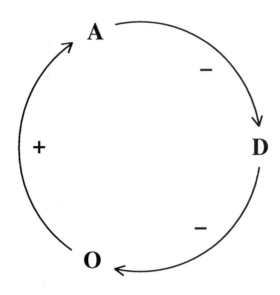

Figure 9.5: Vicious Cycle Influences

loop [A – D – O + A] feeds itself, at least in concept, endlessly. The meaning of this loop is that there is a potential loss of all of the firm's largest customers, to whom smaller quantity discounts are being extended and who can get better deals elsewhere. Only if the process is *countervailed* by another loop will the process be prevented. The loop that is needed is a sensitivity by the firm to competitor policy-matching reactions, and a corresponding influence to adjust its policy [O + Q]. Figure 9.6 shows both the potentially vicious positive loop and the negative loop that can countervail it.

The impact of the strategy depends on the strength of these influences, which an influence diagram cannot determine. What the influence diagram *does* help determine is the existence of other influences in the firm, of chains and loops that clearly complicate the strategy decision.

Time-Process Diagrams. Because many of the aspects of the environment around us involve processes with non-trivial timing or triggering linkages, the more specialized flow chart forms illustrated in Figure 9.7 may be useful analytical devices. Panel A of Figure 9.7 portrays a Gantt chart [84], a highly general form to juxtapose process in one dimension with time in the other dimension. Such charts have found common use in scheduling applications, using critical path method (CPM) and program evaluation and review technique (PERT) methodologies [174;336]. Panels B and C of Figure 9.7 show these project-based networks, in their traditional and time-scaled formats. The critical path [0 – 3 – 7 – 8] is identified as the one requiring the most sequential time.

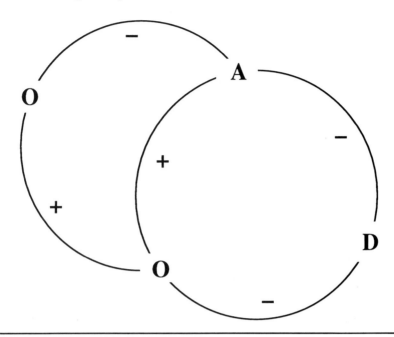

Figure 9.6: Vicious Cycle Resolved by a Countervailing Force

Two-dimensional approaches such as these permit illustration of time dependency (sequencing, triggering) as well as time absorption in the completion of a process or set of processes. In its more general application to environmental scanning, the two-dimensional approach to flow chart mapping permits better predictions to be formulated about future outcomes. That is, the set of possible and probable future events that are evaluated in the process of developing scenarios could be shaped and refined using two-dimensional flow charting. Just as morphological analysis identifies some shape-dimension combinations to be impossible states of nature (see p. 158), time precedence flow charts can identify impossible or implausible sequences or combinations of events. Moreover, just as morphological analysis can assist the analyst in uncovering possible undiscovered or unexploited states of nature, time-process flow charts can help identify possible event convergences, where parallel processes in political, social, technological and economic dimensions of the environment may reach future time-states more or less simultaneously.

Tree Diagrams. Tree diagrams are useful in describing *linkages* in systems and processes. These could be probability linkages from one state of the system to another, which are referred to as decision trees [58;174;218;234;383;489]. In Figure 9.8, the decision is whether to undertake a test market for a new product. The path to each node is a possible outcome to which some finite probability is attached. Some of these outcomes represent decisions (the square nodes in Figure 9.8), and some represent outcomes. Each ultimate outcome of the decision/outcome tree is associated with a payoff or cost. The expected value of the decision process can be computed as the probability-weighted value of those possible outcomes.

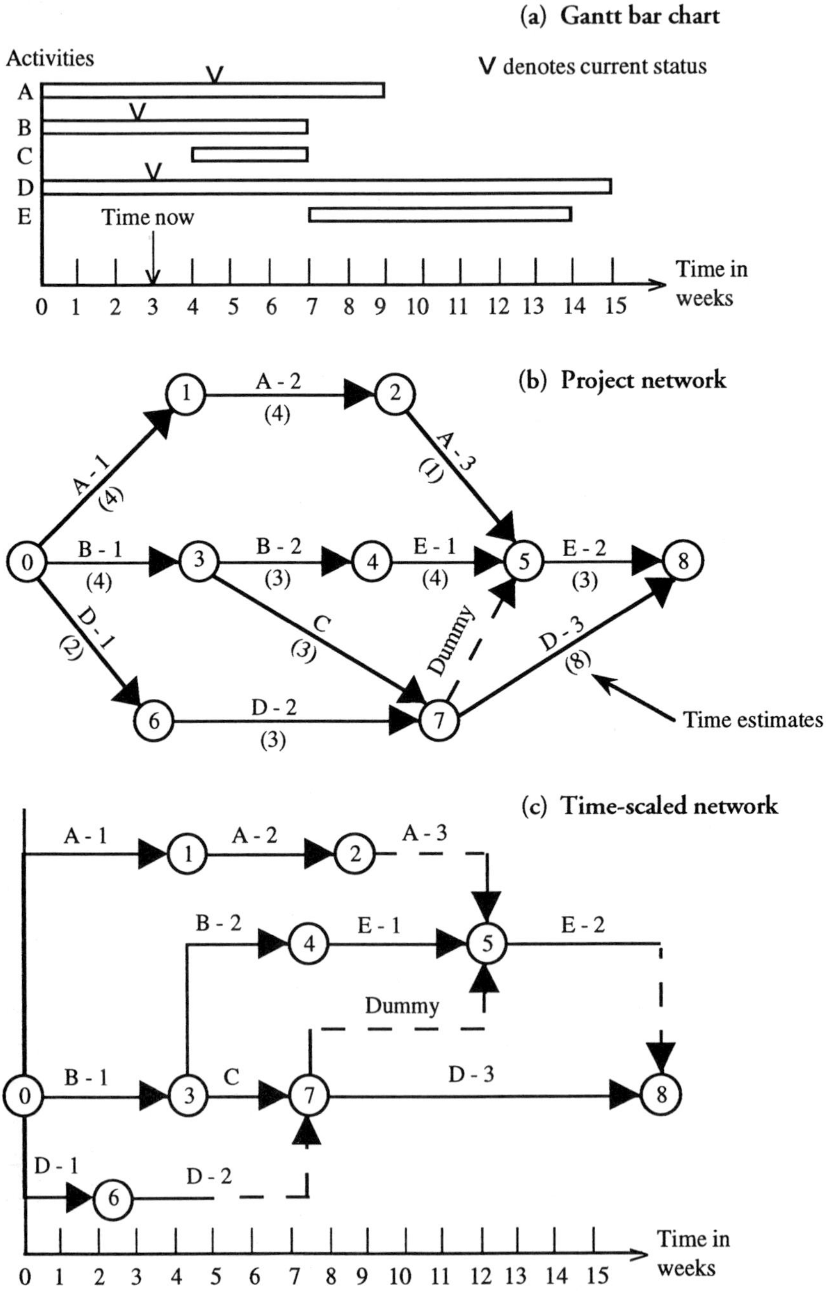

Figure 9.7: Examples: Gantt Chart, Project Network, and Time-Scaled Network

(Reprinted by permission from Joseph Moder, et al., Project Management with CPM, PERT and Precedence Diagramming. *© 1983 by Van Nostrand Reinhold.)*

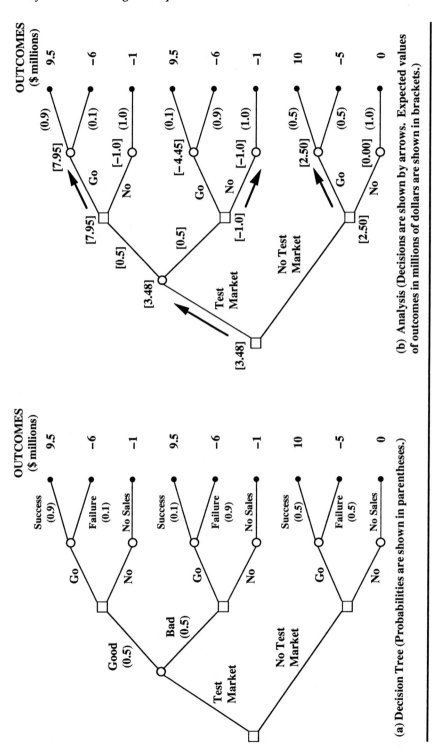

Figure 9.8: Decision Analysis for the Decision Whether or Not to Test Market

(*Source: Urban [489,421]. Reprinted by permission.*)

Linkages can also be from one level of complexity in a system to another (Figure 9.9); in this example, components, sub-assemblies, labor and materials come together through several levels of process to form a product. Finally, a tree diagram can portray relationship linkages across levels of hierarchy in a system. Figure 9.10 shows a hierarchy describing the market for coffee. Such hierarchies are not simply organizational; they imply a higher degree of substitution (or communication) *across* the hierarchy at any level than vertically. The relevance tree is a specialized type of tree diagram [405,255].

The basic difference between tree diagrams and other flow charts is that each node of a tree diagram represents a set of increasingly detailed components or events at the next level of the tree. When such maps are used to portray uncertainty or complexity across multiple dimensions of a system, they become more intricate than other forms of flow charts.

Input-Output Analysis. Input-output analysis involves creating a flow chart of the economy, a sector of the economy, or even of a large company within the economy. The purpose of the analysis is to determine the sales to, and revenues from, any two elements of an economic system. Knowing these supply/demand relationships permits one to predict the impact of marginal changes in demand in one place in the economic system under study upon the required supply from other places in that system. Input-output analysis was undertaken for the U.S. economy over 20 years ago. (See Leontief [273; 274].) Such a national economic map can be used to predict the future positions of industries and sub-industries, given assumptions about overall economic growth and about marginal shifts in GNP distribution across industries. Applied to a company, input-output analysis is a methodology for a company to apply to better understand *its own* structure.

In American industry, practices of transfer pricing and absorption costing have often obscured the fundamental demand cross-elasticities across elements of integrated and diversified organizations. Input-output analysis cuts through these conventional smoke screens. Yet, existing input-output linkages depend on a reasonably stable industrial structure. If the discontinuities of the 1980s represent the evidence of the coming of a new industrial order, as Toffler suggests, much existing input-output work will have to be reformulated if it to be useful. For more information on the application of input-output analysis, see Ayres [24], Carter [71], and Smith and Walsh [436].

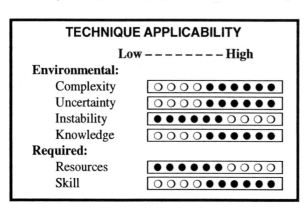

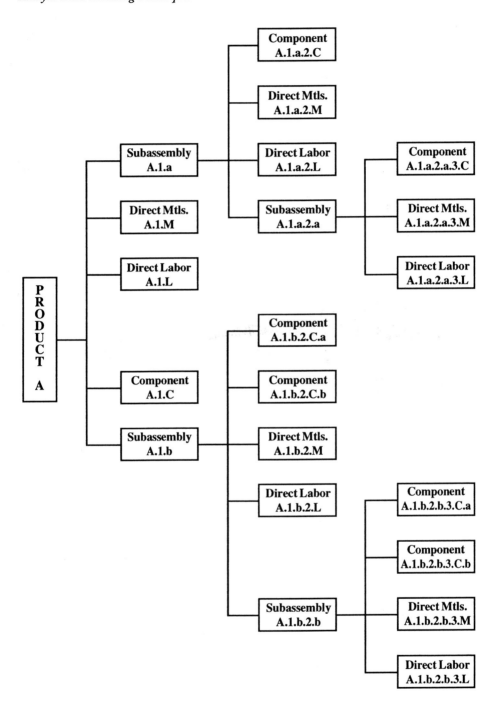

Figure 9.9: Process Hierarchy Flow Chart

Limit Envelopes. Some systems and processes may defy detailed mapping, especially where they exhibit signs of instability, or where uncertainty is high because of our lack of knowledge (reducible uncertainty) or because of the system's fundamental characteristics (irreducible uncertainty). In such cases, the best action may be to characterize that aspect of the environment in terms of *limiting cases,* or best case/worst case terms, using theory as the guide. See Lebel [262].

To construct limit envelopes, identify a set of related variables and estimate their outcomes assuming a defined set of most favorable circumstances in the relevant dimensions of the environment. Then identify a comparable set of outcomes in the event of a combined occurrence of least favorable circumstances. This process can continue to the limit of available knowledge about linkages between the variables and the environment, about the linkages between the variables, and about the linkages within the environment.

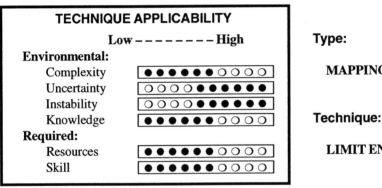

There are similar limits on our ability to fine-tune the prospective impact of more specialized environments on our chosen environmental variables. These limits result from the application of theoretical linkages in defining limiting circumstances. Rarely are there quantitative guidelines to supplement that theoretical exercise; if there were, modeling techniques rather than mapping techniques might yield a better analysis.

Impact Analysis. Impact analysis is similar to limit envelopes in that it relates environmental circumstances to outcomes. Rather than dealing with limiting best or worse case environments, a firm conducting impact analysis first selects a set of *independent critical events* by quantitatively or subjectively assessing the probability of occurrence and the resultant impact of possible future events. Second, the firm specifies a group of input or outcome measures within its task environment, important to the goals of projects, products or divisions. Third, the firm arrays each target measure in its own Cartesian probability-impact space, such as shown in Figure 9.11. Fourth, each event is assigned an *impact position* within each target "space," with positive impacts being favorable and negative impacts unfavorable.

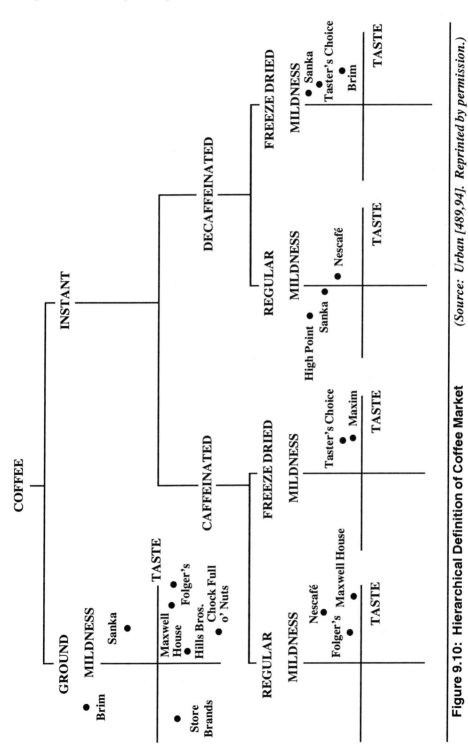

Figure 9.10: Hierarchical Definition of Coffee Market   *(Source: Urban [489,94]. Reprinted by permission.)*

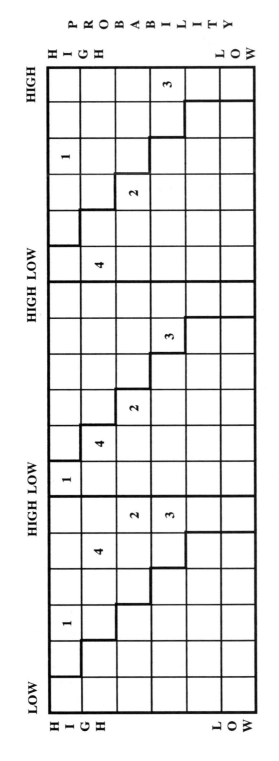

Figure 9.11: Multi-Target Impact Assessment

Event or Issue
1. Negative GNP growth Q1-Q2
2. Inflation above 10 percent this year
3. Strike at contract expiration
4. Foreign competition

The meanings to be attached to these impact data are clear only in a general sense. The highest impact (+ and –) events for any measure are most critical for that measure *to the extent that all events are equally probable.* The highest impact (+ and –) measures for any event are the most sensitive to that event *assuming that the measures are independent of one another.* In general, high-priority issues emerge in the upper right quadrant of each target space. Note that there is a bias in assigning importance (the bold dividing lines in Figure 9.11), toward high-impact, low-probability outcomes (unlikely but devastating), and against high-probability, low-impact outcomes (commonplace irritants).

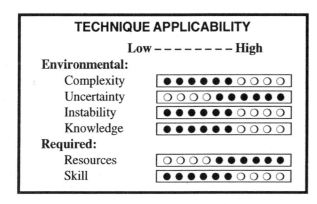

TECHNIQUE APPLICABILITY

Low – – – – – – – High

Environmental:
Complexity
Uncertainty
Instability
Knowledge
Required:
Resources
Skill

Type:

MAPPING

Technique:

IMPACT ANALYSIS

The visual format of this analysis has two benefits. First, it can be used readily as a consensus-building device for group assessment of critical issues. Second, the visual and qualitative nature of the analysis obviates summation of probability-impact values into event or measure "totals." These summary totals are inevitably calculated when a quantitative cross impact analysis is conducted, but they have questionable meanings. The sum of impacts for a given measure in some way reflects the overall impact on that measure if *all* of the critical events occurred. The sum of the impacts for a given critical event indicates the overall impact of the event on the firm, or on the measures the firm chooses to assess, *assuming that measure impacts are additive.* Assume a case where two of the measures were: 1) risk-adjusted net present value of new product "A," and 2) number of years for product "A" to achieve positive cumulative cash flow. If a particular critical event yielded summary, probability-weighted impacts of +30 for measure 1) and –30 for measure 2), it is doubtful that the product manager, or his or her boss, would consider the net impact of that critical event to be zero.

Impact analysis is best used in relatively placid environments where, even if the firm does not have a high degree of knowledge about environment-firm or environment-environment relationships, those relationships are fairly straightforward and stable. Impact analysis assumes a significant degree of uncertainty; otherwise there would be few if any critical events to assess. It is a method with quantitative outcomes that must be interpreted with caution; firms do not need a high degree of skill to apply it successfully, but do need to commit the resources necessary to gather opinions about events and outcomes in a structured way, involving as many thoughtful participants as possible in seeking consensus.

In more complex and less stable environments, other techniques may be better; e.g., cross-impact analysis and trend impact analysis. More information on impact analysis can be found in Ashley [20], Camillus [65], Smith/Walsh [436], and Stoffels [451].

Morphological Models. A morphology is a study of form and structure. Traditionally associated with linguistics, biology, chemistry and physical geography, morphological analysis became associated with environmental scanning through its use to support technological forecasting. The concept of morphological analysis is to associate a subject, object or idea with as many dimensions as necessary to describe it, and with as many shapes as the subject can take within any dimension. It should then be possible to describe all of the possible shapes the subject can take, with an upper limit of the number of shapes times the number of dimensions. Some combinations will be self-evident, some novel or undiscovered, and some impossible. A list of present and plausible combinations, called "events," is the principal outcome of a morphological model.

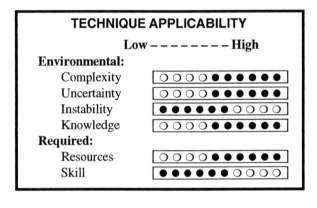

Wissema [525] presents several examples of the application of the technique, principally to product and process development problems. Cardboard is one of his examples: First, consider all of the possible functions, described in their most general sense, that cardboard can serve. It can separate one "thing" from another, or can encase an object, as well as restrain an object or serve as a barrier. When mixed with other materials its abilities are extended, and Wissema calls these the dimensions of the subject.

Cardboard as a separator most frequently serves the purpose of keeping solid objects from bumping into one another, such as wine bottles in a case. More broadly, such objects are a form of matter, and matter exists as solids, liquids and gases. Setting aside preconceptions, as scanners should, it is at least conceivable that cardboard could separate any of the conceivable combinations of matter, that is:

Solid from Solid	Solid from Liquid
Solid from Gas	Liquid from Liquid
Liquid from Gas	Gas from Gas

In other dimensions, cardboard serves other purposes. It can surround its object completely (the wine case is sealed) or partially (once the case has been opened). Cardboard can stand alone or be combined with other materials, by laminating, coating, impregnating or assembling. The pairing materials are many; Wissema's example included paper, plastic, wood and paint. Cardboard can act as a barrier against gravity (wine cases are stacked in a warehouse), against mechanical forces (the forklift that stacks the cases), against heat (a cardboard sleeve insulates chilled wine for a picnic), radiation (cardboard protects the wine from ultraviolet light), and sound (cardboard mutes a soprano's high C).

The combination of dimensions or functions with shapes or purposes leads to a two-dimensional matrix, or morphological space, for the object. For cardboard, that space is described in Table 9.2, with 300 (6 x 2 x 5 x 5) possible combinations in which cardboard could be applied.

Table 9.2: Morphological Space for Cardboard

Possible Dimensions	Possible Shapes					
	1	2	3	4	5	6
A. Separation between	solid-solid	solid-liquid	solid-gas	liquid-liquid	liquid-gas	gas-gas
B. Surrounding one	completely	partly				
C. Barrier against	gravity	mechanical forces	heat	radiation	sound	
D. Combined with	paper	plastic	wood	paint	alone	

(Source: Wissema [525,147]. Reproduced by permission of Butterworth and Co. [Publishers] Ltd.)

A sampling of these combinations is enumerated in Table 9.3. For example, the combination A1,B2,C3,D4 assigns painted cardboard the task of protecting a hot solid from a cold solid while only partly surrounding one of them. The combination A3,B1,C2,D5 is a newly purchased case of wine in the trunk of a car on the way home.

Some of these combinations are impossible; as Wissema observes, cardboard is useless in a liquid environment unless coated with plastic, so that any combination including A2, A4 or A5 must also include D2. Some of the combinations are merely unfamiliar or implausible, but possible. For cardboard, this could mean new uses; for ideas and issues,

---

Table 9.3: Sample Combinations from a Morphological Space
_____

Subject: Cardboard

A1,B2,C3,D4   A partly open cardboard separator between hot and cold solids.

A3,B1,C2,D5   A solid encased completely to protect contents from mechanical forces exerted in a gas: *a case of wine in the trunk of a car.*

A5,B1,C1,D2   A closed carton coated with plastic protecting a liquid from
gravity in a gas: *a box of frozen fruit juice.*

A4,B1,C3,D5   A plain closed carton separating a hot liquid from a cold one: *a
soggy mess — this is an impossible combination.*

(Note: Letters and numbers refer to Dimensions and Shapes in Table 9.2.)

---

this could imply previously unforeseen turns of events. Some of the combinations are not yet even identified, because the space is incomplete. For example, one of the barriers cardboard can provide is from sight, as when the container is intended to convey an image distinct from its contents, or simply to hide them.

Morphological analysis involves four steps beyond initial creation of the morphological space. One must first describe all possible combinations of shapes and dimensions; second, carefully identify all impossible combinations; third, review the space for shapes or dimensions that were missed but could create still more possible combinations; and fourth, assess the outcomes for novelty and potential as opportunities or threats.

The future assessment potential associated with morphological analysis is in discovering previously unarticulated combinations. In technological forecasting, this approach can lead to new product or process discoveries. In environmental forecasting, the approach has promise for uncovering possible future events and trends. For more information on morphological models, see Cetron and Ralph [75], Gregory [185] and Zwicki [537].

Cross-Impact Analysis. Cross-impact analysis is a variant of impact analysis. The concept involves identifying relationships between environmental events and using those relationships to derive through iteration a set of probabilities of events occurring at any of several points into the future. These reflect the compound probability of the event itself, and the probabilities of other events to which that event's occurrence is related. Events can then be further related to impacts on the firm using conventional techniques. See Gordon and Hayward [180], Jantsch [210], and Cetron and Ralph [75].

```
┌─────────────────────────────────────────┐
│         TECHNIQUE APPLICABILITY          │           Type:
│           Low ──────── High              │
│  Environmental:                          │           MAPPING
│     Complexity    ○○○○●●●●●●              │
│     Uncertainty   ○○○○●●●●●●              │
│     Instability   ○○○○●●●●●●              │
│     Knowledge     ○○○○●●●●●●              │           Technique:
│  Required:                               │
│     Resources     ○○○○●●●●●●              │           CROSS-IMPACT
│     Skill         ○○○○●●●●●●              │           ANALYSIS
└─────────────────────────────────────────┘
```

In applying cross-impact analysis ideally, several steps are involved. First, a set of relevant possible future events (RPFEs) is identified. Second, a year is associated for each event with three probabilities of occurrence: .1, .5 and .9. Third, an occurrence matrix is formed to describe the direction and intensity of impact on each RPFE if each of the other RPFEs independently occurs. Fourth, as a means of validating the occurrence matrix, a second matrix is formed indicating the impact of the non-occurrence of each of the RPFEs on all of the others. Fifth, a Monte Carlo simulation is run through multiple trials; in each a "real outcome" is simulated in the future, and the probabilities of future events at each level of time are recalculated. The outcome of this process is a revised estimate of the probability of the occurrence of each event in the initially specified (.1, .5, and .9) years. In most cases, the probabilities are different from their initial levels.

While cross-impact analysis requires considerable skill to apply independently or resources to acquire commercially, it does seek to take command over the most elusive aspects of the environment — complexity and instability. Turbulent environments may be so because of the occurrence of several events that are importantly, but not obviously related to one another; the turbulence might have been predicted with a better understanding of those underlying phenomena. Moreover, few other techniques interrelate the causes of events; most focus on plausible cause-and-effect. For further information on the application of the technique, see Cetron and Ralph [75,259-73], and Gordon and Hayward [180].

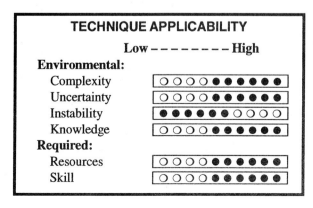

```
┌─────────────────────────────────────────┐
│         TECHNIQUE APPLICABILITY          │           Type:
│           Low ──────── High              │
│  Environmental:                          │           MAPPING
│     Complexity    ○○○○●●●●●●              │
│     Uncertainty   ○○○○●●●●●●              │
│     Instability   ●●●●●○○○○○              │
│     Knowledge     ○○○○●●●●●●              │           Technique:
│  Required:                               │
│     Resources     ○○○○●●●●●●              │           TREND IMPACT
│     Skill         ○○○○●●●●●●              │           ANALYSIS
└─────────────────────────────────────────┘
```

Trend Impact Analysis. Trend impact analysis is a variant of cross-impact analysis. Its focus is on assessing the multivariate impact of the environment on broad environmental trends, rather than in assessing the probability of environmental outcomes or the impact of those outcomes on the firm's operations. For more information on trend impact analysis, see Jain [207].

Modeling Techniques

As used here, the category of models includes techniques that are more comprehensively quantitative than maps. Except for that difference, maps also represent bona-fide models. Models may be explanatory or predictive. They are explanatory if they seek to explain the relationships embedded in an accumulation of experimental data. They are predictive if they utilize such explanatory variables to predict the future outcome of a dependent variable. Evaluating variables across time represents a *time-series* approach to modeling; where experimental data observations are obtained independent of time, the model is a *cross-section*.

If the future course of a model variable is solely dependent on time advancing, it is a simple *extrapolation* where only the rate or pattern of growth is at issue. If a time series model depends for its resolution on the value of multiple variables in the future, it is a *causal* model. When at least some of those multiple variables are uncertain, and subject to probability distributions, the model is *stochastic*. Should the model depend for its resolution on the simultaneous solution of multiple submodels, where, in general, there are at most as many unknown predictive variables as model equations, the model is *econometric*. In the special case where relationships are policy driven rather than experientially or statistically derived, the model is referred to as a *response* model because the outcomes are a result of policy choices of the limits or definitions assigned to certain variables.

Trend Extrapolation. The simplest approach to predicting the value of a variable is to assume that it will continue its course through time following the same path as it has in the past. Trend extrapolation involves applying two steps to historical information about a single variable. First, determine what time-related model best describes the historical behavior of the variable. Second, predict the future course of that variable by allowing time to advance beyond the present, solving the model for the "emerging future."

The first step is experimental. The past behavior of the variable may best be described by a linear least squares model, or by a nonlinear model that describes the variable as following a life cycle, a growth rate or a repeating, harmonic cycle (see Figure 9.12). Because of statistical or economic noise, the data may not exhibit any pattern relationship at all until it is expressed as a moving average or subjected to cyclical or exponential smoothing. The best model of the variable's behavior is the one that explains the variable's behavior against time with the highest percentage of correlation.

If historical analysis ended at time period 20, a future prediction is obtained by solving the chosen model for time periods 21 and beyond. This extrapolation technique is

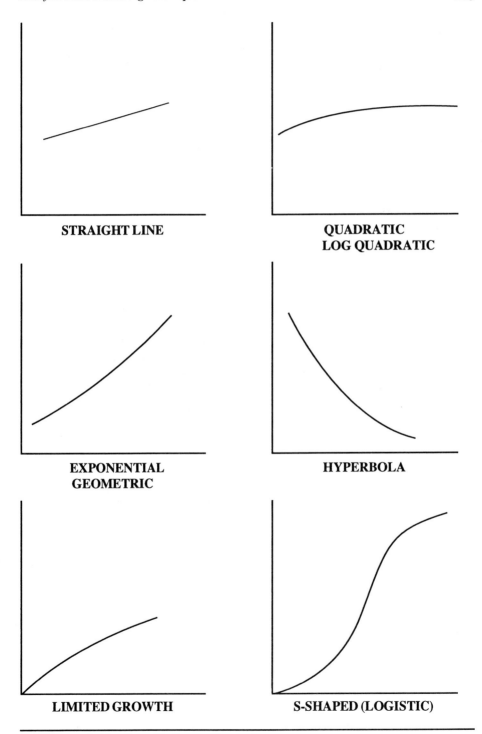

STRAIGHT LINE

QUADRATIC
LOG QUADRATIC

EXPONENTIAL
GEOMETRIC

HYPERBOLA

LIMITED GROWTH

S-SHAPED (LOGISTIC)

Figure 9.12: Growth Curve Examples

based on the assumption that the future is a continuing unfolding of the history that was properly described by the model chosen in the first step. The accuracy of the predictions obtained through extrapolation thus depends on the future being shaped by the same processes that determined the past. In particular, the methodology allows for no future changes in other unspecified variables that would influence the nature of this variable's relationship with advancing time. Extrapolation is applicable only in the most placid of circumstances, where complexity is at a minimum and uncertainty is low. Little knowledge about either the environment or the technique is required; one needs to assume only that time will continue to advance and to apply a set of readily available computer programs to a set of historical data observations.

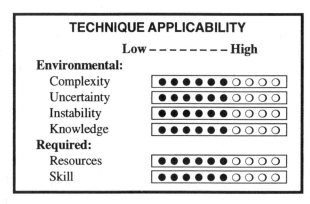

The simplicity of trend extrapolation belies the robustness of methodologies used to develop underlying models on which the extrapolation is based. A substantial body of research in the field of technological forecasting has developed around the effort to explain the diffusion of research into development and into products; see, for example, Bright [54], Jantsch [210], Linstone and Sahal [282], DeBresson and Lampel [113], and Cetron and Ralph [75]. The S-curve, product life cycle or logistic curve shown in Figure 7.2 is one of the outgrowths of this research. Additionally (see Rosenfield [403]), statistical modifications of extrapolation models can be made to enhance their predictive power where underlying processes are subject to both environmental and individual event uncertainty, as where the environment might remain stable in an overall sense, but individual event and behavior probabilities might shift over time (being nonhomogeneous).

Because of its ease of use, trend extrapolation is a popular means for describing the behavior of environmental variables. Survey data presented later in this chapter show that the use of the technique has not diminished in recent years, even considering the general acceptance of the notion that environments are becoming more turbulent in virtually all dimensions, and for virtually all participants. Because of this heightened turbulence, implying growth in complexity and uncertainty along with instability, the meaning of extrapolated variables in most cases is highly questionable. For more information on the techniques of data analysis, least squares regression of single time series and trend forecasting, see Blackman [41], Chambers, etal. [76], Cetron and Ralph [75,14-17], Lenz [268], Tukey [483], and Zwicky and Wilson [538].

Time Series Analysis. Time series analysis, as used here, comprises the building of multivariate models to explain the behavior of a dependent variable. Data series making up the model may be averaged, deseasonalized or transformed. The model may be linear or may involve power series of the variables, and should explain the behavior of the dependent variable successfully and in terms that are consistent with theory, or with our understanding of the behavior of the environment.

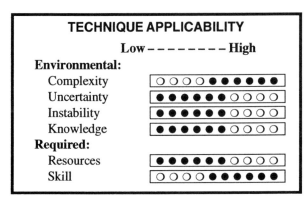

TECHNIQUE APPLICABILITY	
Low – – – – – – – – High	**Type:**
Environmental:	
Complexity ○○○○●●●●●●	**MODELS**
Uncertainty ●●●●●●○○○○	
Instability ●●●●●●○○○○	
Knowledge ●●●●●●○○○○	**Technique:**
Required:	
Resources ●●●●●●○○○○	**TIME SERIES**
Skill ○○○○●●●●●●	**ANALYSIS**

Time series models are typically developed on computers using multiple linear or quadratic regression routines and software such as SPSS, SAS or BMD. Numerous excellent references to time series modeling at various levels of sophistication exist [16;79;299;300;307;324;340;371;442;517;518]. More comprehensive treatment of the subject is contained in Taylor [464]. The special topic of ordinal time series analysis, where variables are ranks rather than values, is treated by Ruefli and Wilson [409].

The success of a time series model is measured by the multiple correlation coefficient, R^2, a measure that indicates the proportion of total variation in the dependent variable that is explained by the model. Further, there should be an absence of a pattern to the residual variation in the model or model errors — the difference between the actual value of the dependent variable and the value predicted by the model. Models that are successful in explaining a high degree of the past variation in a dependent variable may be useful predictive devices (see Causal Models). Often, the impetus for undertaking time series analysis is to seek to develop such a predictive relationship.

What series analysis does however, is describe the relationship between independent, explanatory variables and the variable one is interested in explaining or modeling in the context of past data. Therefore, time-series analysis is a useful analytical tool where uncertainty and instability are both low, and the past has some reliable continuity with the future. Time-series analysis can successfully describe complex relationships, if the analyst's knowledge about the techniques of such analysis is reasonably thorough.

Cross-Section Analysis. There are times when multiple observations of a variable can be made within a time period, and modeled in the cross-section, so that the model explains the value of a dependent variable regardless of its position in time. The gathering

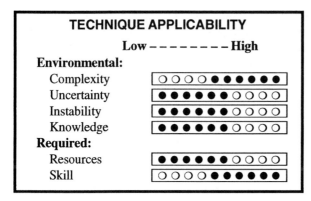

of atmospheric and geophysical observations at 100 cities across the Midwest United States creates a cross-section database. The gathering of the same information hourly at one of the cities from January through June of a given year creates a time-series database. Cross section models are sometimes useful in helping to develop an understanding of the behavior of time series variables, and to predict them. Many of the references for time series models (above), also treat cross-section analysis.

Causal Models. By adopting a time-series or cross-section model as a predictor of the future value of a dependent variable, one creates a causal model. To apply such a model, estimates are formulated for the emerging values of the explanatory variables, and the model equation is solved to obtain a prediction of the dependent variable.

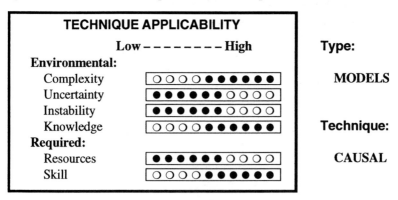

The models decision makers adopt for predictive purposes were developed using time-series and cross-section analysis techniques to explain the past successfully. They may have been developed using high sophistication of technique, but with relatively little knowledge about the theory and behavior of relationships in the environment being modeled; such models are described as experimental, and experimental models can successfully explain the past. But such an experimental model may contain explanatory variables that are themselves determined by other relationships, referred to by Mueller and Smith [342] as "third variables." When these variables ultimately change, as in the future, the model's performance would break down, because the third variable was not incorporated in the model. Such mis-specification of models is more likely to occur when knowledge about the environment being modeled is low. Mis-specification and lack of knowledge about theory and behavior of environments thus become serious impediments once a model is to be used for prediction purposes, as through a causal model.

Stochastic Models. Stochastic models are models that incorporate one or more variables whose outcomes are expected values that result from probability distributions. A classic article by Hertz [195] illustrates how uncertainty, in the form of probability distributions of variables, can be incorporated into business decision making. One begins by specifying appropriate model variables as probability distributions; perhaps variable X is normally distributed with a mean of 200 and a standard deviation of 20, rather than as single point estimates or predictions. The variable's form within the model changes from X to E(X), the expected value of X.

There may be other such stochastic variables in the model, the expected value of which at any future point in time is probabilistic, rather than deterministic as with causal models. For stochastic models, the dependent variable's outcome is a result of the conduct of a combination of predictions of deterministic variables and experimental outcomes of probabilistic variables. After numerous experiments with the probabilistic variables, the average of outcomes for any of those variables should be the same as its mean or expected value. But for any single experiment with such a variable to determine a future time period estimate, the resulting value could come from anywhere in the probability distribution. And in that same experiment, values will result for all other stochastic variables from somewhere within each of their probability distributions.

TECHNIQUE APPLICABILITY		
Low – – – – – – – High	**Type:**	
Environmental:		
Complexity $\circ\circ\circ\circ\bullet\bullet\bullet\bullet\bullet\bullet$	**MODELS**	
Uncertainty $\circ\circ\circ\circ\bullet\bullet\bullet\bullet\bullet\bullet$		
Instability $\bullet\bullet\bullet\bullet\bullet\circ\circ\circ\circ\circ$		
Knowledge $\circ\circ\circ\circ\bullet\bullet\bullet\bullet\bullet\bullet$	**Technique:**	
Required:		
Resources $\circ\circ\circ\circ\bullet\bullet\bullet\bullet\bullet\bullet$	**STOCHASTIC**	
Skill $\circ\circ\circ\circ\bullet\bullet\bullet\bullet\bullet\bullet$		

When time actually passes into the future, to use terms loosely, there will exist some observed value of the dependent variable. If the model is "correct," this value will have resulted from the combination of parameters and variable values observed in the environment, with deterministic outcomes for deterministic variables, and experimental outcomes from probability distributions for stochastic variables. But, if the intent is to forecast or predict the value of a dependent variable in a future time period, the best estimate of the outcome is not a single experimental value, but a probability distribution of values, determined by the stochastic interaction of the probabilistic explanatory variables in the model.

To estimate the distribution of a future predicted value of the dependent variable in a model, Hertz describes an experimental procedure called Monte Carlo Analysis,where the model is run experimentally through many trials. Each trial contains a single outcome from each stochastic variable, determined from a random process; each results in a value for the dependent variable when the model is solved using the predicted and simulated values of the explanatory variables. All trials together create a frequency distribution of the values for the dependent variable, and this distribution represents the stochastic prediction of the future value of that variable.

Stochastic models are useful in forecasting future environments since they incorporate uncertainty in a way that broadly reflects reality. However, stochastic models have several liabilities. First, it is difficult experimentally to estimate the probability distributions controlling any variable unless the historical database from which the distribution is drawn contains no instability or third-variable influences. Second, one must assume such influences in the future will not invalidate an experimentally determined distribution.

Third, it is necessary to present model outcomes that are future environmental predictions to users in the form of probability distributions, not point estimates. This stochastic communication interface is often a difficult hurdle, because non-mathematicians do not tend to think in terms of distributional outcomes. However, the expected outcome and variability measures generated by stochastic models are the essence of risky decision-making, of which environmental forecasting may be the pre-eminent example.

Modeling languages exist that can readily simulate outcomes using stochastic relationships, including EPS-FCS [147;330], IFPS [203;204], and SYSTEM W [138;459]. The risk analysis and decision support literature begun by Hertz has grown; authors who have dealt with these subjects from an applications and communications viewpoint include Bidgoli [38], Carter [72], Hertz and Thomas [196], Raiffa and Schlaifer [383], Wagner [505;516] and Wriston [529].

Econometric Models. The causal and stochastic models described above have principally been of the "single equation" type, where there is one equation and one unknown. The explanatory variables are estimated, and the dependent variable is determined as a result. Environments rarely are so simple, but they may be made to seem simple so that a manageable set of "partial equilibrium" predictions can be made. In partial equilibrium, elements of the system not incorporated in the model are assumed to remain constant.

Econometric models adopt a more expansive view of their environments. Basically, they combine sectorial equations as a system of models with as many unknowns as equations, and seek to determine equilibrium of the system simultaneously. Very large models of the U.S. and world economies exist, such as the FRB-MIT econometric model of the U.S. economy, the Wharton model and others. Extremely expensive to develop, these models can quite effectively deliver precise predictions and tests of policy parameters, as long as structures in existence when the models were built and tested remain unchanged.

```
┌──────────────────────────────────────────┐
│        TECHNIQUE APPLICABILITY             │
│          Low – – – – – – – – High          │
│   Environmental:                           │
│     Complexity    [○ ○ ○ ● ● ● ● ● ● ●]    │
│     Uncertainty   [○ ○ ○ ● ● ● ● ● ● ●]    │
│     Instability   [● ● ● ● ● ● ○ ○ ○ ○]    │
│     Knowledge     [○ ○ ○ ● ● ● ● ● ● ●]    │
│   Required:                                │
│     Resources     [○ ○ ○ ● ● ● ● ● ● ●]    │
│     Skill         [○ ○ ○ ● ● ● ● ● ● ●]    │
└──────────────────────────────────────────┘
```

Type:

MODELS

Technique:

ECONOMETRIC

Econometric models can thus handle every curve the environment can pitch at us — high degrees of complexity and uncertainty — except instability. This limitation plus the cost and time for development reduces the value of econometric models in turbulent times; see, "Where Big Econometric Models Go Wrong" [519]. Econometric modeling techniques are explored in some of the same references provided for time series analysis. Additional applications-oriented references include Ayres [23], Chang [77], and Klein and Young [245]. Comprehensive references include Box, etal. [50], and Pindyck and Rubinfeld [371].

Response Models. Response models exist principally as "planning models" within the context of the firm. They may contain stochastic linkages with the external environment that are quite robust, and they are capable of reflecting a high degree of complexity in their environmental interfaces. An important further purpose of response models is to translate predicted conditions of market size, market growth and market share in customer markets, along with conditions in supply markets, into three outcomes: operating results, financing outcomes and value creation (see Table 9.4).

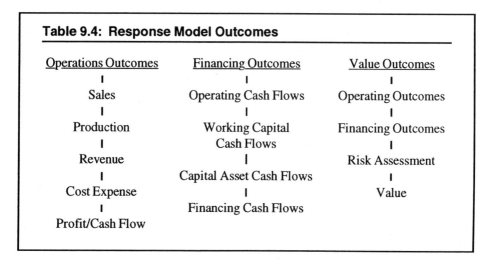

Table 9.4: Response Model Outcomes

Operations Outcomes	Financing Outcomes	Value Outcomes
I	I	I
Sales	Operating Cash Flows	Operating Outcomes
I	I	I
Production	Working Capital Cash Flows	Financing Outcomes
I		I
Revenue	I	Risk Assessment
I	Capital Asset Cash Flows	I
Cost Expense	I	Value
I	Financing Cash Flows	
Profit/Cash Flow		

These models project financing and operating cash flows that are intended to assist the firm in making strategic management judgments about products and markets, and in funding those strategic judgments. The models are interactive with the environment to the extent the firm makes them so. Demand, supply, production, terms of trade and cost of funds functions can all be made highly interactive, even stochastic, to reflect the complexity and uncertainty of the environment. These are causal elements of the firm's planning model.

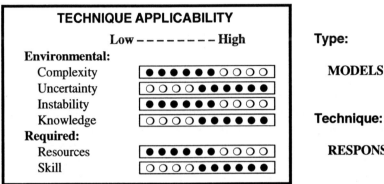

Most such planning models are kept relatively simple in their interactions with the environment because their principal purpose is to determine the cash flow impacts of strategic investment alternatives, plus fund and operating management strategies. And the principal context within which these responses occur is the fundamental accounting identity (assets = liabilities + equity), expressed in terms of some form of balance sheet and income statement. The response mechanisms these models contain may include policy parameters on working capital turnover (receivables, payables, inventories, cash), debt ratios, expense ratios and the like.

The value of response models is twofold. First, the firm seeks, through the model, to illustrate the consequences of strategy and policy decisions in terms of highly local interest in the income statement, the balance sheet and cash flows. Second, the firm seeks through connections with the environment to make the model "realistic" in its responses and outcomes. As a group, response models probably imply a greater control over the impact of policy and strategy than is justified. They also suppose a greater insight into the form of linkages of the firm with its environment than probably is justified. As a consequence, response models have elements of the hypothetical about them. Yet they are worthy of development and enhancement, because they interface the environment and the firm at a level closer to the locus of the firm decision process than more generic forms of predictive and forecasting models.

Research-Based Application Models. Commercial and academic researchers have developed and tested models, or models linked with databases, with application to environmental scanning. For example, Strebel [452] proposes a methodology using stock valuation models to assess the relative competitive position and future growth value of companies. The Strategic Planning Institute's database, PIMS, has spawned considerable strategy research (see Lubatkin and Pitts [288], Ramanujam and Venkatraman [385]). A newer project, OASIS, seeks to integrate strategy, human resources practices and organization characteristics with financial performance [Ulrich, etal.: 488]. These application model approaches can be useful in both determining environmentally sensitive variables and in synthesizing environmental information for strategic decision-making purposes.

Subjective Techniques

Subjective techniques tend to be the most judgemental and least quantitatively driven of analysis and forecasting techniques and are likely to be most useful where environmental complexity or uncertainty are high. As a group, they tend to require less skill to apply. Some of these techniques may be helpful in building the firm's knowledge about the environment, especially interview techniques. Other subjective methods are useful only where the firm already has a good understanding of its circumstances; intuition, role playing and scenario development are techniques for expressing that environmental knowledge creatively. As a group, subjective techniques are dismissed as "conjectural" by some critics, but proponents respond with a record of success in building sensitivity to environmental options when more quantitative approaches are confounded for lack of data. Subjective techniques are described and classified below.

Brainstorming. Brainstorming is a technique for eliciting ideas and insights about a problem or issue about which an assembled group may individually have very little or incomplete knowledge. Individuals are encouraged to contribute ideas or idea fragments in a non-judgmental atmosphere based on what they know, or based on a free association of thought which has been triggered by the ideas of others. The technique has been extensively documented and evaluated; for a sample of the literature on the application of brainstorming, see Gregory [185,194-200] and Sage [411].

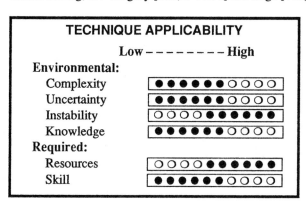

The brainstorming process is initiated by asking a series of open-ended questions about a targeted issue. "What" and "how" questions are particularly useful, as opposed to "why" and "who" questions which tend to generate accusative statements and diminish a non-judgmental atmosphere. Two main benefits emerge from successful brainstorming. The level of general knowledge within the group is raised by incorporating what was previously only the specific knowledge of individuals, and the synthesis of such knowledge contributes to a new and broader understanding of the issue.

Brainstorming can generate new insights about the environment. If group knowledge is limited at the outset, the insights might form only an initial understanding of the environment. If brainstorming is applied in a group setting where environmental sensitivity is already high, it may lead to a synthesis of insights about emerging changes, as signals from various sources, however weak, are shared and freely analyzed.

Brainstorming is thus a flexible vehicle for seeking knowledge and understanding. It requires little skill, but utilizes human resources intensively. The more the group knows about its environmental issue beforehand, the greater the potential payoff through recognizing impending change, that is, in detecting the consequences of instability.

Brainstorming begins to break down if the issue becomes too big or broad. Specific ideas either get lost in the broader discussion or accumulate to such a degree that the process is overwhelmed. More commonly, the level of generality increases to the point where, even if a synthesis occurs, the significance and interpretation of that synthesis becomes difficult to express. For these reasons, the issue must be defined quite narrowly if brainstorming is to be used in complex or uncertain environments. Indeed, brainstorming should not be used to develop base knowledge about such environments.

Role Playing. Role playing is a highly specialized extension of brainstorming. If an environment is too complex or uncertain to describe accurately and quantitatively, but has been subjected to enough study so that knowledge levels are high, insight about the behavior of environmental participants may be gained by acting out their understood roles in a dynamic simulation. Such a simulation represents role playing.

Assume the firm wanted to simulate the behavior of its competition using a variety of assumptions about future product and pricing strategies. Teams would be formed from among the firm's employees to represent relevant groups of customers and competitors. Team members would establish operating roles to allow them to evaluate and react to

TECHNIQUE APPLICABILITY		
Low – – – – – – – – High	**Type:**	
Environmental:		
Complexity	○○○○●●●●●●	**SUBJECTIVE**
Uncertainty	○○○○●●●●●●	
Instability	●●●●●●○○○○	
Knowledge	○○○○●●●●●●	**Technique:**
Required:		
Resources	○○○○●●●●●●	**ROLE-PLAYING**
Skill	●●●●●●○○○○	

competitive conditions in the marketplace. The firm would interpose a strategy, perhaps through a pricing announcement or a new product advertising campaign. The teams would enact their roles as objectively as possible, reflecting what must be an already high degree of accumulated knowledge about that role of customer groups or competitors. Interaction would continue through several iterations or time periods with outcomes analyzed for both expected and unexpected results.

Role playing does not require a high degree of skill, but it does require some depth of knowledge about the environment being simulated, and does require participation by a significant number of people. Its principal benefit is in bringing to bear the collective creative interpretation of all of the people in the simulated environment. It is through that creative interpretation that bona-fide surprises about the environment can sometimes be discovered. Although this technique has not been classified as useful in environments exhibiting high degrees of instability, because existing knowledge in such environments becomes obsolete, role playing may uncover the elements that could contribute to impending instability, through the unexpected behavior of environmental participants.

Scenario Development. As subjective techniques, brainstorming and role playing seek to enhance knowledge about how uncertain environments will evolve and behave in the future. The process of scenario development recognizes this uncertain future more explicitly since a scenario is a depiction of the possible future. If it is a story about future conditions and circumstances, it is a cross-sectional scenario. If it includes a logical development of the events and interactions that occur to cause such a future to emerge, it is a path (or sequence-of-event) scenario. The best of scenarios incorporate elements of both, although they may balance toward one or the other.

TECHNIQUE APPLICABILITY		
Low – – – – – – – – High		**Type:**
Environmental:		
Complexity	○ ○ ○ ○ ● ● ● ● ● ●	**SUBJECTIVE**
Uncertainty	○ ○ ○ ○ ● ● ● ● ● ●	
Instability	○ ○ ○ ○ ● ● ● ● ● ●	
Knowledge	○ ○ ○ ○ ● ● ● ● ● ●	**Technique:**
Required:		
Resources	● ● ● ● ● ● ○ ○ ○ ○	**SCENARIO**
Skill	○ ○ ○ ○ ● ● ● ● ● ●	**DEVELOPMENT**

Scenarios may be based on predictions of change in social conditions, attitudes, beliefs, preferences or behaviors: consider the scenario of the "starved and stretched philanthropies" as increasing needs of the underclass, dwindling government and corporate support, negative growth in real wealth, and diminished personal giving all combine to create a crisis for charities. Scenarios may also be triggered by predictions of technological transformation: the scenario of "global customization" in the automotive industry, as a knowledge and communications network linking human and physical resources worldwide, and producing advanced, customized products with rapid turnaround. Whatever triggers the scenario, it explores the impact of resulting conditions on social, political, economic and competitive outcomes. Because of their explicit purpose in reflecting uncertainty through plausible future conditions, scenarios rarely are created singly. By assimilating the outcomes of multiple plausible scenarios, environmental scanners and corporate strategists obtain an appreciation for the range and locus of impacts of uncertainty on the firm. Multiple scenarios motivate contingent strategy development.

Planning at Atlantic Richfield Company involves multiple scenario development, each scenario spanning a 20-year future and encompassing its own set of values for growth, elasticity and productivity variables. The variables themselves are chosen by determining which influence the critical decisions and areas of concern facing top management. As a starting point for any scenario, the current forces from all dimensions of the environment influencing the variables are described. The scenario is created by assuming certain "forces for change" impact current trends and change outcomes from what they otherwise might have been. Each scenario describes those changes and outcomes in the environment and in the organization's markets. The issues, risks and opportunities that emerge from the scenarios cause management to rethink its fundamental areas of concern, its evaluation of current trends and its choice of the forces and impacts of change. Through this feedback and refinement process, the value of multiple scenarios emerges; the process leads to a greater consistency in management's understanding of strategic issues/options [220].

To avoid being dismissed as wild, unscientific speculation, scenarios must develop several types of linkages: from the present to the future; from behavior to outcome; from imagination to structured forecasts. To be accepted as worthy vehicles around which strategy can be developed, scenarios must be plausible, internally consistent and relevant to the firm. The Atlantic Richfield example can be made relevant by associating the scenarios with forecasts of oil prices, thus driving those forecasts with the conditions and variables that are the outcomes of each developing scenario.

Most closely associated with a firm is the assumption set scenario. The firm establishes a set of assumptions with respect to product and raw material pricing, product demand, interest rates and perhaps the timing of new available technology, and tests the impacts of these assumptions on the firm's financial outcomes. Multiple scenarios in this context take the form of "what-if" analyses. These may not fully fit the definition of scenarios because such assumption sets rarely incorporate a logical, interconnected development of the conditions leading the assumptions to emerge from the environment.

Other scenario types include the global scenario, popularized in the 1960s by Herman Kahn [222]. This was a means to speculate about the impacts of political and technological events and trends. More limited industry scenarios may focus principally on the conditions of demand and supply in customer and raw material markets, and of technology in changing the economics of production. Issue scenarios became popular in the 1970s, especially in relation to three issues: energy cost and availability, government spending for goods and services, and government financing impacting on interest rates. All of these scenario examples are much more remote from the firm in general than the assumption set scenario. Yet, to the extent that they are linked to the firm's success, these scenario types are useful analytical devices for understanding the environment, because they focus on the processes and probabilities of the emergence of such conditions in the broader environment, not just on the values of a set of variables that affect the firm.

For a comprehensive, recent study of scenario usage, see Linneman, etal. [244;278; 279;280], and Zentner [533]. These authors report on the extent, characteristics and trends of scenario usage among U.S. corporations. Scenarios can be used to describe and assess environments with high degrees of complexity, uncertainty and instability. They require extensive knowledge about the environment in its possible as well as plausible shapes, and call for skillful development to achieve a proper balance between the quantitative and the qualitative. More resources may be needed to achieve thoughtful integration into the firm's strategic management process than are required in research or writing. Scenarios are both more and less than future forecasts of the environment, because they analyze and project the fabric of the future, and open the imaginations of planners and executives.

Interview Techniques. Unlike most of the other analytical techniques described in this chapter, interviewing represents a direct method of obtaining environmental information, and therefore cannot be applied to an existing environmental database. Interview techniques can be used to learn about the opinions of others on chosen issues, in seeking a consensus of others on the course of a chosen issue and in learning about the intentions of others in regard to certain behaviors. In complex and unstable environments, opinions about people's attitudes and beliefs might best be obtained through opinion-gathering, in anticipation of learning about emerging social changes before the experts have articulated them. However, opinions about future events and conditions in unstable environments are probably best collected by experts using consensus-generating techniques.

Opinion Surveys. Opinion surveys can be conducted in a *structured* manner, using scientifically-designed questions and a scientifically-selected sample population. Statistical analysis can be applied to the results, and measures of reliability of the data can be determined. Survey research firms and institutions and market research firms conduct such opinion surveys for clients, and also periodically for general distribution [30].

TECHNIQUE APPLICABILITY	Type:
Low – – – – – – – High	
Environmental:	**SUBJECTIVE**
Complexity ○ ○ ○ ○ ● ● ● ● ● ●	
Uncertainty ○ ○ ○ ○ ● ● ● ● ● ●	
Instability ● ● ● ● ● ○ ○ ○ ○	**Technique:**
Knowledge ● ● ● ● ● ○ ○ ○ ○	
Required:	**INTERVIEW**
Resources ○ ○ ○ ○ ● ● ● ● ●	**(UN)STRUCTURED**
Skill ● ● ● ● ● ● ○ ○ ○	**OPINION**

Market and opinion research can also be conducted in an *unstructured* fashion at less expense, but at the cost of reduced reliability. One can obtain unstructured opinion input by asking a few of the same questions of everyone one meets. The questions asked could be about attitudes, beliefs, preferences and concern for possible future events. The non-scientific data may still show subjective patterns of meaning upon analysis; analysis naturally can be conducted only if the results of these informal survey efforts are documented as to timing, type and source of response.

Delphi Technique. Opinion surveys tend to generate response frequency distributions. If the issue is quantitative, one could calculate a mean response and a standard deviation from the mean. Such a distribution could be used as an independent variable in a model estimating some future outcome. If the issue is qualitative, it may not be useful to learn that 40 percent of respondents agreed and 60 percent disagreed with the prospect of a given outcome. In such cases, and wherever a refined, expert opinion is desirable, the Delphi Technique offers a way of structuring the interview process so that experts are sequentially resurveyed with refined information in search of a consensus, or at least a refined average. The technique, originally articulated by Olaf Helmer [181], has wide use in its original and modified forms for quantitative predictions as well as political and social forecasts. For additional research on the subject, see Campbell and Hitchin [67], Cetron and Ralph [75], and Smith/Walsh [436]. For an application of the technique in the property and casualty insurance industry, see Clouser [87].

TECHNIQUE APPLICABILITY		
Low – – – – – – – High	**Type:**	
Environmental:		
Complexity ○○○○●●●●●●	**SUBJECTIVE**	
Uncertainty ○○○○●●●●●●		
Instability ○○○○●●●●●●		
Knowledge ●●●●●○○○○	**Technique:**	
Required:		
Resources ○○○○●●●●●●	**DELPHI**	
Skill ○○○○●●●●●●	**TECHNIQUE**	

The essential steps in the Delphi technique are:

1. Group issues about which you want to survey opinions into categories by type of expertise;
2. Constitute a panel of experts who can see both the narrow and broad aspects of the issues;
3. Survey the experts anonymously;
4. Gather and summarize survey results; report results to the entire panel, again anonymously;
5. Steps 3 and 4 can be repeated again; repetition can be avoided by engaging experts in open debate on the issue, but anonymity is then typically lost;
6. Resurvey;
7. Compile revised results; accept mean or median as the single point estimate of the experts.

For the Delphi technique to be successful, the survey panel must be experts. The need for such expertise makes Delphi expensive, but the cost of such resources may well be justified if the technique is applied to aspects of environments which are complex, uncertain and unstable.

Intention Surveys. A final purpose in interviewing others is to learn the intentions of decision makers. Purchasing agents and treasurers are asked about their plans for capital expenditures. Politicians and legislators are surveyed for their legislative intentions. Consumers are asked about their plans for spending on brands, products and product categories. No single response to an intention survey is valuable, but the combined result can be a useful forecast. Often, large samples are used to improve reliability.

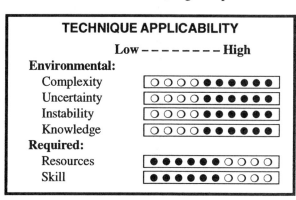

Surveys such as these are easier to conduct than are general opinion surveys, because they involve asking specific questions of the decision makers themselves. Access to the population may require the services of a survey firm or the cooperation of a peer group association. The surveys themselves could be conducted informally by an individual firm if it had respondent access.

Intuition and Conjecture. Some individuals have a good record of making correct intuitive judgments about the future course of events. They apparently have developed internal models of their environments through study, observation and experience. Many

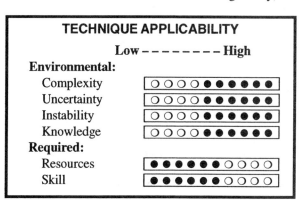

CEOs, especially those with deep experience in a single industry, can make judgments on the basis of such models. Their success is evidenced by their position.

If you asked these intuitive experts how their forecasting success is achieved, few would tell you, and most could not tell you. These intuitive assets are the target of expert systems builders, and the greatest challenge faced by the expert system builders is in learning how the intuitive expert makes decisions.

The input of some intuitive experts is probably available to the firm, perhaps by asking the right question of senior officers and staff members, or perhaps through industry association and government contacts. One of the most difficult aspects of making these contacts is in determining what signals the presence of the expertise. Risks are high in making commitments based upon an intuitive judgment. However, there are few environmental analysis and forecasting techniques where the risks are low. Expert intuition is one of many imperfect sources this chapter has identified for obtaining and conducting environmental analysis.

Applicability and Use: Evidence and Summary

In this chapter, approximately 22 techniques and approaches to environmental analysis and forecasting have been described. Each has been rated on a six-way classification scheme to suggest applicable environments and the resource requirements for their use. Table 9.5 ranks these techniques in one of four groups, according to a combined measure of environmental complexity, uncertainty and instability. Group I contains techniques that are limited in use to what we may call low-intensity environments. Groups II and III include approaches applicable to moderate intensity environments. Group IV comprises techniques that can be effectively employed in high intensity environments, where conditions are least stable, most complex and most risky.

Finally, Figures 9.13 and 9.14 contain indicative survey result data on the use of environmental analysis techniques by U.S. firms during two periods of time: 1975-77 and 1981-82. In 1975 McHale and McHale [315] surveyed 400 firms; in 1977 Diffenbach [116] surveyed 66 of the Fortune 500; in 1981 Klein and Linneman [243] surveyed 215 of the top 1000 U.S. industrial firms; and in 1982 Jain [207] surveyed 186 firms. Because of the differing nature of the samples used in these surveys and the inconsistency of questions regarding technique across survey designs, it is not possible directly to compare survey results. For indicative purposes, comparable survey results from the two earlier surveys and the two later surveys have been averaged to present some evidence on the recent changes that seem to have occurred in the use of environmental analysis techniques.

The figures present results on the use of individual techniques of environmental analysis, grouped by category into mapping, modeling and subjective techniques. Comparing 1975-77 to 1981-82 by these categories, there was a decline in the use of modeling from 50 to 45 percent, where percentages generally mean percent of firms reporting at least some use. There were corresponding increases in the other two categories of tech-

Table 9.5: Intensity Ranking of Environmental Analysis and Forecasting Techniques

Type	Technique	Environmental:				Resources Required to Use	Skill Required to Use
		Com-plexity	Uncer-tainty	Insta-bility	Knowledge Required		
GROUP I. Low Intensity							
Models	Time series analysis	L	L	L	L	L	H
Models	Trend extrapolation	L	L	L	L	L	L
Subjective	Brainstorming	L	L	L	L	H	L
GROUP II. Moderately Low Intensity							
Mapping	Flow Charting	H	L	L	H	L	L
Models	Causal	H	L	L	H	L	H
Models	Response	L	H	L	H	L	H
Models	Cross-section Analysis	H	L	L	L	L	H
GROUP III. Moderately High Intensity							
Mapping	Impact Analysis	L	H	L	L	H	L
Mapping	Tree Diagrams	H	H	L	H	L	H
Mapping	Input-Output Analysis	H	H	L	H	L	H
Mapping	Limit Envelopes	L	H	H	L	L	L
Mapping	Cross Impact Analysis	H	H	L	H	H	H
Mapping	Trend Impact Analysis	H	H	L	H	H	H
Mapping	Morphological Models	H	H	L	H	H	L
Models	Stochastic	H	H	L	H	H	H
Models	Econometric	H	H	L	H	H	H
Subjective	Interview:						
	Unstructured Opinion	H	H	L	L	H	L
Subjective	Role-Playing	H	H	L	H	H	L
GROUP IV. High Intensity							
Subjective	Intuition and Conjecture	H	H	H	H	L	L
Subjective	Interview:						
	Survey Intentions	H	H	H	H	L	L
Subjective	Scenario Development	H	H	H	H	L	H
Subjective	Interview:						
	Delphi Technique	H	H	H	L	H	H

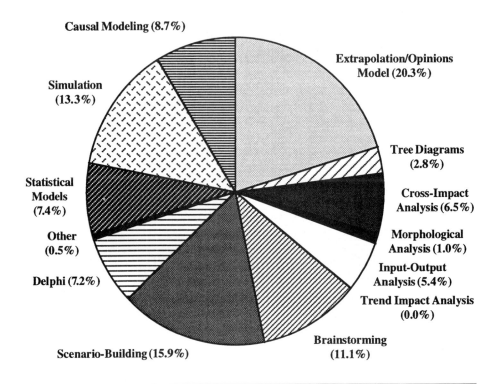

**Figure 9.13: Environmental Analysis Techniques:
Combined 1975–77 Survey Results**

nique, from 34 percent to 36 percent for subjective techniques, and from 16 percent to 18 percent for mapping techniques. Overall, these results are consistent with increasing turbulence in the environment over the period. As Table 9.5 suggests, mapping techniques, and particularly subjective techniques, are more appropriate when environmental intensity is high.

Ironically, the modeling technique that predominates in the survey data — both in the early and later periods — is extrapolation, including operations models, which are associated most closely with the response model technique identified in previous sections of this chapter. Neither extrapolation nor response modeling is particularly useful in intense or turbulent environments. However, as indicated in the discussion earlier in this chapter, extrapolation models are easy to develop and use, while response models are closely tied to the firm's internal strategy evaluation activity. Neither of these environmental analysis techniques is likely to disappear from the corporate tool chest.

With these descriptions of mapping, modeling and subjective techniques for analyzing the environment, the final threads of the fabric of environmental scanning have been woven. Rationale, methodology, sources and technique have been explored. Effective

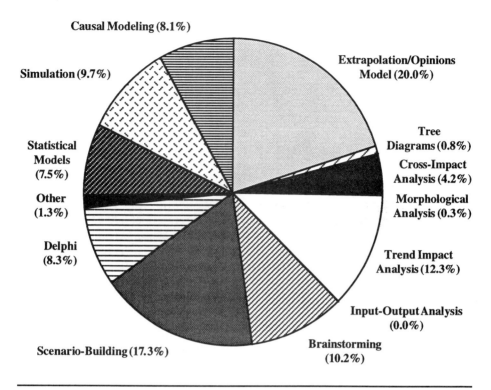

**Figure 9.14: Environmental Analysis Techniques:
Combined 1981–82 Survey Results**

management of environmental scanning has been described, as well as the people, the process, and the communication of environmental intelligence throughout the organization. These are the materials from which an organization can tailor an intelligence system that will permit maximum effective advantage to be gained from the subtle signals of an uncertain future. The methodology of environmental scanning positions the firm to manage its responses and outcomes, create and capture opportunities, and avoid becoming a victim of change.

APPENDIX

INFORMATION SOURCES FOR
ENVIRONMENTAL SCANNING

This appendix contains source listings for information to support the environmental scanning effort. While published documentary sources predominate, the listings include references to personal sources such as conferences and organizations providing consulting and database services. Sources are categorized broadly by class of information content, type of source, and frequency of updating or publication. A guide to the meaning of these categories appears below.

While the number of source listings included here is in excess of eight hundred, and while the scope of these sources is comprehensive, the database is nevertheless incomplete. Only limited sources are included for most industries, and for international, national, and regional economic and demographic data. Yet the inclusions are indicative of the information available and should serve as a framework on which to build knowledge of additional specialized sources to meet the needs of a particular firm or organization.

Of particular importance as sources of strategically valuable environmental scanning information are the growing number of computer-readable databases that can be scanned rapidly for environmental signals. One-fourth of the listings, with type codes beginning with the letters "DB," are for computer databases. These databases are available from one or more network database providers or consulting service organizations. Five years ago only a few such sources existed. Five years from now, databases may well dominate the pool of information sources that scanners utilize.

The best computer-readable databases for environmental scanners are full-text versions of publications that otherwise are, or could be, distributed in print. This includes all databases whose type is "DBTXT" and many of those typed as "DBAS." These may be speeches, news releases, regulatory filings, analyst reports, newsletters, research studies, newspaper or magazine articles. Searched with the proper software tools and contextual search skills, such databases can yield information for strategic inferences much more efficiently and accurately than reading. According to one estimate, about 18 percent of the 3,010 databases extant at the end of 1985 stored full-text data. That percentage had increased to 28 percent by 1989, causing the number of full-text databases to nearly triple to 1412 [521].

Other forms of computer-readable databases are riskier for scanners to use, but still potentially quite valuable. Some specialized databases provide information in limited or pre-digested form. They may present abstracts of the original source article (type ="DBABS"), or subject keywords characterizing the article. They may simply provide bibliographic information (type="DBIDX"). They may represent the outputs of some proprietary methodology intended to provide the client user with inference-level data that has already been subjected to some form of integration and synthesis. In these cases, the scanner must rely on the ability of the abstracter, keyword assigner, or analyst to have captured the *flavor of the data or information* in the same way that the scanner or scanning organization would have captured it by reading and digesting the same material. As this book has demonstrated, scanning requires divergent thinking and the effort to make new thought connections and build new models of "what is." If the person who intervenes between the data and the scanner to create a database applies convergent thinking to fit the data to known models, something vital may be lost in the process. For an illustration of risks of reliance on abstracts, see *The Environment Speaks XIII* (page 134).

Even if they must be used with caution, these index and abstract databases are excellent reference resources for the environmental scanner. Many of them are updated more frequently than printed sources and can provide the scanner more rapid access to the information than would otherwise be possible. Computerized scanning skills should be built or acquired by the organization to permit this rapid access.

A third category of databases comprise mainly data or statistics on production, finance, demographics, and other subjects. These databases may be useful in building and maintaining the knowledge base of the organization; they are not typically available on a timely basis that contributes to future scanning methodologies.

The database source *Database of Databases* is a good reference for refining and extending knowledge about available databases. In addition, both Compuserve and Dialog Information Services maintain online or published directories of the databases they support, including descriptions of content and suggested use.

Sources Categorized by Futurity

The main classification of the source database is from the perspective of the type of information sources typically contain. The categories are these:

Contemporaneous Sources are published with both the intent *and* the timeliness to allow the source to provide information about what is happening now.

Contemporaneous Sources with Future Content make forecasts or predictions of future environments as part of their reporting and analysis of current conditions.

Future-focused Sources focus primarily on the content of the future in at least part of the publication, and perhaps in all of it.

For and About Key Subpopulations are publications read by change agents and advocates, and those that report on precursor environments.

Guides are reference sources to general information about the past, the present, the future, or the process of scanning, including sources of sources.

Retrospective Sources provide information on what has happened, chronicling, consolidating and explaining as a base for building and maintaining knowledge about the state of the environment.

Services includes organizations providing sources or services of information and expertise to support environmental scanning; this category includes both database providers and consultants.

These categories are explained and exemplified in more detail in Chapter 8. As the organization selects resources to support its scanning effort, some representation from each of these categories should be sought, with balance away from the retrospective.

Sources Categorized by Type

The type classification in the listings that follow is intended to convey the form of information availability. Some of the sources may be available in either print or computer-readable database form. Some sources are textual, some bibliographic. The type classification also identifies organization sources and media sources in addition to publications.

Type Code	Meaning
DB____	Databases, as a general category refers to computer-readable databases, either accessible on-line from a remote computer database vendor, or available on magnetic or laser-readable media for loading onto a user's computer system. There are four subset categories:
DBAS	the most general category, includes database service organizations (e.g., *Compuserve* or *Cedocar*) integrated databases providing information from a variety of sources (e.g., *Citibase* or *Japan Computer Industry Scan*), online newsletters (e.g., *Charitable Giving, Forex Commentary*), and databases that could not readily be classified below; the original source databases in this category may be presented in full-text;

DBABS   for databases that consist of abstracts or short summaries of information from other sources, with or without keywords;

DBIDX   for databases that index other sources bibliographically, normally with subject keywords for directed search (e.g., *Business Periodicals Index*), or that contain indexed source information directly (e.g., *World Patents Index*);

DBTXT   for databases that provide the full text of publications from a collection of sources (e.g., *Magazine ASAP*), or from a single source (e.g., *Chicago Tribune*).

PUB   Publications, refers to journals, magazines, newspapers, newsletters, reports, statistical releases and other serial publications that appear in printed form either regularly or intermittently.

IDX   Indexes, refers to printed publications that provide bibliographic references to source materials, by subject matter keywords, with or without abstracts (indexes and abstracts are not separated for printed publications as with computer databases, above).

ORG   Organizations, refers to foundations, associations, institutions and consultancies that provide scanning-related services, except for database vendors, which are classified under the DBAS type.

Other   Other source types, including *books, conferences,* and *media broadcasts.*

Sources Categorized by Frequency of Publication

Information sources are also classified according to their publication frequency. The numbers in the frequency column refer to the number of times the source is published (or updated) over the course of a year. The most common frequencies that appear in the database are translated as follows:

FREQ Code	Meaning
1	Annual
2	Semi-annual
4	Quarterly
6	Bi-monthly
12	Monthly

FREQ

Code	Meaning
24	Twice monthly
26	Biweekly
52	Weekly
104	Twice weekly
DLY	Daily (or periodically during day)
VAR	Varies (usually with availability of new information)
REG	Regularly (but no set schedule)
IRR	Irregular (could be less frequent than annual)
QQ	Quinquennial (5-year intervals)

In general, the frequency of publication is related to the currency or futurity of its content. However, the separation of frequency from content class in the listings below is intentional and necessary. Some periodicals frequently publish information about what *has been,* for example, the *Federal Reserve Bulletin,* published monthly. Other sources may appear or occur infrequently, yet deal almost exclusively with the *future,* for example, the American Council on Life Insurance's *TAP Reports,* published annually, or the annual Planning Forum International Conference.

The sources appear below alphabetically in groups according to their futurity classification. Other arrangements of the list may be of interest to the reader, and can readily be obtained using computer spreadsheet or database programs. Interested readers may obtain the source list on diskette from the author (5-1/4", double density, files in .WK1 and ASCII formats; from Source Diskette, College of Business, Marquette University, Milwaukee, WI 53233; $10 postpaid.)

Contemporaneous Sources

Source	*Type*	*Freq.*
ABLEDATA	DBAS	12
Access Reports/Freedom of Information	DBIDX	52
Across The Board	PUB	12
ADWEEK	DBTXT	52
Administrative Management	PUB	12
Advertising Age	PUB	104
Agrochemicals Handbook	DBIDX	2
American Banker	DBTXT	DLY
American Metal Market	PUB	DLY
American Management Association	CONF	VAR

Source	Type	Freq.
Antitrust FOIA Log	DBAS	12
Aquatic Sciences and Fisheries Abstracts	DBABS	12
Asahi News Service	DBAS	DLY
Asian Business	PUB	12
Asian Economist (Toyo Keizai)	PUB	52
Asian Finance	PUB	12
Asian Wall Street Journal	PUB	52
Associated Press (Europe Edition)	DBTXT	DLY
Associated Press (U. S. Edition)	DBTXT	DLY
Australian Business	DBTXT	52
Automotive News	PUB	52
BBC External Services News	DBAS	DLY
BBC Summary of World Broadcasts	DBAS	DLY
Bio Business	DBABS	12
Bio Commerce Abstracts	DBABS	24
Biological & Agricultural Index	DBIDX	104
Biomedical Technology Info Service	DBAS	26
Biosis Previews	DBABS	24
BIS Infomat World Business	DBABS	52
BNA Congressional/Presidential Calendar	DBAS	DLY
BNA Daily Report for Executives	DBAS	DLY
BNA Daily Tax Report	DBAS	DLY
Bond Buyer	DBTXT	DLY
Bond Week	PUB	52
British Business	PUB	52
Broadcasting	DBTXT	52
Business and Health	PUB	10
Business Computer Digest	PUB	12
Business Periodicals Index	DBIDX	104
Business Software	PUB	12
CA Search	DBABS	26
CAB Abstracts	DBABS	12
Campaign	DBTXT	52
Canadian Business	DBTXT	12
Canadian Business and Current Affairs	DBIDX	12
CENDATA	DBTXT	DLY
Chemical Business Newsbase	DBAS	52
Chemical Industry Notes	DBABS	52
CHEM-INTELL	DBABS	12
Chinese Patent Abstracts in English	DBABS	26
Code of Federal Regulations	PUB	12
Columbia Journal of World Business	PUB	4

Contemporaneous Sources cont.

Source	Type	Freq.
Commerce Business Daily	DBTXT	DLY
Commerce Clearinghouse Pubs	PUB	VAR
Commodity Trade Statistics, UN	PUB	28
Communications Daily	DBAS	DLY
COMPUSTAT PC-Plus	DBAS	12
Computer Contents	INDX	26
Computing Today	DBAS	52
Conference Board Seminars	CONF	VAR
Congress in Print	PUB	52
Congress Watcher	PUB	6
Congressional Activities	DBAS	52
Construction Reports	PUB	12
Consumer Attitudes & Buy Plans, Conference Board	PUB	12
Consumer Reports	PUB	12
Country Facts Database (Frost & Sullivan)	DBAS	4
Country Facts (Frost & Sullivan)	PUB	4
Crain's Chicago Business	DBTXT	52
Crain's New York Business	DBTXT	52
Credit Market Analysis	DBAS	DLY
Current Business Reports:		
Monthly Retail Trade, Sales, Inventory	PUB	12
Current Digest of the Soviet Press	DBTXT	52
Current Population Reports	PUB	12
Current Technology Index	DBIDX	12
Current Wage Developments, Bureau of Labor Statistics	PUB	12
Daily Industrial Index Analyzer	DBAS	DLY
Daily Industrial Times (Nikkan Kogyo)	PUB	DLY
Daily Metals Report	DBAS	DLY
Daily Newspapers in Relevant Markets	PUB	DLY
Data User News	PUB	12
Dialog Quotes and Trading (NYSE, AMEX, NASDAQ)	DBAS	DLY
Diogenes	DBTXT	52
Disclosure Financials	DBAS	52
DJNEWS	DBABS	DLY
DJTEXT	DBTXT	DLY
DJTRACK	DBABS	DLY
DOE Energy	DBAS	26
Dollars and Sense (Chicago)	PUB	6
Dun's Business Monthly	PUB	12
D&B Canadian Dun's Market Identifiers	DBAS	4
D&B Donnelly Demographics	DBAS	1

Source	Type	Freq.
D&B Dun's Financial Records	DBAS	4
D&B Dun's Market Identifiers	DBAS	4
D&B International Dun's Market Identifiers	DBAS	4
Economic Literature Index	DBIDX	4
Economic Week	PUB	52
Education Index	DBIDX	104
El Commercio	PUB	DLY
El Mercurio	PUB	DLY
El Pais	PUB	DLY
El Universal	PUB	DLY
Electric Vehicle Progress	DBAS	26
Electronic Business	PUB	23
Electronic Publishing Abstracts	DBABS	26
EMBASE	DBABS	52
Energy Research Abstracts	IDX	24
Engineered Materials Abstracts	DBABS	12
EuroMoney	DBTXT	12
Expansion (France)	PUB	6
Expansion (Mexico)	PUB	26
Facts on File	DBTXT	52
Facts On File World News Digest	IDX	52
Family Resources	DBAS	12
FCC Week	DBAS	52
Federal Register	PUB	DLY
Federal Research Report	DBAS	52
Federal Reserve Bank Reviews	PUB	VAR
Fiber/Optics News	DBAS	52
Financial Post	PUB	52
Financial Times	DBTXT	DLY
Financial Times Company Abstracts	DBABS	52
Financial World	DBTXT	26
Findex Reports and Studies Index	DBIDX	4
FIND/SVP Information Catalog	PUB	12
FINIS: Financial Industry Information Service	DBABS	26
FLUIDEX	DBABS	12
Food Science and Technology Abstracts	DBABS	12
Food Technology	PUB	12
FOODS ADLIBRA	DBAS	12
Foreign Trade & Economic Abstracts	DBAS	24
Foreign Trade, USD Comm. (Numerous Subtitles)	PUB	12
FOREX Commentary	DBAS	DLY
Frankfurter Allgemeine	PUB	DLY

Contemporaneous Sources cont.

Source	*Type*	*Freq.*
Friday Memo	DBTXT	26
Friday Report	PUB	52
General Science Index	DBIDX	104
German Business Weekly	DBAS	52
Globe and Mail	PUB	DLY
Handelsblatt	DBTXT	DLY
Health	PUB	12
Health Care Financing Review	PUB	4
Health Facts	PUB	12
Health Planning and Administration	DBIDX	12
High-Tech Marketing	PUB	12
Hoppenstedt Directory of German Companies	DBAS	4
Hospital Management Review	PUB	12
Humanities Index	DBIDX	104
ICC British Company Financial Datasheets	DBAS	52
Industrial Production Index, FRB	PUB	4
Industry Data Sources	DBABS	12
Industry Week	PUB	26
InfoWorld	PUB	52
Investment Dealer's Digest	PUB	52
Investor's Daily	DBTXT	DLY
Iron Age	PUB	12
Japan Computer Industry Scan	DBAS	52
Japan Economic Journal	DBTXT	52
Japan Economic Newswire	DBTXT	DLY
Japan Weekly Monitor	DBAS	52
Journal of Consumer Affairs	PUB	2
Labor and investments	PUB	9
Land Use Planning Report	DBAS	52
Le Monde	PUB	DLY
Le Soir	PUB	DLY
Les Echos	PUB	DLY
London Times	PUB	DLY
Lotus One Source CD/Banking	DBAS	12
Lotus One Source CD/Corporate	DBAS	12
Lotus One Source CD/Corptech	DBAS	12
Lotus One Source CD/International	DBAS	12
Lotus One Source CD/Private+	DBAS	12
M & A Database	DBAS	12
Management and Marketing Abstracts	PUB	8
Management and Marketing Abstracts	DBABS	24

Source	*Type*	*Freq.*
Management Review	PUB	12
Materials Business File	DBAS	12
MathSci	DBIDX	12
McGraw Hill News	DBTXT	DLY
Media and Methods	PUB	6
Medical World News	PUB	24
Modern Healthcare	DBTXT	26
Money	PUB	12
Monthly Labor Review, U.S. Department of Labor	PUB	12
Monthly Vital Statistics Report	PUB	12
Moody's Corporate News — International	DBTXT	52
Moody's Corporate News — U.S.	DBTXT	52
Moody's Corporate Profiles	DBAS	52
Nation's Business	PUB	12
NewSearch	DBIDX	DLY
Newspaper Abstracts	DBABS	52
Newswire ASAP	DBTXT	DLY
Nexis	DBAS	DLY
Nikkei Business	PUB	12
Nikkei Byte	PUB	12
Nikkei Computer	PUB	12
Nikkei Sangyo Shimbun (Japan Manufacturing Times)	PUB	DLY
Nikkei Venture	PUB	12
Nikkei Watcher IBM Edition	PUB	26
OECD Observer	PUB	60
Omni	PUB	12
Packaging Science and Technology Abstracts	DBABS	12
Pascal	DBABS	12
Pensions and Investment Age	PUB	26
Personal Computing	PUB	12
Personnel Journal	PUB	12
Points de Vente	PUB	6
Politics Today	PUB	12
Population and Development Review	PUB	4
Population Bulletin	PUB	4
Population Today	PUB	11
Predicasts Basebook	PUB	1
Presidents Weekly Activities Report	PUB	52
Prevention	PUB	12
Product Safety Letter	PUB	52
PTS International Forecasts	DBABS	12
PTS New Product Announcements	DBTXT	52

Contemporaneous Sources cont.

Source	Type	Freq.
PTS U.S. Forecasts	DBABS	12
Public Interest	PUB	4
Public Opinion	PUB	6
Public Relations Journal	PUB	12
Public Relations News	PUB	52
RANDATA (Rand McNally)	DBAS	1
Reuters	DBTXT	DLY
Scan (Shell Oil Newsletter)	PUB	4
Social Sciences Index	DBIDX	104
Society	PUB	6
Software Magazine	PUB	12
Soviet Science and Technology	DBIDX	12
Standard Rate & Data: Newspapers	PUB	52
Standard Rate & Data: Spot Radio	PUB	52
Standard Rate & Data: Television	PUB	52
Standard & Poor's News	DBTXT	DLY
Supertech	DBABS	12
Survey of Current Business, USDC	PUB	12
Sylvia Porter's Personal Finance	PUB	6
Telemarketing	PUB	6
Trade Opportunities Weekly	DBAS	52
Tris	DBABS	12
U S News & World Report	PUB	52
UK News	DBTXT	DLY
United States Banker	PUB	12
UPI News	DBTXT	DLY
USA Today	PUB	DLY
U.S. Long-Term Review (Data Resources)	PUB	4
VDI Nachrichten	PUB	52
Ward's Auto World	DBTXT	12
Washington Business Journal	PUB	52
Washington Presstext	DBTXT	DLY
Wharton (The)	PUB	1
World Affairs Report	DBABS	12
World Press Review	PUB	12
WorldWatch Papers	PUB	IRR
W&V Werben und Verkaufen	PUB	52

Contemporaneous Sources with Future Content

Source	*Type*	*Freq.*
Advanced Military Computing	DBAS	26
Aging	PUB	6
Agribusiness USA	DBABS	26
Agricola	DBABS	12
AI Magazine	PUB	4
Air/Water Pollution Report	DBAS	52
All Things Considered (NPR)	BDCST	DLY
American Demographics	PUB	12
American Enterprise Institute Economist	PUB	12
American Marketplace	DBAS	26
Applied Science & Technology Index	DBIDX	104
Art Index	DBIDX	104
Art of M&A Update	PUB	52
Arthur D. Little/Online (Available Reports, Forecasts)	DBIDX	12
Aviation Week and Space Technology	PUB	52
Biotechnology Investment Opportunities	DBAS	12
Book Review Digest	DBABS	104
Breakthrough (Boardroom Reports)	PUB	24
Brookings Papers on Economic Activity	PUB	2
Bureau of National Affairs Publications	PUB	VAR
Business Computer	DBAS	104
Business Conditions Digest, U.S. Dept. of Commerce	PUB	12
Business Dateline	DBTXT	52
Business International Weekly Report	PUB	52
Business Week	PUB	52
Business Wire	DBTXT	DLY
Catalyst (Montpelier)	PUB	6
Chilton's Food Engineering	PUB	12
Christian Science Monitor	DBIDX	DLY
Christian Science Monitor	PUB	DLY
Claims/U.S. Patent Abstracts Weekly	DBABS	52
Coming Boom, The; Herman Kahn (1982)	BOOK	
COMPENDEX PLUS	DBABS	12
Conference Papers Index	DBIDX	12
Congressional Insight	PUB	52
Congressional Monitor	PUB	DLY
Congressional Research Service Review	PUB	12
Corporate and Industry Research Reports OnLine	DBIDX	12
Corporate Exposure	PUB	26
Council Review	PUB	8

Contemporaneous Sources with Future Content cont.

Source	Type	Freq.
Country Risk Update	PUB	12
Current Biotechnology Abstracts	DBABS	12
Data Channels	DBAS	52
Demography	PUB	4
DISCLOSURE	DBAS	52
Disclosure Spectrum Ownership	DBAS	4
DMS Defense Newsletters	DBTXT	52
DMS Market Intelligence Reports	DBTXT	52
ECONBASE	DBAS	12
Economic Indicators, JEC; CEA	PUB	12
Economic Projection Series, National Planning Assn.	PUB	IRR
Economist	DBTXT	52
Economist (London)	PUB	52
Electronic Business Forecast	PUB	24
Electronic Design	DBTXT	26
Energyline	DBABS	12
Enviroline	DBABS	12
Executive Update	PUB	24
Finance and Development	PUB	4
Financial Market Trends	PUB	IRR
Financial Planning	PUB	12
Food Industry Intelligence (Strategic Intell. Systems)	DBAS	12
Food Industry Futures	PUB	24
Footnotes (Future Problem Solving Program)	PUB	4
Forbes	PUB	50
Forecast (United Califoria Bank)	PUB	1
Fortune	PUB	26
Frankfurter Allgemeine Magazine	PUB	52
Future Abstracts, Strategic Information Service	PUB	12
Future Survey Annual (World Future Society)	PUB	1
Futuribles: Analyse-Prevision-Prospective	PUB	4
Futurics: Quarterly Journal of Futures Research	PUB	4
Goldsmith-Nagan Bond & Money Market Letter	PUB	26
Haner's Bus. Environment Risk Index (42 Countries)	PUB	1
Harris Surveys	PUB	10
Harvard Medical School Health Letter	PUB	12
High Technology	PUB	12
High-Tech Materials Alert	DBTXT	12
INC	PUB	12
INPANEW: Patents	DBAS	52
Inside R & D	PUB	12

Source	Type	Freq.
Institute for the Future Perspective	PUB	IRR
Interaction (Global Tomorrow Coalition)	PUB	4
International Demographics	PUB	12
International Economic Indicators	PUB	12
InvesText	DBAS	52
Issues Management Letter	PUB	24
Japan Technology	DBABS	12
Journal of American Medical Association	PUB	52
Journal of Business Forecasting Methods & Systems	PUB	4
Journal of Forecasting	PUB	4
Journal of International Economics	PUB	8
Kami Strategic Assumptions	PUB	4
Kiplinger Tax Letter	PUB	52
Kiplinger Washington Letter	PUB	52
Looking Ahead, National Planning Association	PUB	4
Los Angeles Times	PUB	DLY
Los Angeles Times	DBIDX	12
Management World	PUB	12
Managerial Technology	PUB	4
Manas	PUB	52
McGraw-Hill Publications Online	DBTXT	52
McNeil Lehrer News Hour (CPB)	BDCST	DLY
Media General Databank	DBAS	52
Monitor Radio (Syndicated)	BDCST	DLY
Moody's Investor Service	PUB	52
M&A Filings	DBAS	DLY
National Media Index	DBAS	52
National Science Foundation Bulletin	PUB	12
National Planning Association Economic & Demographic Data Base	DBAS	6
New Product Report	PUB	26
New Republic	PUB	24
New Scientist	DBTXT	52
New Times	PUB	52
New York Times	PUB	DLY
Newsweek	PUB	52
Next 200 Years, The; Herman Kahn (1976)	BOOK	
Numbers News	PUB	12
ORC Public Opinion index	PUB	24
OTC Newswire Daily	DBTXT	DLY
Policy Review	PUB	12
Political Risk Database (Political Risk Services)	DBAS	4

Contemporaneous Sources with Future Content cont.

Source	Type	Freq.
Political Risk Letter (Political Risk Services)	PUB	12
Political Risk Reports 85 Countries		
(Political Risk Services)	PUB	1
Political Risk Yearbook (Political Risk Services)	PUB	1
PR Newswire	DBTXT	DLY
Preview	PUB	52
Probe	PUB	5
PTS Newsletter Database	DBTXT	12
PTS Promt	DBABS	DLY
Public Pulse (Roper Organization)	PUB	IRR
P/E Petroleum/Energy News	DBABS	52
Rain (Portland)	PUB	6
Research & Development	DBTXT	12
Science Digest	PUB	12
Science News	PUB	52
Sciences	PUB	6
Science, Technology & Human Values	PUB	4
Signs	PUB	4
SIS Financial Industry Abstracts	DBAS	12
Social Policy	PUB	4
Space Daily	DBAS	DLY
Spectrum (Journal Brasileiro Ciencias)	PUB	6
Spin	DBABS	12
Standard & Poor's Industry Surveys	PUB	52
Standard & Poor's Outlook	PUB	52
Standard & Poor's Economic Report	DBAS	24
Sunday Morning (APR)(CBC Radio)	BDCST	52
Sustainable Societies	PUB	4
Technology	PUB	52
Technology Management News	DBAS	26
Technology Review (MIT)	PUB	8
Technology Strategies	PUB	12
Technology Update	PUB	52
Technology Week	PUB	52
Tech-Scan (Technical Journals) Strategic		
Intelligence Systems	DBAS	12
Third Wave, The; Alvin Toffler (1980)	BOOK	
Thomas New Industrial Products	DBAS	52
Time	PUB	52
Toxic Materials News	DBAS	52
Turning Points	PUB	12

Source	Type	Freq.
Urban Outlook	PUB	26
Urban & Social Change Review	PUB	2
U.S. Census Report	PUB	26
U.S. Dept. of Agriculture Economic & Statistics Service	PUB	REG
U.S.Industrial Outlook, USDC	PUB	1
Value Line Investment Service	PUB	52
Venture	PUB	12
Wall Street Journal	PUB	DLY
Wall Street Journal Online	DBTXT	DLY
Wall Street Monitor: Weekly Market Digest	DBABS	52
Wall Street Transcript	DBTXT	52
Washington Post Online	DBTXT	DLY
Washington Report (U.S.Chamber of Commerce)	PUB	52
Washington Week in Review (CPB)	BDCST	52
World Information Services (Bank of America)	PUB	12

Future-Focused Sources

Source	Type	Freq.
Actualites Prospectives (Futurables Assoc)	PUB	12
Aerospace Database	DBABS	24
Alternative Futures: Journal of Utopian Studies	PUB	4
Business Tomorrow	PUB	6
Changing Family: Its Function & Future, Schultz (1982)	BOOK	
Current	PUB	10
Emerging Trends	PUB	4
Expert Systems: Artificial Intelligence in Business	BOOK	
Fusion	PUB	4
Future Search, Institute of the Future	DBAS	12
Future Shock, Toffler, Bantam (1971)	BOOK	
Future Survey (World Future Society)	PUB	12
Futures	PUB	10
Futures Research Quarterly (World Future Society)	PUB	4
Futurist, The; World Future Society	PUB	6
Global Futures Digest	PUB	4
Global Futures Network	PUB	4
Global Perspective Quarterly	PUB	4
IAPS (International Affiliation of Planning Societies) Conferences	CONF	IRR
Institute F/T Future Ten Year Forecast	PUB	1
John Naisbitt's Trend Letter	PUB	26
Journal of Businss Strategy	PUB	4
Leading Edge	PUB	4

Future-Focused Sources cont.

Source	*Type*	*Freq.*
Long Range Planning	PUB	6
Naisbitt Group Trend Report	PUB	4
Next	PUB	12
OECD Economic Outlook	PUB	2
Planning Forum International Conference	CONF	1
Planning Review	PUB	6
Predicasts Forecasts	PUB	4
Revue Futuribles (Futuribles Association)	PUB	12
Scan (SRI International)	PUB	12
Strategic Management Journal	PUB	4
Strategic Management Society Annual Meeting	CONF	1
Strategic Moves	PUB	12
Technological Forecasting & Social Change	PUB	8
Technology Forecasts	PUB	12
Trend Analysis Reports, American Council of Life Ins.	PUB	1
U.S. Long Term Economic Growth Prospects, JEC	PUB	1
What's Next? (Congressional Clearinghouse on the Future)	PUB	4
World Future Society Bulletin	PUB	4
Worldcasts	PUB	4
Year 2000, The; Herman Kahn (1976)	BOOK	

Sources For and About Key Subpopulations

Abstracts of Working Papers in Economics	DBABS	12
AFL-CIO News	PUB	52
Ageline	DBABS	6
American Education	PUB	12
American Journal of Public Health	PUB	12
American Journal of Sociology	PUB	6
American Medical News	PUB	52
American Scholar	PUB	4
American Scientist	PUB	6
American Sociological Review	PUB	6
Architectural Record	PUB	12
Arizona Republic	DBTXT	DLY
Atlantic	PUB	12
Banker (UK)	PUB	12
Bankers Magazine	PUB	6
Banking World	PUB	12
Behavior Today Newsletter	PUB	IRR

Source	Type	Freq.
Black Enterprise	PUB	12
Blue Chip Economic Indicators	PUB	12
Boston Globe	DBTXT	104
Brain Mind Bulletin	PUB	17
Breakthrough (San Francisco)		3
Bulletin of the Atomic Scientist	PUB	12
Business Horizons	PUB	6
Byte	PUB	12
California Business	PUB	12
California Magazine	PUB	12
California Management Review	PUB	4
Center Magazine	PUB	12
Challenge	PUB	6
Change	PUB	4
Changing Times	PUB	12
Channels	PUB	12
Channels of Communication	PUB	6
Chicago Tribune	DBTXT	DLY
Chronicle of Higher Education	PUB	52
College Press Service	DBAS	52
Columbia Journalism Review	PUB	6
Communication Briefings	PUB	12
Communication News	PUB	12
Computer World	PUB	6
Daedalus	PUB	4
Datamation	PUB	12
East West Journal	PUB	12
Ebony	PUB	12
Editor & Publisher	PUB	52
Education Week	PUB	52
Elle	PUB	52
Esquire	PUB	12
Essence	PUB	12
Executive Fitness Newsletter	PUB	26
Fifty Plus	PUB	12
Financial Analysts Journal	PUB	6
Financial Executive	PUB	6
Folio	PUB	4
Footnotes	PUB	4
Foreign Affairs	PUB	12
Free Lance	PUB	24
Gallup Poll Release	PUB	104

Sources For and About Key Subpopulations cont.

Source	Type	Freq.
Geo	PUB	12
Gerontologies	PUB	6
Glamour	PUB	12
Good Housekeeping	PUB	12
Handgun Control: Semi-Annual Progress Report	PUB	2
Harper's Bazaar	PUB	4
Harper's Magazine	PUB	12
Harvard Business Review/Online	DBTXT	6
Harvard Educational Review	PUB	4
Hastings Center Report	PUB	6
Heavy Metal	PUB	12
High Times	PUB	12
House Beautiful	PUB	12
Human Events	PUB	52
Humanist	PUB	6
In Context	PUB	4
In These Times	PUB	52
Inquiry	PUB	4
Insight (Washington Times)	PUB	52
Institutional Investor	PUB	12
Jet	PUB	52
Journal of Business	PUB	4
Journal of Communication	PUB	4
Journal of Consumer Research	PUB	4
Journal of Contemporary Business	PUB	4
Journal of Health & Social Behavior	PUB	4
Journal of Marketing	PUB	4
Journal of Political Economy	PUB	6
Journal of Product Innovation Management	PUB	4
Journal of Social Issues	PUB	4
Ladies Home Journal	PUB	12
Life	PUB	12
Living Single	PUB	12
Mademoiselle	PUB	12
McCall's	PUB	12
Mortgage Banking	PUB	12
Mosaic	PUB	4
Mother Jones	PUB	12
Ms.	PUB	12
NAACP Report	PUB	12
National Journal	PUB	52

Source	Type	Freq.
New Age Journal	PUB	12
New England Journal of Medicine	PUB	12
New Management	PUB	4
New York Review of Books	PUB	26
New Yorker	PUB	52
Off Our Backs	PUB	12
PC Magazine	DBTXT	26
PC Tech Journal	PUB	12
PC Week	PUB	52
PC World	PUB	12
People Magazine	DBTXT	52
Policy Studies Journal/Review	PUB	5
Popline	PUB	12
Popular Science	PUB	12
Progressive	PUB	12
Psychology Today	PUB	12
Reason	PUB	12
Redbook	PUB	12
Resurgence	PUB	12
Rolling Stone	PUB	26
San Francisco Chronicle	DBTXT	DLY
Savvy	PUB	12
Science	PUB	51
Scientific American	PUB	12
Sierra Club Bulletin	PUB	2
Smithsonian	PUB	12
Social Indicators Research	PUB	4
South (UK)	PUB	12
Sweden Now	PUB	6
Swedish Journal of Social Change	PUB	4
Teacher Education Quarterly	PUB	4
Technovation	PUB	4
Teen	DBTXT	12
Union of Concerned Scientists Nucleus	PUB	4
Utne Reader (Digests Small Circulation Periodicals)	PUB	12
Village Voice	PUB	52
Vital Speeches of the Day	PUB	26
Vogue	PUB	12
Whole Earth Review	PUB	6
Wilson Quarterly	PUB	4
Working Papers for New Society	PUB	4
Working Woman	PUB	12

Guides to Sources and Information

Source	Type	Freq.
ABI/Inform	DBABS	12
Abstracts of Health Care Management Studies	IDX	1
Abstracts on Health Effects of Environmental Pollution	IDX	12
ASI/American Statistics Index	DBIDX	12
Automatic Subject Citation Alert	DBAS	52
Basic Bibliography on Marketing Review, American Marketing Association (1984)	BOOK	
Behavioral Abstracts	IDX	4
Bibliographie Prospective (Futuribles Association)	PUB	12
BRS/Search Service Database Catalog	PUB	1
Business Information Sources (Univ. of Calif. Press)	BOOK	
Business International Master Key Index	IDX	12
Business Periodicals Index	IDX	12
Business Statistics, USDComm	PUB	1
Canadian Periodicals Index	IDX	12
Catalog of New Industry Studies (Bus. Trend Analysts)	IDX	IRR
CIS Federal Register Index	IDX	52
Computer Abstracts	IDX	12
Computer-Readable Databases: Directory/Sourcebook	IDX	IRR
Congressional Directory	BOOK	
Congressional Information Service (CIS)	DBIDX	12
Congressional Record Abstracts	DBABS	52
Congressional Staff Directory	BOOK	
Current Contents (Editions in various fields)	IDX	52
Current Sources of Marketing Information: Bibliography of Primary Data	BOOK	
Current Technology Index	IDX	12
Database	PUB	4
Database End-User	PUB	12
Database of Databases	DBAS	4
Datasolve (British)	DBAS	12
Dialog Information Services Database Catalog	PUB	1
Dowline	PUB	6
Energy Information Abstracts	IDX	50
Federal Register Abstracts	DBABS	52
Findex Directory of Market Research Reports, Studies	IDX	12
Frost & Sullivan Market Research Reports	DBAS	12
Future Survey, World Future Society	IDX	12
Futurist Bookstore Catalog	PUB	IRR
F&S Index (Company Information)	IDX	52

Source	Type	Freq.
Industrial Arts Index	IDX	12
Information Catalog (FIND/SVP)	IDX	6
Information Today	PUB	12
Information & the Future: Handbook of Sources, Strategy	BOOK	
Knowledge Executive: Leadership in an Information Society	BOOK	
Left Index	IDX	4
Magazine ASAP	DBTXT	12
Magazine Index	DBIDX	12
Magazines for Libraries (Bowker)	BOOK	
Management Contents	DBIDX	12
Microcomputers for the OnLine Searcher	BOOK	
Middle East Abstracts	IDX	4
Mideast File (340 Journals and Other Sources)	DBIDX	52
Monthly Catalog of Gov't. Publications, U.S. GPO	PUB	12
National Newpaper Index	DBIDX	12
New York Times Index	IDX	12
NTIS/National Technical Information Service	DBIDX	26
Off-The-Shelf	IDX	IRR
Online	PUB	6
PAIS Foreign language Index	IDX	4
PAIS International	DBIDX	12
PAIS Bulletin	IDX	24
Political Handbook of the World	PUB	1
Popular Magazine Review	PUB	52
Predibriefs	PUB	12
Predicasts — SEE PTS (Predicasts)	DBAS	
Readers' Guide to Periodical Literature	DBIDX	104
Research and Development Directory	PUB	1
Rules of the U.S.House of Representatives	BOOK	
Science Abstracts Computers and Control	IDX	12
Science Abstracts Electrical & Electronic	IDX	12
Science Abstracts Physics	IDX	6
Science Citation Index	IDX	6
Science Fiction Review	IDX	4
Science Research Abstracts	IDX	10
SciSearch	DBIDX	12
Social Science Citation Index	IDX	3
Social Sciences Index	IDX	4
Social SciSearch	DBIDX	12
Sources of European Economic Information (Gower)	BOOK	

Guides to Sources and Information cont.

Source	Type	Freq.
Spectrum (Olathe)	PUB	1
Standard Periodical Directory	BOOK	
Statistical Sources, Wasserman	BOOK	
Statistics Europe: Statistics for Social, Economic & Market Research	PUB	IRR
Statistics of Africa: Sources for Market Research	PUB	IRR
Superindex	DBIDX	12
Television News Index & Abstracts	IDX	12
Thinking Strategically: Planning for Your Company's Future	BOOK	
Trade and Industry Index	DBIDX	12
Ulrich's International Periodicals Directory	BOOK	
Ulrich's International Periodicals Directory	DBAS	12
U.S. Senate Manual	BOOK	
Wall Street Journal Index	IDX	12
Washington Information Directory	BOOK	

Retrospective Information Sources

Source	Type	Freq.
Agricultural Abstract, USDA	PUB	12
Almanac of Business & Industry Financial Ratios, Troy	PUB	1
American Education Research Journal	PUB	4
American Health	PUB	12
America: History and Life	DBABS	3
Annual Reports of Co's, Org's	PUB	1
Annual Statement Studies, Robert Morris Assoc.	PUB	1
Business	PUB	4
Business and Society Review	PUB	4
Business Economics	PUB	4
Business Education Forum	PUB	4
Business Quarterly	PUB	4
Census of Agriculture	PUB	QQ
Census of Government	PUB	QQ
Census of Housing	PUB	QQ
Census of Manufactures	PUB	QQ
Census of Population	PUB	QQ
Census of Mineral Industries	PUB	QQ
Census of Retail Trade	PUB	QQ
Census of Service Industries	PUB	QQ
Census of Transportation	PUB	QQ
Census of Wholesale Trade	PUB	QQ

Source	Type	Freq.
CITIBASE	DBAS	12
Commercial Atlas & Marketing Guide	PUB	1
Comparative Data, Major Dept. Stores, Harris Bank	PUB	1
Concentration Ratios in Manufacturing	PUB	1
Conference Board Statistical Bulletin	PUB	12
Construction Review	PUB	6
Consumer Price Index Detail	DBAS	12
Consumer Price Index Detail Report,		
Bureau of Labor Statistics; U.S. Dept. of Labor	PUB	12
Cost of Doing Business in 185 Lines, D&B	PUB	1
County and City Data Book, U.S. Dept. of Commerce	PUB	1
County Business Patterns, U.S. Dept. of Commerce	PUB	1
Current Housing Reports: Vacancies	PUB	4
Current Housing Reports: Market Absorption of Apts.	PUB	4
Federal Reserve Bulletin	PUB	12
Federal Reserve Chart Book	PUB	4
Flow of Funds Statistics, Federal Reserve Board	PUB	4
Gas Facts, American Gas Association	PUB	1
Guide to Foreign Trade Statistics,		
U.S. Department of Commerce	PUB	1
Handbook of Basic Economic Statistics	PUB	12
Highway Statistics, Federal Highway Administration;		
U.S. Department of Transportation	PUB	1
Historical Statistics of the U.S.,		
U.S. Deptartment of Commerce	BOOK	
Industrial Distribution: Survey Distributor Opns.	PUB	1
International Financial Statistics, IMF	PUB	12
Journal of Economic Literature	PUB	4
Journal of Insurance	PUB	4
Journal of Money, Credit & Banking	PUB	4
Journal of Portfolio Management	PUB	4
Journal of Risk & Insurance	PUB	4
Key Business Ratios in 125 Lines, D&B	PUB	1
Location of Manufacturing Plants,		
U.S. Department of Commerce	PUB	4
Market Guide, Rand McNally	PUB	6
Marketing and Transportation Situation, USDA	PUB	12
Marketing Economics Guide	PUB	1
Metropolitan Toronto (example publication)	PUB	IRR
Moody's Manuals	PUB	1
NBER Reporter	PUB	4
NFIB Quarterly Report for Small Business	PUB	4

Retrospective Information Sources cont.

Source	Type	Freq.
Places Rated, Rand McNally	PUB	1
Pocket Data Book USA, USDC	PUB	IRR
Progressive Grocer: Industry Annual Report	PUB	1
Quarterly Failure Report, D&B	PUB	4
Regulated Company Filings (Federal, State)	PUB	VAR
Research Council's Handbook (Washington)	PUB	IRR
SEC Monthly Statistical Review	PUB	12
Securities & Exchange Commission 10-K'S	PUB	VAR
Social Indicators 1976, U.S. Department of Commerce, GPO (1977)	BOOK	
Sociological Methods and Research	PUB	4
Standard & Poor's Corporation Records	PUB	52
Statistical Abstract of Illinois (example publication)	PUB	1
Statistical Abstract of the U.S., U.S. Dept. of Commerce	PUB	1
Statistical Pocketbook Sri Lanka (example publication)	PUB	IRR
Statistical Yearbook, UN	PUB	1
Statistical Yearbook of Turkey (example publication)	PUB	IRR
Statistical & Marketing Report, Merchandise Week	PUB	1
Statistics of Income Bulletin	PUB	4
Statistics of Income: Individual Income Tax Returns, U.S. Department of the Treasury	PUB	1
Survey of Buying Power, Sales & Marketing Mgmt.	PUB	2
Survey of Industrial Purchasing Power, Sales & Marketing Management	PUB	1
Trade Association Publications	PUB	VAR
Transportation Statistics in the US, ICC	PUB	IRR
Treasury Bulletin	PUB	12
U.S. Geological Survey Water Supply Papers	PUB	IRR
U.S. Geological Survey Yearbook	PUB	1
U.S. Lodging Industry: Annual Report	PUB	1
Vermont Facts and Figures	PUB	1
Vital Statistics of the U.S., , U.S. Department of Health and Human Services	PUB	1
Vital and Health Statistics, Public Health Service, U.S. Department of Health and Human Services	PUB	IRR
Washington Monthly	PUB	11
World Bank Technical Data Sheets	PUB	52
World Development	PUB	12
Yearbook of International Trade Statistics, UN	PUB	1
Yearbook of National Accounts Statistics, UN	PUB	1

Database and Consulting Service Organizations

Source	Type
ADP Network Services	DBAS
Arthur D. Little Decision Resources	ORG
Arhtur D. Little International Developmental Forecasts	ORG
AUSINET (Australia)	DBAS
Battelle Memorial Institute	ORG
BELINDIS (Belgium)	DBAS
Bibliographic Retrieval Services, Inc.	DBAS
Brain-Reserve	ORG
Brookings Institution	ORG
BRS	DBAS
Bureau of National Affairs	DBAS
Bureau of National Affairs	ORG
Business International	ORG
Business Trends Analysts	ORG
CEDOCAR (France)	DBAS
Chase Econometrics	ORG
CISTI (Canada)	DBAS
Competitor Intelligence Group	ORG
Compuserve	DBAS
Conference Board	ORG
Congressional Clearinghouse on the Future	ORG
Corporate Priorities Program (Yankelovich, Skelly & White)	ORG
Data Resources, Inc.	ORG
Data-Star (UK)	DBAS
Dialog Information Services, Inc.	DBAS
DIMIDI (Germany)	DBAS
Dow Jones News Retrieval	DBAS
DRI Data Resources	ORG
European Space Agency (Italy, UK)	DBAS
Evans Economics	ORG
FIND/SVP	ORG
FIZ Technik (Germany)	DBAS
Fuld & Co.	ORG
Futures Network (UK)	ORG
Futures Research Institute (Oregon)	ORG
Futuribles, International Association (France)	ORG
Global Futures Network (Canada, India)	ORG
Hudson Institute	ORG

Database and Consulting Service Organizations cont.

Source	Type
Human Resources Information Network	DBAS
Inferential Focus	ORG
Information Data Search	ORG
Institute for Alternative Futures	ORG
Institute for Strategic Studies	ORG
Institute for the Future	ORG
Ist-Informatheque (Canada)	DBAS
Japan Information Processing Company	ORG
JICST (Japan)	DBAS
Mead Data Central	DBAS
Naisbitt Group	ORG
National Library of Medicine	ORG
National Planning Association	ORG
NewsNet	DBAS
Orbit Information Technologies	DBAS
Pergamon Infoline	DBAS
Planning Forum Research & Education Foundation	ORG
Policy Analysis Co., Inc.	ORG
Political Risk Services	ORG
Probe International	ORG
QL Systems Ltd (Canada)	DBAS
SDC Search Service, System Development Corp.	DBAS
Signal Program (Yankelovich, Skelly & White)	ORG
SRI Business Intelligence Program	ORG
STN International	DBAS
Strategic Intelligence Systems	ORG
Strategic Planning Institute	ORG
Technical Insights, Inc.	ORG
Technology Futures, Inc.	ORG
Telesystemes-Questel (France)	DBAS
United Communication Group	DBAS
VU/Text Information Services	DBAS
Washington Researchers, Ltd.	ORG
WEFA	ORG
Weiner•Edrich•Brown, Inc.	ORG
West Services, Inc.	DBAS
Wilsonline	DBAS
World Future Society	ORG
World Futures Studies Federation	ORG

BIBLIOGRAPHY AND REFERENCES

Numerical notations in the text refer to the sources listed below; as, [5] would refer to the Aguilar reference below. Where more than one source is indicated, these are separated by semicolons; as, [5;6] would indicate both the Aguilar and Allio references. Where it is desirable to show specific pages in that source, the reference number is followed by a comma and the appropriate page citation; as, [5,6-7] would indicate pages 6 and 7 of the Aguilar reference.

1. Abdelsamad, M.H. "Planning and Budgeting in Interesting Times." *Management World,* July 1980, pp. 28-29.

2. Abell, Derek F., and Hammond, John S. *Strategic Market Planning.* Englewood Cliffs, New Jersey: Prentice-Hall, 1979).

3. Achrol, Ravi S., and Stern, Louis W. "Environmental Determinants of Decision-Making Uncertainty in Marketing Channels." *Journal of Marketing Research,* Feb. 1988, pp. 36-50.

4. Ackoff, Russell L., "Beyond Prediction and Preparation." *Journal of Management Studies* (UK), Jan. 1983, pp. 59-69.

5. Aguilar, Francis. *Scanning the Business Environment.* New York: Macmillan, 1967.

6. Allio, Robert J. "Forecasting: The Myth of Control." *Planning Review,* May 1986, pp. 6-11.

7. Allett, E. J. "Environmental Impact Assessment and Decision Analysis." *Journal of the Operational Research Society* (UK), Sept. 1986, pp. 901-910.

8. Ambrosio, Johanna. "Databases Reach Out to Text and Images." *Software Magazine,* Feb. 1988, pp. 44-49.

9. Amit, Raphael; Domowitz, Ian; and Fershtman, Chaim. "Thinking One Step Ahead: The Use of Conjectures in Competitor Analysis." *Strategic Management Journal* (UK), Sept./Oct. 1988, pp. 431-442.

10. Anderson, Wayne C. "Issues Management: Conflicting Interests Within a Multidivisional Organization." *Vital Speeches,* 1 Mar. 1984, pp. 308-311.

11. Ansoff, H. Igor. "Conceptual Underpinnings of Systematic Strategic Management." *European Journal of Operational Research* (Netherlands), Jan. 1985, pp. 2-19.

12. Ansoff, H. Igor. *Implanting Strategic Management.* Englewood Cliffs, New Jersey: Prentice-Hall, 1984.

13. Ansoff, H. Igor. "Strategic Issue Management." *Strategic Management Journal* (UK), April/June 1980, pp. 131-148.

14. Ansoff, H. Igor. "Strategic Management." *Practising Manager* (Australia), April 1988, pp. 4-14.

15. Armstrong, Richard A. "The Concept and Practice of Issues Management in the United States: The Corporation Must Be Prepared." *Vital Speeches,* Oct. 1, 1981, pp. 763-765.

16. Armstrong, S. Scott. *Long Range Forecasting.* New York: Wiley-Interscience, 1978.

17. Arrington, Charles B., Jr., and Sawaya, Richard N. "Issues Management in an Uncertain Environment." *Long Range Planning* (UK), Dec. 1984, pp. 17-24.

18. Arrington, Charles B., Jr., and Sawaya, Richard N. "Managing Public Affairs: Issues Management in an Uncertain Environment." *California Management Review,* Summer 1984, pp. 148-160.

19. Ascher, William, and Overholt, William H. *Strategic Planning and Forecasting: Political Risk and Economic Opportunity.* New York: Wiley-Interscience, 1983.

20. Ashley, William C. "Issues Management — New Tool for New Times." *Bank Marketing,* Aug. 1983, pp. 10-14.

21. Attanasio, Dominick B. "The Multiple Benefits of Competitor Intelligence." *Journal of Business Strategy,* May/June 1988, pp. 16-19.

22. At-Twaijri, Mohamed Ibrahim Ahmad, and Montanari, John R. "The Impact of Context and Choice on the Boundary-Spanning Process: An Empirical Extension." *Human Relations,* Dec. 1987, pp. 783-797.

23. Ayres, Robert U. *Resources, Environment & Econometrics: Application of the Materials/Energy Balance Principle.* New York: Wiley, 1978.

24. Ayres, Robert U., and Shapanka, Adele. "Explicit Technological Substitution Forecasts in Long Range Input-Output Models." *Technological Substitution.* Edited by Harold Linstone and Devendra Sahal. New York: Elsevier, 1976, pp. 143-168.

25. Ball, Ben C., and Lorange, Peter. "Managing Your Strategic Responsiveness to the Environment." *Managerial Planning,* Nov./Dec. 1979, pp. 3-9, 27.

26. Ball, Richard. "Assessing Your Competitor's People and Organization." *Long Range Planning* (UK), April 1987, pp. 32-41.

27. Band, William A. "How to Evaluate Competitors' Marketing Strategies." *Sales & Marketing Management in Canada* (Canada), Sept. 1986, pp. 19-21.

28. Barrett, Stephanie S. "An IS* Case: The Closed Loop Scenario." *Information & Management* (Netherlands), May 1985, pp. 263-269.

29. Barret, Timothy. "When the Market Says 'Beware'." *Management Decision* (UK), Vol. 24 No. 6 (1986), pp. 36-40.

30. Bartos, Rena. "George Gallup: Mr. Polling." *Journal of Advertising Research,* Feb./ Mar. 1986, pp. 21-25.

31. Bates, Constance S. "Mapping the Environment: An Operational Environmental Analysis Model." *Long Range Planning* (UK), Oct. 1985, pp. 97-107.

32. Baysinger, Barry D. "Domain Maintenance as an Objective of Business Political Activity: An Expanded Typology." *Academy of Management Review,* April 1984, pp. 248-258.

33. Beazley, J. Ernest, and Hymowitz, Carol. "Strike at USX Shows How Far Steelmaker Has Fallen From Glory." *The Wall Street Journal,* 7 August 1986, p. 1.

34. Bell, D. *The Coming of Post-Industrial Society.* New York: Basic Books, 1973.

35. Belohlav, J., and Sussman, L. "Environmental Scanning and Dialectical Inquiry." *Managerial Planning,* Sept./Oct. 1983, pp. 46-49.

36. Bennet, David H., and Bushnell, David S. "Management is an Unnatural Act." *Bureaucrat,* Spring 1984, pp. 37-41.

37. Betts, Mitch. "Snoopers See MIS as Dr. No." *Computerworld,* 20 Feb 1989, pp. 1, 113.

38. Bidgoli, Hossein, and Attaran, Mohsen. "Improving the Effectiveness of Strategic Decision Making Using an Integrated Decision Support System." *Information & Software Technology* (UK), June 1988, pp. 278-284.

39. Binsted, Don. "Learning to Cope with Change." *Management Decision* (UK), 1986, pp. 32-36.

40. Binsted, Don. "Learning to Cope with Change in the 80s." *Journal of Management Development* (UK), 1984, pp. 66-75.

41. Blackman, A.W. "A Mathematical Model for Trend Forecasts." *Technological Forecasting and Social Change,* Vol. 3 (1972), pp. 441-452.

42. Blair, Cassandra. "Scanning the Corporate Horizon: Public Affairs in the Strategically Managed Organization." *Canadian Business Review* (Canada), Autumn 1986, pp. 33-36.

43. Blair, Cassandra. "The C.E.O.'s View of Political and Social Change." *Canadian Business Review* (Canada), Spring 1985, pp. 18-20.

44. Blandin, J.S., and Brown, W.B. "Uncertainty and Management's Search for Information." *IEEE Transactions on Engineering Management,* Nov. 1977, pp. 114-119.

45. Boschee, J. Arthur. "Simple Report Plugs PR into Management Mainstream." *Communication World,* Feb. 1987, p. 40.

46. Boulton, W.R., and Lindsay, W.M. "Strategic Planning: Determining the Importance of Environmental Characteristics and Uncertainty." *Academy of Management Journal,* Sept. 1982, pp. 500-509.

47. Bourgeois, L.J. III. "Strategic Goals, Perceived Uncertainty, and Economic Performance in Volatile Environments." *Academy of Management Journal,* Sept. 1985, pp. 548-573.

48. Bourgeois, L.J. III. "Strategy and Environment: A Conceptual Integration." *Academy of Management Review,* Jan 1980, pp. 25-39.

49. Bower, Catherine Downes, and Hallett, Jeffrey J. "Issues Management at ASPA." *Personnel Administrator,* Jan. 1989, pp. 40-43.

50. Box, George E.P.; Hunter, William G.; and Hunter, J. Stuart. *Statistics for Experimenters.* New York: Wiley, 1978.

51. Bracker, S.J., and Pearson, J.M. "Planning and Financial Performance of Small Mature Firms." *Strategic Management Journal* (UK), Nov./Dec. 1986, pp. 503-522.

52. Briggs, Barton S. "Competition vs. Growth." *Barrons,* 28 Oct. 1968, p. 5.

53. Briggs, Warren and Coleman, James. "Compact Discs: New Tool for Competitive Analysis." *Planning Review,* Nov./Dec. 1987, pp. 32-37.

54. Bright, James R., ed. *Technological Forecasting for Industry and Government.* Englewood Cliffs, New Jersey: Prentice-Hall, 1968.

55. Brock, John J. "Competitor Analysis: Some Practical Approaches." *Industrial Marketing Management,* Oct 1984, pp. 225-231.

56. Brown, J.K. "This Business of Issues: Coping With The Company's Environments." *The Conference Board Report,* No. 758, 1979.

57. Brown, Arnold and Weiner, Edith. *Supermanaging: How to Harness Change for Personal and Organizational Success.* New York: McGraw-Hill, 1984.

58. Brown, Rex V.; Kahr, Andrew S.; and Peterson, Cameron. *Decision Analysis for the Manager.* New York: Holt Rinehart, 1974.

59. Burack, Elmer H. "A Strategic Planning and Operational Agenda for Human Resources." *Human Resource Planning,* 1988, pp. 63-68.

60. Burack, Elmer H. "Linking Corporate Business and Human Resource Planning: Strategic Issues and Concerns." *Human Resource Planning,* 1985, pp. 133-145.

61. Burack, Elmer H., and Mathys, Nicholas J. "Environmental Scanning Improves Strategic Planning." *Personnel Administrator,* Apr. 1989, pp. 82-87.

62. Burns, Mark, and Mauet, Alfred R. "Patrolling the Turbulent Borderland: Managerial Strategies for a Changing Health Care Environment." *Health Care Management Review,* Winter 1989, pp. 7-12.

63. Burton, Richard M., and Obel, Borge. "Environmental-Organizational Relations: The Effects of Deregulation." *Technovation* (Netherlands), Oct. 1986, pp. 23-34.

64. Calori, Roland. "Designing a Business Scanning System." *Long Range Planning* (UK), Feb. 1989, pp. 69-82.

65. Camillus, John C., and Venkatraman, Nataraja. "Dimensions of Strategic Choice." *Planning Review,* Jan. 1984, pp. 26-31.

66. Campbell, Donald T. "Systematic Error on the Part of Human Links in Communication Systems." *Information and Control,* Dec. 1958, pp. 334-369.

67. Campbell, Robert, and Hitchin, David. "The Delphi Technique." *Management Services,* Nov./Dec. 1968, pp. 37-42.

68. Campbell, Thomas W. "Identifying the Issues." *Public Relations Journal,* Aug. 1983, pp. 19-20.

69. Capon, Noel, and Hulbert, James M. "The Integration of Forecasting and Strategic Planning." *International Journal of Forecasting* (Netherlands), 1985, pp. 123-133.

70. Cardinale, Val. "Wholesalers Discover A Little Planning Won't Hurt Anyone." *Drug Topics,* 7 Jan. 1985, pp. 41-42.

71. Carter, Anne P. *Structural Change in the American Economy.* Cambridge: Harvard University, 1970.

72. Carter, E. Eugene. "What Are the Risks in Risk Analysis." *Harvard Business Review,* July/Aug. 1972, pp. 72-82.

73. Cathey, Paul. "Industry Has A New Advance Guard — Issue Managers." *Iron Age,* 23 Apr. 1982, pp. 69-70.

74. Cerne, Frank. "External Data Can Improve Strategic Planning." *Hospitals,* 20 Apr. 1988, pp. 85-86.

75. Cetron, Marvin J., and Ralph, Christine A. *Industrial Applications of Technological Forecasting.* New York: Wiley-Interscience, 1971.

76. Chambers, J.C.; Mullick, S.K.; and Smith, D.D. "How To Choose the Right Forecasting Technique." *Harvard Business Review,* July/Aug. 1971, pp. 45-74.

77. Chang, Semoon. *Practitioners Guide to Econometrics.* Lanham, Maryland: University Press of America, 1984.

78. Channon, Derek F. and Jalland, Michael. *Multinational Strategic Planning.* New York: AMACOM, 1979.

79. Chao, Lincoln L. *Statistics for Management.* Palo Alto, California: Scientific Press, 1984.

80. Chase, W. Howard. *Issue Management: Origins of the Future.* Stamford, Connecticut: Issue Action Publications, Inc., 1984.

81. Checkland, P. *Systems Thinking, Systems Practice.* New York: Wiley-Interscience, 1981, pp. 161-183.

82. Christopher, William F. *Management for the 1980's.* Revised ed. Ann Arbor, Michigan: UMI Books on Demand, n.d.

83. Christopher, William F. *The Achieving Enterprise.* New York: AMACOM, 1974.

84. Clark, Wallace. *The Gantt Chart: A Working Tool of Management.* Second ed. London: Pitman &Sons, Ltd., 1942.

85. Cleave, John. "Environmental Assessments." *Finance & Development,* Mar. 1988, pp. 44-47.

86. Cleland, David, and King, William. "Competitive Business Intelligence Systems." *Business Horizons,* Dec 1975, pp. 19-28.

87. Clouser, E. Randall. "How the Delphi Panel Prognosticates the Future." *Risk Management,* Sept. 1986, pp. 30-41.

88. Cohen, William, and Czepiec, Helena. "The Role of Ethics in Gathering Corporate Intelligence." *Journal of Business Ethics* (Netherlands), Mar. 1988, pp. 199-203.

89. Cohen, William A. "Strategic Marketing: The Case for Strengths, Weaknesses." *Direct Marketing,* Mar. 1985, pp. 72-80.

90. Cohn, Theodore, and Lindberg, Roy A. *Survival & Growth for Small Business.* New York: AMACOM, 1980.

91. Camillus, John C., and Armstrong, W.J., Jr. "Strategic Vision and the Real World." *Conference Proceedings.* Oxford Ohio: The Planning Forum, 1989.

92. Coleman, E.R., and Tunstall, W.R. *Bell System Emerging Issues Program.* Basking Ridge, New Jersey: AT&T, 1980.

93. Cole, Harold Linh. "Comment: General Competitive Analysis in an Economy with Private Information." *International Economic Review,* Feb 1989, pp. 249- 252.

94. Collings, Robert. "Scanning the Environment for Strategic Information." Unpublished dissertation. Boston: Harvard University, 1968.

95. Combs, Richard and Moorhead, John. "The Quest for Corporate Excellence Begins with Competitive Intelligence." *Marketing News,* 9 May 1988, pp. 11, 20- 21.

96. Cornish, Edward S. *Planting Seeds for the Future.* Stamford, Connecticut: Champion International Corporation, 1979.

97. "Cotton Shortages Crop Up As Demand and Exports Climb." *Industry Week,* 3 Dec. 1973, p. 57.

98. Cox, Connie A. "The Art of Prying Out Information." *Journal of Management Consulting* (Netherlands), 1985, pp. 22-25.

99. Crable, Richard E. and Vibbert, Steven L. "Managing Issues and Influencing Public Policy." *Public Relations Review,* Summer 1985, pp. 3-16.

100. Crane, Teresa Yancey. "How to Prevent a Crisis." *New Management,* Summer 1987, pp. 35-37.

101. Crouch, Carolyn J. and Crouch, Donald B. "The Impact of External Factors on Productivity in an Engineering Support Organization." *IEEE Transactions on Engineering Management,* Aug. 1988, pp. 147-157.

102. Culnan, Mary J. "Environmental Scanning: The Effects of Task Complexity and Source Accessibility on Information Gathering Behavior." *Decision Sciences,* Apr. 1983, pp. 194-206.

103. Cyert, R.M., and March, J.G. *Behavioral Theory of the Firm.* Englewood Cliffs, New Jersey: Prentice-Hall, 1963.

104. Daft, Richard L.; Sormunen, Juhani; and Parks, Don. "Chief Executive Scanning, Environmental Characteristics, and Company Performance: An Empirical Study." *Strategic Management Journal* (UK), Mar./Apr. 1988, pp. 123-139.

105. Daneke, Gregory A., and Lemak, David J. "Integrating Strategic Management and Social Responsibility." *Business Forum,* Summer 1985, pp. 20-25.

106. Darrow, R. Morton. "Confessions of a Corporate Futurist." *New Management,* Spring 1983, pp. 16-19.

107. Davidson, William R., and Sheppard, Jeanne L. "Retailing Challenges for the 80s."*Business Forum,* Fall 1982, pp. 20-24.

108. de Bergerac, Cyrano. *Voyages to the Moon and the Sun.* Trans. by Richard Aldington. New York: Orion Press, 1962.

109. de Bono, Edward. *Lateral Thinking for Management.* New York: American Management Association, 1971.

110. de Carbonnel, Francois E., and Donance, Roy G. "Information Sources for Planning Decisions." *California Management Review,* Summer 1973, pp. 42-53.

111. de Neufville, Judith Innes. *Social Indicators and Public Policy.* Amsterdam: Elsevier, 1975.

112. De Noya, Louis E. "The Federal Government as a Source of Strategic Planning Information." *Long Range Planning* (UK), Oct. 1980, pp. 100-105.

113. DeBresson, Chris, and Lampel, Joseph. "Beyond the Life Cycle: Organizational and Technological Design. I. An Alternative Perspective." *Journal of Product Innovation Management,* Sept. 1985, pp. 170-187.

114. Deming, B.W. "Strategic Environmental Appraisal." *Long Range Planning* (UK), Mar. 1973, pp. 22-27.

115. Devasconcellos, Filho P. "Environmental Analysis for Strategic Planning." *Managerial Planning,* Jan./Feb. 1985, pp. 23-20.

116. Diffenbach, John. "Corporate Environmental Analysis in Large U.S. Corporations." *Long Range Planning* (UK), June 1983, pp. 107-116.

117. Diffenbach, John. "Influence Diagrams for Complex Strategic Issues." *Strategic Management Journal* (UK), Apr./June 1982, pp. 133-146.

118. Dill, W.R. "Environment As An Influence on Managerial Autonomy." *Administrative Science Quarterly,* Mar. 1958, pp. 409-443.

119. Dirsmith, Mark, and Covaleski, Mark A. "Strategy, External Communication and Environmental Context." *Strategic Management Journal* (UK), Apr./June 1983, pp. 137-151.

120. Dixit, Mukund R. "Environmental Scanning for Corporate Planning." *Productivity,* July-Sept. 1984, pp. 217-229.

121. Dollinger, Marc J. "Environmental Boundary Spanning and Information Processing Effects on Organizational Performance." *Academy of Management Journal,* Vol. 27 (1984), pp. 351-368.

122. Dollinger, Marc J. "Environmental Contacts and Financial Performance of the Small Firm." *Journal of Small Business Management,* Vol. 23 No. 1, pp. 24-30.

123. Dollinger, Marc J., and Kolchin, Michael G. "Obtaining Strategic Information from Suppliers." *Advanced Management Journal,* Autumn 1987, pp. 42-46.

124. Downey, H. Kirk; Hellriegel, D.; and Slocum, J., Jr. "Environmental Uncertainty: The Construct and its Application." *Administrative Science Quarterly,* Dec. 1975, pp. 613-629.

125. Downey, H. Kirk, and Ireland, R. Duane. "Quantitative Versus Qualitative: Environmental Assessment in Organizational Studies." *Administrative Science Quarterly,* Dec. 1979, pp. 630-637.

126. Drucker, Peter. *The Age of Discontinuity.* New York: Harper & Row, 1978.

127. Dumaine, Brian. "Corporate Spies Snoop to Conquer." Fortune, 7 Nov. 1988, pp. 68-76.

128. Duncan, Robert B. "Characteristics of Organizational Environment and Perceived Environmental Uncertainty." *Administrative Science Quarterly,* Sept. 1972, pp. 313-327.

129. "DuPont Stubs Its Toe." *Dun's Review,* June 1967, p. 61.

130. Dutta, Biplab K., and King,William R. "A Competitive Scenario Modeling System." *Management Science,* Mar. 1980, pp. 261-273.

131. Dutton, Jane E., and Ottensmeyer, Edward. "Strategic Issue Management Syttems: Forms, Functions, and Contexts." *Academy of Management Review,* Apr. 1987, pp. 355-365.

132. Dutton, Jane E., and Webster, Jane. "Patterns of Interest Around Issues: The Role of Uncertainty and Feasibility." *Academy of Management Journal,* Sept. 1988, pp. 663-675.

133. Edmunds, Stahrl W. "Environmental Impacts: Conflicts and Tradeoffs." *California Management Review,* Spring 1977, pp. 5-11.

134. Edmunds, Stahrl W. "Futures Research and Its Application to Business Policy." *Los Angeles Business & Economics,* Summer 1981, pp. 16-19.

135. Edmunds, Stahrl W. "Role of Futures Studies in Business Strategic Planning." *Journal of Business Strategy,* Fall 1982, pp. 40-46.

136. Edrich, Harold. "Keeping a Weather Eye on the Future." *Planning Review,* Jan. 1980, pp. 11-14.

137. Eells, Richard, and Nehemkis, Peter. *Corporate Intelligence and Espionage.* New York: Macmillan, 1984.

138. EIS: *Executive Information System.* IBM Edition. Ann Arbor, Michigan: Comshare Inc., 1987.

139. Eliashberg, Jehoshua, and Chatterjee, Rabikar. "Analytical Models of Competition with Implications for Marketing: Issues, Findings, and Outlook." *Journal of Marketing Research,* Aug. 1985, pp. 237-261.

140. El-Sawy, Omar A. "Personal Information Systems for Strategic Scanning in Turbulent Environments: Can the CEO Go On-Line?" *MIS Quarterly,* Mar. 1985, pp. 53-60.

141. El-Sawy, Omar A., and Pauchant, Thierry C. "Triggers, Templates and Twitches in the Tracking of Emerging Strategic Issues." *Strategic Management Journal* (UK), Sept./Oct. 1988, pp. 455-473.

142. Emery, F.E., and Trist., E. "The Causal Texture of Organizational Environments." *Human Relations,* Feb. 1965, pp. 21-31.

143. Engel, Alan K. "Number One in Competitor Intelligence." *Across the Board,* Dec. 1987, pp. 43-47.

144. Engledow, Jack L., and Lenz, R.T. "What Ever Happened to Environmental Analysis." *Long Range Planning* (UK), Apr. 1985, pp. 93-106.

145. "Environmental Scanning #1." *Manpower Planning,* Vol. 3 No. 11 (1980), p. 1.

146. "Environmental Scanning #2." *Manpower Planning,* Vol. 3 No. 12 (1981), p. 1.

147. *EPS-FCS.* IBM and DEC-VAX Editions. Chelmsford, Mass.: Thorn EMI Computer Software, 1986.

148. Evans, Martin. "Marketing Intelligence: Scanning the Marketing Environment." *Marketing Intelligence & Planning* (UK), 1988, pp. 21-29.

149. "Expert at Univ. of Illinois Sees Data Bases Multiplying." *Government Computer News,* 31 Jan. 1986, n.p.

150. Fahey, Liam, and King, William. "Environmental Scanning for Corporate Planning." *Business Horizons,* Aug 1977, pp. 61-71.

151. Fahey, Liam; King, William R.; and Narayanan, Vandake K. "Environmental Scanning and Forecasting in Strategic Planning: The State of the Art." *Long Range Planning* (UK), Feb. 1981, pp. 32-39.

152. Fahey, Liam, and Narayanan, Vandake K. *Macroenvironmental Analysis for Strategic Management.* St. Paul: West Publishing Co., 1986.

153. Farh, J.L.; Hoffman, R.C.; and Hegarty, W.H. "Assessing Environmental Scanning at the Subunit Level: A Multitrait-Multimethod Analysis." *Decision Sciences,* Spring 1984, pp. 197-220.

154. Farmer, David. "Competitive Analysis — Its Role in Purchasing." *Long Range Planning* (UK), June 1984, pp. 72-77.

155. Feuer, M.J. "From Environmental Scanning to Human Resources Planning: A Linkage Model Applied to Universities." *Human Resource Planning,* June 1983, pp. 69-82.

156. Fleming, John E. "Linking Public Affairs with Corporate Planning." *California Management Review,* Winter 1980, pp. 35-43.

157. Ford, Jeffrey D. "Management of Organizational Crises." *Business Horizons,* May/June 1981, pp. 10-16.

158. Franklin, Stephen. "USX, Steelworkers Dig In as Industry Teeters." *Detroit Free Press,* 17 August 1986, p. 1.

159. Franklin, Stephen G.; Rue, Leslie W.; Boulton, William R.; and Lindsay, William M. "A Grass Roots Look At Corporate Long Range Planning Practices." *Managerial Planning,* May/June 1981, pp. 13-18.

160. Fredericks, Peter, and Venkatraman, N. "The Rise of Strategy Support Systems." *Sloan Management Review,* Spring 1988, pp. 47-54.

161. Freeman, Harry L. "Eight Forces of Change." Economic Review of the Federal *Reserve Bank of Atlanta,* Sept. 1981, pp. 42-43.

162. Free, Valerie. "How Ogilvy & Mather Is Shaping Its Future." *Marketing Communications,* May 1988, pp. 24-43.

163. Friedmann, Roberto, and French, Warren A. "Beyond Social Trend Data." *Journal of Consumer Marketing,* Fall 1985, pp. 17-21.

164. Friedmann, Roberto, and French, Warren A. "Pricing Augmented Commercial Services." *Journal of Product Innovation Management,* Mar. 1987, pp. 33-42.

165. Friedman, Hershey H., and Friedman, Linda W. "Applying Warfare to Business Competition." *Business Forum,* Winter 1986, pp. 8-12.

166. Friend, David. "Benefits of an Executive Information System." *Information Management Review,* Winter 1989, pp. 7-15.

167. Fuld, Leonard M. "How to Get the Scoop on Your Competition." *Working Woman,* Jan. 1989, pp. 39-42.

168. Galbraith, John. *The New Industrial State.* 4th Ed. Boston: Houghton, Mifflin, 1985.

169. Gearing, C.E.; Swart, W.W.; and Var, T. "Establishing a Measure of Touristic Attractiveness." *Journal of Travel Research,* Spring 1974, pp. 1-18.

170. Gerstenfeld, Arthur. "Technological Forecasting." *Journal of Business,* Jan. 1971, pp. 10-18.

171. Gerwin, Donald, and Tuggle, Francis. "Modeling Organizational Decisions Us-ing the Human Problem Solving Paradigm." *Academy of Management Review,* Oct. 1978, pp. 762-773.

172. Ghoshal, Sumantra. "Environmental Scanning in Korean Firms: Organizational Isomorphism in Action." *Journal of International Business Studies,* Spring 1988, pp. 69-86.

173. Ghoshal, Sumantra, and Kim, Seok Ki. "Building Effective Intelligence Systems for Competitive Advantage." *Sloan Management Review,* Fall 1986, pp. 49-58.

174. Gibson, John E. *Managing Research and Development.* New York: Wiley-Interscience, 1981.

175. Gilad, Benjamin, and Gilad, Tamar. "Strategic Planning: Improving the Input." *Managerial Planning,* May/June 1985, pp. 10-13,17.

176. Glasser, Alan. "Technical Role in Competition Analysis, Part 1: Key Concepts." *International Journal of Technology Management* (Switzerland), 1986, pp. 231-242.

177. Glueck, W.F., and Jauch, L.R. *Business Policy and Strategic Management.* 4th Ed. New York: McGraw-Hill, 1984.

178. Godiwalla, Yezdi M.; Meinhart, Wayne A.; and Warde, William D. "Environ-mental Scanning — Does It Help the Chief Executive?" *Long Range Planning* (UK), Oct. 1980, pp. 87-99.

179. Goeldner, C.R., and Kirks, Laura M. "Business Facts: Where to Find Them." *MSU Business Topics,* Summer 1976, pp. 23-76.

180. Gordon, T.J., and Hayward, H. "Initial Experiments with the Cross Impact Method of Forecasting." *Futures,* Vol. 1 (1968), p. 100.

181. Gordon, T.J., and Helmer, Olaf. *Report on a Long-Range Forecasting Study.* Santa Monica, Cal.: Rand Corporation, 1964.

182. Grabowski, Daniel P. "Building an Effective Competitive Intelligence System." *Journal of Business & Industrial Marketing,* Winter 1987, pp. 39-43.

183. Grandstaff, Peter J.; Ferris, Mark E.; and Chou, Shuh S. "Forecasting Competitive Behavior: An Assessment of AT&T's Incentive to Extend Its U.S. Network." *International Journal of Forecasting* (Netherlands), 1988, pp. 521-533.

184. Gregg, Leigh. "Four Trends to Watch." *Credit Union Magazine,* June 1988, pp. 44-50.

185. Gregory, Carl E. *The Management of Intelligence.* New York: McGraw-Hill, 1967.

186. Gup, Benton E. *Guide to Strategic Planning.* New York: McGraw-Hill, 1980.

187. Haegele, Monroe. "Financial Deregulation and the Commercial Account Officer." *Journal of Commercial Bank Lending,* Dec. 1982, pp. 30-43.

188. Hainsworth, Brad, and Meng, Max. "How Corporations Define Issue Management." *Public Relations Review,* Winter 1988, pp. 18-30.

189. Hambrick, Donald C. "Environmental Scanning and Organizational Strategy." *Strategic Management Journal* (UK), Apr./June 1982, pp. 159-174.

190. Hambrick, Donald C. "Specialization of Environmental Scanning Activity Among Upper Level Executives." *Journal of Management Studies* (UK), July 1981, pp. 299-320.

191. Hawkins, Michael D. "A Strategic Look at Competitors' HR Data." *Information Strategy: The Executive's Journal,* Winter 1989, pp. 14-20.

192. Hedberg, B., and Jonsson, S.. "Designing Semi-Confusing Systems for Organizations in Changing Environments." *Accounting, Organizations & Society,* Vol. 1 (1978), pp. 47-64.

193. Hedley, Barry. "A Fundamental Aproach to Strategy Development." *Long Range Planning* (UK), Dec. 1976, pp. 2-11.

194. Hershey, Robert. "Commercial Intelligence on a Shoestring." *Harvard Business Review,* Sept./Oct. 1980, pp. 22-30.

195. Hertz, David B. "Risk Analysis in Capital Investment." *Harvard Business Review,* Jan./Feb. 1964, pp. 95-106.

196. Hertz, David B., and Thomas, Howard. "Risk Analysis: Important New Tool for Business Planning." *Journal of Business Strategy,* Winter 1983, pp. 23-29.

197. Hirsch, Robert L. "Reorienting an Industrial Research Laboratory." *Research Management,* Jan./Feb. 1986, pp. 26-30.

198. Hitt, Michael A., and Ireland, R. Duane. "Strategy, Contextual Factors, and Performance." *Human Relations,* Aug. 1985, pp. 793-812.

199. Holroyd, P. "Some Recent Methodologies in Futures Studies: A Personal View." *R & D Management,* Vol. 3 (1979), pp. 107-116.

200. House, William C. "Environmental Analysis — Key to More Effective Dynamic Planning." *Managerial Planning,* Jan./Feb. 1977, pp. 25-29.

201. *How TAP Works.* Washington, D.C.: American Council of Life Insurance, 1985.

202. Hussey, David. *Corporate Planning Theory & Practice.* 2nd Ed. New York: Pergamon, 1982.

203. *IFPS Version 11.* IBM and DEC-VAX Editions. Austin, Texas: Execucom Systems Corporation, 1987.

204. *IFPS/Personal Version 3.* IBM-PC Edition. Austin, Texas: Execucom Systems Corporation, 1986.

205. Ireland, R.; Hitt, M.; Bettis, R.; and DePorras, D. "Strategy Formulation Processes: Differences in Perceptions of Strength and Weaknesses Indicators and Environmental Uncertainty." *Strategic Management Journal* (UK), Sept./Oct. 1987, pp. 469.

206. Iverson, J. Richard, and Albertine, James J. "Managing Change: Two Case Studies in Government Relations." *Association Management,* Dec. 1987, pp. 34-38.

207. Jain, Subhash C. "Environmental Scanning in U.S. Corporations." *Long Range Planning* (UK), Apr. 1984, pp. 117-128.

208. Jain, Subhash C. "Self-Appraisal and Environmental Analysis in Corporate Planning." *Managerial Planning,* Jan./Feb. 1979, pp. 16-18+.

209. James, Philip N. "A Framework for Strategic and Long-Range Information Resource Planning." *Information Strategy: The Executive's Journal,* Fall 1985, pp. 4-12.

210. Jantsch, Erich. *Technological Forecasting in Perspective.* Paris: OECD, 1967.

211. Jauch, Lawrence R, and Kraft, Kenneth L. "Strategic Management of Uncertainty." *Academy of Management Review,* Oct. 1986, pp. 777-790.

212. Javidan, Mansour. "The Impact of Environmental Uncertainty on Long-Range Planning Practices of the U.S. Savings and Loan Industry." *Strategic Management Journal* (UK), Oct./Dec. 1984, pp. 381-392.

213. Javidan, Mansour. "Where Planning Fails — An Executive Survey." *Long Range Planning* (UK), Oct. 1985, pp. 89-96.

214. Jennings, Daniel F. and Lumpkin, James R. "Insights Into the Relationship Between Strategic Momentum and Environmental Scanning: An Empirical Analysis." *Akron Business and Economic Review,* Spring 1989, pp. 84-93.

215. Jennings, Marian C. "What Is Financially Driven Strategic Planning?" *Topics in Health Care Financing,* Fall 1988, pp. 1-8.

216. Jensen, Daniel R. "Unifying Planning and Management in Public Organizations." *Public Administration Review,* Mar./Apr. 1982, pp. 157-162.

217. Johnston, H. Russell, and Carrico, Shelley R. "Developing Capabilities to Use Information Strategically." *MIS Quarterly,* Mar. 1988, pp. 37-48.

218. Jones, J. Morgan. *Introduction to Decision Theory*. Homewood, Illinois: Richard D. Irwin, 1977.

219. Jones, Lou. "Competitor Cost Analysis at Caterpillar." *Management Accounting,* Oct. 1988, pp. 32-38.

220. Jones, Scott T. "Multiple Scenario Planning — Atlantic Richfield's Experience." *Journal of Business Forecasting,* Fall 1985, pp. 19-23.

221. Kahn, Herman. *The Coming Boom*. New York: Simon and Schuster, 1982.

222. Kahn, Herman. *The Next 200 Years: A Scenario for America and the World*. New York: Wm.Morrow & Co., 1976.

223. Kallman, Ernest A. *Information System for Planning and Decision Making*. New York: Van Nostrand Reinhold, 1984.

224. Kallman, Ernest A., and Shapiro, Jack. "The Motor Freight Industry — A Case Against Planning." *Long Range Planning* (UK), Feb. 1978, pp. 81-86.

225. Kami, Michael. *Trigger Points*. New York: McGraw-Hill, 1988.

226. Karagozoglu, Necmi, and Brown, Warren B. "Adaptive Responses by Conservative and Entrepreneurial Firms." *Journal of Product Innovation Management,* Dec. 1988, pp. 269-281.

227. Karlsson, Christer. "Challenges for the Organization of Technical Functions in the Automotive Industry." *International Journal of Technology Management* (Switzerland), 1987, pp. 405-416.

228. Kastens, Merritt L. *Long Range Planning for Your Business: An Operating Manual*. New York: AMACOM, 1976.

229. Kast, Fremont. "Scanning the Future Environment: Social Indicators." *California Management Review,* Fall 1980, pp. 22-32.

230. Katz, D.L., and Kahn, R.L. . *The Social Psychology of Organizations*. New York: Wiley, 1966.

231. Kaufman, Jerome L., and Jacobs, Harvey M. "A Public Planning Perspective on Strategic Planning." *Journal of the American Planning Association,* Winter 1987, pp. 23-33.

232. Kay, N.M., and Diamantopoulos, A. "Uncertainty and Synergy: Towards a Formal Model of Corporate Strategy." *Managerial & Decision Economics* (UK), June 1987, pp. 121-130.

233. Keegan, Warren. "Multinational Scanning." *Administrative Science Quarterly,* Sept. 1974, pp. 411-421.

234. Keeney, R.L. and Raiffa, Howard. *Decisions with Multiple Objectives.* New York: Wiley, 1976.

235. Kefalas, A.G. "Analyzing Changes in the External Business Environment." *Policy, Strategy & Implementation: Readings & Cases.* Edited by Milton Leontiades. New York: Random House, 1983.

236. Kefalas, A.G. "Environmental Management Information Systems (ENVIMIS): A Reconceptualization." *Journal of Business Research,* July 1975, pp. 253-266.

237. Kefalas, A.G. "Toward a Sustainable Growth Strategy." *Business Horizons,* Apr. 1979, pp. 34-40.

238. Kefalas, A.G., and Schoderbek, P.P. "Scanning the Business Environment: Some Empirical Results." *Decision Sciences,* Jan. 1973, pp. 63-74.

239. Keiser, Barbie E. "Practical Competitor Intelligence." *Planning Review,* Sept./Oct. 1987, pp. 14-18.

240. Kennedy, Charles R., Jr. "External Environment — Strategic Planning Interface: U.S. Multinational Corporate Practices in the 80's." *Journal of International Business Studies,* Fall 1984, pp. 99-108.

241. Kennedy, Charles R., Jr. "Political Risk Management: A Portfolio Planning Model." *Business Horizons,* Nov./Dec. 1988, pp. 26-33.

242. King, William R., and Cleland, David I. *Strategic Planning and Policy.* New York: Van Nostrand Reinhold, 1978.

243. Klein, Harold E., and Linneman, R. E. "Environmental Assessment: An International Study of Corporate Practice." *Journal of Business Strategy,* Summer 1984, pp. 66-75.

244. Klein, Harold E., and Linneman, R. E. "The Use of Scenarios in Corporate Planning: Eight Case Histories." *Long Range Planning* (UK), Oct. 1981, pp. 69-77.

245. Klein, Lawrence R., and Young, Richard M.. *An Introduction to Econometric Forecasting and Forecasting Models.* Lexington, Mass.: Lexington Books, 1980.

246. Kloman, H. Felix. "Risk Management . . . By Many Other Names." *Risk Management,* June 1987, pp. 56-62.

247. Koberg, Christine S., and Ungson, Gerardo R. "The Effects of Environmental Uncertainty and Dependence on Organizational Structure and Performance: A Comparative Study." *Journal of Management,* Winter 1987, pp. 725-737.

248. Koberg, Christine S. "Resource Scarcity, Environmental Uncertainty, and Adaptive Organizational Behavior." *Academy of Management Journal,* Dec. 1987, pp. 798-807.

249. Koco, Linda. "Who Watches the Product Watchers?" *National Underwriter (Life/Health/Financial Services),* 29 Feb. 1988, pp. 13, 30.

250. Korey, George. "Linear Responsibility Charting: A Technique for Strategic Management." *Management Decision* (UK), 1988, pp. 11-21.

251. Kovach, Jeffrey L. "Competitive Intelligence." *Industry Week,* 12 Nov. 1984, pp. 50-53.

252. Krijenen, Hans G. "The Flexible Firm." *Long Range Planning* (UK), Apr. 1979, pp. 63-67.

253. Kudla, Ronald. "The effects of Strategic Planning on Common Stock Returns." *Academy of Management Journal,* Vol. 23 (1980), pp. 5-20.

254. Laczniak, Gene R. and Lusch, Robert F. "Environment and Strategy in 1995: A Survey of High-Level Executives." *Journal of Consumer Marketing,* Spring 1986, pp. 27-45.

255. Lamb, Robert B., ed. *Competitive Strategic Management.* Englewood Cliffs, New Jersey: Prentice-Hall, 1984.

256. Lancaster, F.W. and Lee, Ja-Lih. "Bibliometric Techniques Applied to Issues Management: A Case Study." *Journal of the ASIS,* Nov. 1985, pp. 389-397.

257. Landford, H.W., and Cleary, M.J. "Data Sources for Trend Extrapolation in Technological Forecasting." *Long Range Planning* (UK), Feb. 1972, pp. 72-76.

258. Langton, James F., and Lewin, Arie Y. "Dinosaurs Did Not Survive." *Enterprise,* Winter 1982, pp. 14-19.

259. Lasden, Martin. "MIS/DP Espionage: The Inside Story." *Computer Decisions,* 8 Apr. 1986, pp. 66-71.

260. Lawrence, P.R., and Lorsch, J.W. *Organization and Environment.* Boston: Harvard Business School, 1967.

261. Lazer, William; Luqmani, M.; and Quraeshi, Z. "Product Rejuvenation Strategies." *Business Horizons,* Nov./Dec. 1984, pp. 21-28.

262. Lebel, Don, and Krasner, O.J. "Selecting Environmental Forecasting Techniques from Business Planning Requirements." *Academy of Management Review,* July 1977, pp. 373-83.

263. Lederman, Leonard L. "Foresight Activities in the U.S.A.: A Time for Reassessment?" *Long Range Planning* (UK), June 1984, pp. 41-51.

264. Lee-Kwang, Chul, and Kwok, Chuck. "Multinational Corporations vs. Domestic Corporations: International Environmental Factors and Determinants of Capital Structure." *Journal of International Business Studies,* Summer 1988, pp. 19.

265. Leidecker, J.K., and Bruno, A.V. "Identifying and Using Critical Success Factors." *Long Range Planning* (UK), Feb. 1984, pp. 23-32.

266. Leifer, Richard and Delbecq, Andre. "Organizational-Environmental Interchange: A Model of Boundary Spanning Activity." *Academy of Management Review,* Jan. 1978, pp. 40-50.

267. Leifer, Richard, and Huber, R.L. "Relations Among Perceived Environmental Uncertainty, Organizational Structure, and Boundary Spanning Behavior." *Administrative Science Quarterly,* Mar. 1977, pp. 235-248.

268. Lenz, Ralph C., Jr. "Technological Forecasting." paper presented at U.S. Air Force Symposium on Long Range Forecasting and Planning, Colorado Springs, Colorado, Aug. 1966.

269. Lenz, R.T. "Environment, Strategy, Organizational Structure and Performance." *Strategic Management Journal* (UK), Vol. 2 (1981), pp. 131-154.

270. Lenz, R.T., and Engledow, Jack L. "Environmental Analysis Units and Strategic Decision-Making: A Field Study of Selected 'Leading-Edge' Corporations." *Strategic Management Journal* (UK), Jan./Feb. 1986, pp. 69-89.

271. Lenz, R.T., and Engledow, Jack L. "Environmental Analysis: The Applicability of Current Theory." *Strategic Management Journal* (UK), July/Aug. 1986, pp. 329-346.

272. Leontiades, James C. *Multinational Corporate Strategy.* Lexington, Massachusetts: Heath & Company, 1985.

273. Leontief, Wassily. *Input-Output Economics.* New York: Oxford University Press, 1966.

274. Leontief, Wassily. *Structure of the American Economy, 1919-1939.* 2nd Ed. New York: Oxford University Press, 1951.

275. Lerner, Linda D. and Fryxell, Gerald E. "An Empirical Study of the Predictors of Corporate Social Performance: A Multi-Dimensional Analysis." *Journal of Business Ethics* (Netherlands), Dec. 1988, pp. 951-959.

276. Levy, Ronald N. "Issues Management: Measuring Your Success." *Public Relations Quarterly,* Fall 1987, pp. 17-18.

277. Lindsay, W.M., and Rue, L.W. "Impact of the Organizational Environment on the Long Range Planning Process: A Contingency View." *Academy of Manage-ment Journal,* Sept. 1980, pp. 385-404.

278. Linneman, Robert E., et al. "Using Multiple Scenarios for Strategic Environmental Assessment: Implications for Marketing Management." *Marketing Intelligence and Planning* (UK), Vol. 1 No. 1 (1983), pp. 67-76.

279. Linneman, Robert E., and Klein, Harold E. "Using Scenarios in Strategic Decision Making." *Business Horizons,* Jan./Feb. 1985, pp. 64-74.

280. Linneman, Robert E.; Klein, Harold E.; and Brightmore, Robert. "Use of Multiple Scenarios by Canadian Firms." *Journal of Business Administration* (Canada), Vol. 14 No. 1 (1983-84), pp. 99-120.

281. Linneman, Robert E., and Thomas, Michael J. "A Commonsense Approach to Portfolio Planning." *Long Range Planning* (UK), Apr. 1982, pp. 77-92.

282. Linstone, Harold A., and Sahal, Devendra, eds. *Technological Substitution.* New York: Elsevier, 1976.

283. Littlejohn, Stephen E. "Competition and Cooperation: New Trends in Corporate Public Issue Identification and Resolution." *California Management Review,* Fall 1986, pp. 109-123.

284. Logsdon, Jeanne M. and Palmer, David R. "Issues Management and Ethics." *Journal of Business Ethics* (Netherlands), Mar. 1988, pp. 191-198.

285. Lorange, Peter. *Corporate Planning.* Englewood Cliffs, New Jersey: Prentice-Hall, 1980.

286. Lorange, Peter, and Vancil, Richard F. *Strategic Planning Systems.* Englewood Cliffs, New Jersey: Prentice-Hall, 1977.

287. Lorange, Peter, and Vancil, Richard F. "How to Design a Strategic Planning System." *Harvard Business Review,* Sept./Oct. 1976, pp. 75-81.

288. Lubatkin, M., and Pitts, M. "PIMS: Fact or Folklore?" *Journal of Business Strategy,* Vol. 3 No. 3 (1983), pp. 38-43.

289. Luconi, F.I.; Malone, T.W.; and Morton, M.S. "Expert Systems: The Next Challenge for Managers." *Sloan Management Review,* Summer 1986, pp. 3-14.

290. Lyles, Marjorie A., and Thomas, Howard. "Strategic Problem Formulation: Biases and Assumptions Embedded in Alternative Decision-Making Models." *Journal of Management Studies* (UK), Mar. 1988, pp. 131-145.

291. Lysonski, Steven. "A Boundary Theory Investigation of the Product Manager's Role." *Journal of Marketing,* Winter 1985, pp. 26-40.

292. Lysonski, Steven; Singer, Alan; and Wilemon, David. "Coping with Environmental Uncertainty and Boundary Spanning in the Product Manager's Role." *Journal of Services Marketing,* Fall 1988, pp. 15-26.

293. Macaulay, S. "Non-Contractual Relations in Business: A Preliminary Study." *Sociological Review,* Feb. 1963, pp. 55-67.

294. Mackenzie, Kenneth D. "Environmental Change and the Search for Organizational Congruency in the U.S.A. Financial Services Industry." *Technovation* (Netherlands), Oct. 1986, pp. 73-93.

295. MacMillan, I.C. "Seizing Competitive Initiative." *Journal of Business Strategy,* Spring 1982, pp. 43-57.

296. MacMillan, I.C., and McCafferty, M.L. "How Aggressive Innovation Can Help Your Company." *Journal of Business Strategy,* Spring 1982, pp. 115-119.

297. Maddox, Nick; Anthony, William P.; and Wheatley, Walt, Jr. "Creative Strate- gic Planning Using Imagery." *Long Range Planning* (UK), Oct. 1987, pp. 118- 124.

298. Mahmood, Syyed T., and Moon, M. Munir. "Competitive Analysis from a Strategic Planning Perspective." *Managerial Planning,* July/Aug. 1984, pp. 37-42.

299. Makridakis, Spyros. *Forecasting Accuracy of Major Time Series Methods.* New York: Wiley, 1984.

300. Makridakis, Spyros, and Wheelwright, Steven C. *Interactive Forecasting.* 2nd Edition. San Francisco: Holden Day, 1978.

301. Mak, Yuen Teen. "Contingency Fit, Internal Consistency and Financial Performance." *Journal of Business Finance & Accounting* (UK), Spring 1989, pp. 273-300.

302. Mangan, Doreen. "None of Your Secrets Are Safe." *Venture,* Feb. 1988, pp. 61-67.

303. Manning, Jeannene. "Decisionmakers Go Online." *Business Software Review,* July 1988, pp. 38-41.

304. Markowitz, Zane N. "Hidden Sector Competitor Analysis." *Planning Review,* Sept./Oct. 1987, pp. 20-24.

305. Martin, M. Dean, and Owens, Stephen D. "Management Change in the Project Environment."*AACE Transactions,* 1988, P.6.1-P.6.7.

306. McCann, Joseph E. "Analyzing Industrial Trends — A Collaborative Approach." *Long Range Planning* (UK), Oct. 1985, pp. 116-123.

307. McCleary, Richard, and Hay, Richard A. *Applied Time Series Analysis for the Social Sciences.* Beverly Hills: Sage, 1980.

308. McConkey, Dale D. "Planning for Uncertainty." *Business Horizons,* Jan./Feb. 1987, pp. 40-45.

309. McConkey, Dale D. "Planning in a Changing Environment." *Business Horizons,* Sept./Oct. 1988, pp. 64-72.

310. McCullough, Robert, and Wolverton, Lincoln. "The Competitor Intelligence Concept Applied to Power Marketing." *Public Utilities Fortnightly,* 18 Sept. 1986, pp. 11-17.

311. McEnery, Jean M., and Lifter, Mark L. "Demands for Change: Interfacing Environmental Pressures and the Personnel Process." *Public Personnel Management,* Spring 1987, pp. 61-87.

312. McFarland, Dalton E. *Management Foundations and Practices.* 5th Ed. New York: Macmillan, 1979.

313. McGaughey, Nick W. "The Logic of Competitive Assessment." *Industrial Management,* July/Aug. 1988, pp. 21-23.

314. McGrane, James M. "Going On-Line for Planning and Competitive Intelligence." *Management Review,* Oct. 1987, pp. 55-56.

315. McHale, John, and McHale, Magda C. "An Assessment of Futures Studies Worldwide." *Futures,* April 1976, pp. 135-147.

316. McLin, Stephen T. "Financial Conglomerates in the 1980's." *Bankers Monthly,* 15 Nov. 1983, pp. 12-19.

317. McNamee, Patrick. "Competitive Analysis Using Matrix Displays." *Long Range Planning* (UK), June 1984, pp. 98-114.

318. McTague, Michael. "Signposts on the Road to Excellence." *Business,* July/Aug./ Sept. 1986, pp. 3-12.

319. Meadows, Donella H., et al. *The Limits to Growth.* Washington, D.C.: Potomac Associates, 1972.

320. Mekata, E., and Watson, B.D. "Japanese View on the Australian Mining Industry (Present and Future)/The Mining Industry in Australia." *Practising Manager* (Australia), Apr. 1985, pp. 11-19.

321. Mendell, Jay S. "The Practice of Intuition." in *Handbook of Futures Research.* Edited by Jib Fowles. Westport, Conn.: Greenwood Press, 1978, pp. 149-161.

322. Mendell, Jay S. "Will the 21st Century Repeal the Laws of Nature?" *Futurist,* Oct. 1968, pp. 91–92.

323. Merriam, John E., and Makower, Joel. Trend Watching: How the Media Create Trends and How to be the First to Uncover Them. Saranac Lake, N.Y.: *American Management Association,* 1988.

324. Merritt, Tom. "Forecasting the Future Business Environment." *Long Range Planning* (UK), June 1974, pp. 54-62.

325. Mesch, Allen H. "Developing an Effective Environmental Assessment Function." *Managerial Planning,* Mar./Apr. 1984, pp. 17-22.

326. Metzger, Robert O. "Internally Managed Market Research." *Financial Manag-ers' Statement,* July 1987, pp. 48-50.

327. Metzger, Robert O. "Strategic Planning Can Sharpen Management's Focus on the Future." *Savings and Loan News,* Nov. 1981, pp. 58-65.

328. Michman, Ronald D. "Linking Ecology and Public Policy with Marketing Planning." *Akron Business & Economic Review,* Fall 1985, pp. 24-29.

329. Michman, Ronald D. "Linking Futuristics with Marketing Planning, Forecasting, and Strategy." *Journal of Business & Industrial Marketing,* Spring 1987, pp. 61-67.

330. *MicroFCS.* IBM-PC Edition. Chelmsford, Mass.: Thorn EMI Computer Software, 1986.

331. Miller, Danny, and Friesen, Peter. "Strategy Making In Context: Ten Empirical Archetypes." *Journal of Management Studies* (UK), Oct. 1977, pp. 253-280.

332. Miller, William H. "Issue Management — 'No Longer a Sideshow'." *Industry Week,* 2 Nov. 1987, pp. 125-129.

333. Milliken, Frances J. "Three Types of Perceived Uncertainty About the Environment: State, Effect, and Response Uncertainty." *Academy of Management Review,* Jan. 1987, pp. 133-143.

334. Mintzberg, H.; Raisinghani, D.; and Theoret, A. "The Structure of Unstructured Decision Processes." *Administrative Science Quarterly,* June 1976, pp. 246-275.

335. Mitroff, Ian I. *Stakeholders of the Organizational Mind.* San Francisco: Jossey-Bass, 1983.

336. Moder, Joseph J. and Phillips, Cecil R. *Project Management with CPM and PERT.* 2nd Edition. New York: Van Nostrand, 1970.

337. Molitor, Graham T.T. "How To Anticipate Public-Policy Changes." *SAM Advanced Management Journal,* Summer 1977, pp. 4-13.

338. Moore, Robert H. "Planning for Emerging Issues." *Public Relations Journal,* Nov. 1979, pp. 42-44.

339. Morrill, Richard L. "Population Redistribution, 1965-1975." *Growth and Change,* April 1978, pp. 35-43.

340. Morrison, James L.; Renfro, William L.; and Boucher, Wayne I. "Applying Methods and Techniques of Futures Research." *New Directions for Institutional Research #39.* San Francisco: Jossey-Bass, 1983.

341. Morris, Elinor. "Vision and Strategy: A Focus for the Future." *Journal of Business Strategy,* Fall 1987, pp. 51-58.

342. Mueller, G., and Smith, James B. "Six Commandments for Successful Futures Studies for Corporate Planning." *Journal of Business Strategy,* Fall 1984, pp. 88-92.

343. Murray, Thomas. "And Now — Futurist." *Dun's Review,* Sept. 1975, pp. 85-86.

344. Naisbitt, John. *Megatrends.* New York: Warner Books, 1984.

345. Nanus, Burt, and Lundberg, Craig. "In Quest of Strategic Planning." *Cornell Hotel & Restaurant Administration Quarterly,* Aug. 1988, pp. 18-23.

346. Narchal, R.M.; Kittappa, K.; and Bhattacharya, P. "An Environmental Scanning System for Business Planning." *Long Range Planning* (UK), Dec. 1987, pp. 96-105.

347. Narin, Francis; Carpenter, Mark P.; and Woolf, Patricia. "Technological Performance Assessments Based on Patents and Patent Citations." *IEEE Transactions on Engineering Management,* Nov. 1984, pp. 172-183.

348. Nelson, Charles R. *Applied Time Series Analysis.* San Francisco: Holden Day, 1973.

349. Nelson, Ken. "Environmental Scan Predicts the Financial Forecast." *Credit Union Executive,* Summer 1982, pp. 12-14.

350. Nelson, Richard Alan, and Heath, Robert L. "A Systems Model for Corporate Issues Management." *Public Relations Quarterly,* Fall 1986, pp. 20-24.

351. Neubauer, F. Friedrich, and Solomon, N.B. "A Managerial Approach to Environmental Assessment." *Long Range Planning* (UK), Apr. 1977, pp. 13-20.

352. "New Multinational Textile Pact May Bring Order to Markets." *Industry Week,* 25 Feb. 1974, p. 29.

353. Newgren, Kenneth E. "Forecasting the Socio-Political Environment: An Assessment of Current Business Practice." *Academy of Management Proceedings,* 1977, pp. 290-294.

354. Nigh, Douglas, and Cochran, Philip L. "Issues Management and the Multinational Enterprise." *Management International Review* (Germany), First Quarter 1987, pp. 4-12.

355. Odiorne, George S. "Human Resources Strategies for the 90's." *Personnel,* Nov./Dec. 1984, pp. 13-19.

356. Odiorne, George S. "The Art of Crafting Strategic Plans." *Training,* Oct. 1987, pp. 94-98.

357. O'Donnell, Joe. "A Planning Process for Hospitals and Service Organizations." *Managerial Planning,* Mar./Apr. 1980, pp. 11-15.

358. Ojala, Marydee. "Business Information on Newswires — Why Wire Watchers Watch All Wires." *Online,* July 1988, pp. 75-79.

359. Patterson, Fred S., and Walter, John D., Jr. "Planning Models and Econometrics." *Managerial Planning,* Mar./Apr. 1980, pp. 11-15.

360. Pearce, John A. II, and Robinson, Richard B., Jr. *Strategic Management.* 2nd Ed. Homewood, Illinois: Richard D. Irwin, 1985.

361. Pearce, John A. II, and Robinson, Richard B., Jr. "Environmental Forecasting: Key to Strategic Management." *Business,* July/Sept. 1983, pp. 3-12.

362. Pearce, John A. II; Chapman, Bruce L.; and David, Fred R. "Environmental Scanning for Small and Growing Firms." *Journal of Small Business Management,* July 1982, pp. 27-34.

363. Peebles, Dwight A. "Planning: Rx For Health Care in North Carolina." *Managerial Planning,* July/Aug. 1984, pp. 9-12.

364. Pekar, Peter P., Jr. "A Strategic Approach to Diversification," *Journal of Business Strategy,* Spring 1985, pp. 99-104.

365. Pekar, Peter P., Jr., "A Topology for Identifying Risk." *Managerial Planning,* Sept./Oct. 1976, pp. 13-17+.

366. Pekar, Peter P., Jr. "New Phase of Strategic Management." *Journal of Business Strategy,* Fall 1984, pp. 96-100.

367. Pekar, Peter P., Jr., and Burack, Elmer H. "Management Control of Strategic Plans Through Adaptive Techniques." *Academy of Management Journal,* Mar. 1976, pp. 79-97.

368. Peters, Tom. "Thriving on Chaos." *Success,* Nov. 1987, pp. 46-48.

369. Pfeffer, J. "Merger As A Response to Organizational Interdependence." *Administrative Science Quarterly,* Sept. 1972, pp. 382-394.

370. Pflaum, Ann M., and Delmont, Timothy J. "External Scanning — A Tool for Planners." *Journal of the American Planning Association,* Winter 1987, pp. 58-68.

371. Pindyck, Robert S., and Rubinfeld, David L. *Econometric Models & Economic Forecasting.* New York: McGraw-Hill, 1976.

372. Pliniussen, John D. "Information Systems Management — The Critical Success Factors." *Cost & Management* (Canada), July/Aug. 1984, pp. 57-59.

373. Porter, Michael E. *Competitive Strategy: Techniques for Analyzing Industries and Competitors.* New York: Free Press, 1980.

374. Porter, Michael E. "How Competitive Forces Shape Strategy." *Harvard Business Review,* Mar./Apr. 1979, pp. 137-145.

375. Preble, John F. "Corporate Use of Environmental Scanning." *Michigan Business Review,* Sept. 1978, pp. 12-17.

376. Preble, John F. "Future Forecasting with L-E-A-P." *Long Range Planning* (UK), Aug. 1982, pp. 64-69.

377. Preble, John F.; Rau, Pradeep A.; and Reichel, Arie. "The Environmental Scanning Practices of U.S. Multinationals in the Late 1980's." *Management International Review* (Germany), Fourth Quarter 1988, pp. 4-14.

378. Prescott, Edward C., and Townsend, Robert M. "General Competitive Analysis in an Economy with Private Information." *International Economic Review,* Feb. 1984, pp. 1-20.

379. Prescott, John E., and Grant, John H. "A Manager's Guide for Evaluating Competitive Analysis Techniques." *Interfaces,* May/June 1988, pp. 10-22.

380. Prescott, John E., and Smith, Daniel C. "A Project-Based Approach to Competitive Analysis." *Strategic Management Journal* (UK), Sept./Oct. 1987, pp. 411-423.

381. Pringle, Charles D. "Managing a Closed System in an Open Systems World." *Business,* Oct./Nov./Dec. 1986, pp. 3-8.

382. Quinn, John J. "How Companies Keep Abreast of Technological Change." *Long Range Planning* (UK), Apr. 1985, pp. 69-76.

383. Raiffa, Howard, and Schlaifer, Robert. *Applied Statistical Decision Theory.* Cambridge: Harvard University, 1961.

384. Ramanujam, Vasudevan, and Venkatraman, N. "Eight Half-Truths of Strategic Planning: A Fresh Look." *Planning Review,* Jan. 1985, pp. 22-27.

385. Ramanujam, Vasudevan, and Venkatraman, N. "An Inventory and Critique of Strategy Research Using the PIMS Database." *Academy of Management Review,* Jan. 1984, pp. 138-151.

386. Rauter, Thomas C. "SPI Versus Spy." *Security Management,* Feb. 1989, pp. 58-62.

387. Reed, J. David, and Hoag, John H. "Regional Coal Mining Employment in the U.S. from 1985 to 2000." *Growth and Change,* July 1984, pp. 43-50.

388. Reif, William E., and Webster, James L. "The Strategic Planning Process." *Arizona Business,* Apr. 1976, pp. 14-20.

389. Reinhardt, C; Lukaszewski, J.E.; and Katz, A.R.. "Workshop: How to Handle a Crisis." *Public Relations Journal,* Nov. 1987, pp. 43-47.

390. Reinhardt, W.A. "An Early Warning System for Strategic Planning." *Long Range Planning* (UK), Oct. 1984, pp. 25-34

391. Renfro, William L. "Environmental Scanning Detects Signals of Change." *Association Management,* Nov. 1983, pp. 140-143.

392. Renfro, William L. "Issues Management: The Evolving Corporate Role." *Futures,* Oct. 1987, pp. 545-554.

393. Renfro, William L. "Managing the Issues of the 1980s." *Futurist,* Aug. 1982, pp. 61-66.

394. Renfro, William L., and Morrison, James L. "Detecting Signals of Change: The Environmental Scanning Process." *Futurist,* Aug. 1984, pp. 49-53.

395. Rhyne, Lawrence C. "Strategic Information: The Key To Effective Planning." *Managerial Planning,* Jan./Feb. 1984, pp. 4-10.

396. Rice, Gillian, and Mahmoud, Essam. "A Managerial Procedure for Political Risk Forecasting." *Management International Review* (Germany), 4th Quarter 1986, pp. 12-21.

397. Richards, Jeff B. "Corporate Videotex System Offers a Window on the Future." *Communication Age,* Dec. 1985, pp. 14-17.

398. Richman, Tom. "Peering Into Tomorrow." *Inc.,* Oct. 1982, pp. 45-48.

399. Ritvo, R.A.; Salipante, Paul, Jr.; and Notz, William W.. "Environmental Scanning and Problem Recognition by Governing Boards." *Human Relations,* Mar. 1979, pp. 227-235.

400. Rizzi, Joseph. "Strategic Analysis: The Neglected Element in the Term Credit Decision." *Journal of Commercial Bank Lending,* July 1984, pp. 2-9.

401. Robinson, Richard B., Jr.; Salem, Moragea Y.; Logan, John E.; and Pearce, John A. II. "Planning Activities Related to Independent Retail Firm Performance." *American Journal of Small Business,* Summer 1986, pp. 19-26.

402. Rosenberg, Larry J., and Schewe, Charles D. "Strategic Planning: Fulfilling the Promise." *Business Horizons,* July/Aug. 1985, pp. 54-62.

403. Rosenfield, Donald. "A Model for Predicting Frequencies of Random Events." *Management Science,* Aug. 1987, pp. 947-954.

404. Ross, Joel E., and Silverblatt, Ronnie. "Developing the Strategic Plan." *Industrial Marketing Management,* May 1987, pp. 103-108.

405. Rothberg, Robert R. *Corporate Strategy and Product Innovation.* New York: The Free Press, 1976.

406. Rothschild, William E. *Strategic Alternatives: Selection, Development & Implementation.* New York: AMACOM, 1979.

407. Rowland, Kendrith M.; and Summers, S.L. "Human Resources Planning: A Second Look." *Personnel Administrator,* Dec. 1981, pp. 73-80.

408. Roy, S. Paul, and Cheung, Joseph K. "Early Warning Systems: A Management Tool For Your Company." *Managerial Planning,* Mar./Apr. 1985, pp. 16-21.

409. Ruefli, Timothy W., and Wilson, Chester L. "Ordinal Time Series Methodology for Industry and Competitive Analysis." *Management Science,* May 1987, pp. 640-661.

410. Rugman, Alan M. "Multinationals and Global Competitive Strategy." *International Studies of Management & Organization,* Summer 1985, pp. 8-18.

411. Sage, A.P. *Methodology for Large-Scale Systems.* New York: McGraw-Hill, 1977.

412. Sanderson, S.M., and Luffman, G.A. "Strategic Planning and Environmental Analysis" *European Journal of Marketing* (UK), 1988, pp. 14-27.

413. Sarin, Sharad. "Industrial Market Research in India." *Industrial Marketing Management,* Nov. 1987, pp. 257-264.

414. Sawers, Peter R. "How to Apply Competitive Analysis to Strategic Planning." *Marketing News,* 18 Mar 1983, pp. 11,14.

415. Sawyer, George C. *Corporate Planning as a Creative Process.* Oxford, Ohio: The Planning Forum, 1983.

416. Schendel, Dan; Patton, G.R.; and Riggs, James. "Corporate Turnaround Strate-gies — Study of Profit Decline and Recovery." *Journal of General Management* (UK), Spring 1976, pp. 3-11.

417. Scheuerman, Janet L., and Fallon, Betsy. "Competitive Analysis: Sizing Up the Shape of Your Opponents." *Healthcare Financial Management,* Sept. 1988, pp. 32-40.

418. Schmid, Hillel. "Managing the Environment: Strategies for Executives in Human Service Organizations." *Human Systems Management* (Netherlands), Vol. 6 No. 4 (1986), pp. 307-315.

419. Schoeffler, Sidney; Buzzell, R.; and Heany, D. "Impact of Strategic Planning on Profit Performance." *Harvard Business Review,* Mar./Apr. 1974, pp. 137-145.

420. Schwenk, Charles R. "The Cognitive Perspective on Strategic Decision Making." *Journal of Management Studies* (UK), Jan. 1988, pp. 41-55.

421. Segev, Eli. "A Framework for a Grounded Theory of Corporate Policy." *Interfaces,* Sept./Oct. 1988, pp. 42-54.

422. Segev, Eli. "How To Use Environmental Analysis in Strategy Making." *Management Review,* Mar. 1977, pp. 4-13.

423. Senkiw, Roman, and Johannson, Roff. "Political Environment Forecasts in an International Banking Environment." *World of Banking,* Jan./Feb. 1986, pp. 24-27.

424. Seth, Satis C. "Environmental Factors and Strategic Planning." Productivity, July-Sept. 1984, pp. 231-242.

425. Sethi, S. Prakash. "A Conceptual Framework for Environmental Analysis of Social Issues and Evaluation of Business Response Patterns." *Academy of Management Review,* Jan. 1979, pp. 63-74.

426. Sethi, S. Prakash. "Corporate Political Activism." *California Management Review,* Spring 1982, pp. 32-42.

427. Sethi, S. Prakash. "Moving Social Responsibility down a Peg." *Public Relations Journal,* Aug. 1982, pp. 25-27.

428. Sharif, M. Nawaz, and Kabir, Chowdhury. "A Generalized Model for Forecast-ing Technological Substitution." in *Technological Substitution.* Edited by Harold A. Linstone and Devendra Sahal. New York: Elsevier, 1976, pp. 9-20.

429. Silverstein, David. "The Litigation Audit: Preventive Legal Maintenance for Management." *Business Horizons,* Nov./Dec. 1988, pp. 34-42.

430. Smeltzer, Larry R.; Fann,; Gail L.; and Nikolaisen, V. Neal. "Environmental Scanning Practices in Small Business." *Journal of Small Business Management,* July 1988, pp. 55-62.

431. Smith, Daniel C., and Prescott, John E. "Couple Competitive Analysis to Sales Force Decisions." *Industrial Marketing Management,* Feb. 1987, pp. 55-61.

432. Smith, Daniel C., and Prescott, John E. "Demystifying Competitive Analysis." *Planning Review,* Sept./Oct. 1987, pp. 8-13.

433. Smith, Maurice L. "Business Planning: Philadelphia Style." *Managerial Planning,* Jan./Feb. 1983, pp. 10-15.

434. Smith, Roger W. "Managing the Spectrum of Competition in Financial Services." *Bankers Magazine,* Jan./Feb. 1985, pp. 32-37.

435. Smith, Shea III. "Approaches to Competitive Analysis." *Planning Review,* Nov. 1981, pp. 14-18.

436. Smith, Shea III, and Walsh, John E., Jr. *Strategies in Business.* New York: Wiley, 1978.

437. Smith, Sherwood H., Jr. "Responding to an Environment of Change in the Electric Utility Industry." *Public Utilities Fortnightly,* 29 May 1986, pp. 15-17.

438. Snyder, Neil H. "Environmental Volatility, Scanning 220.Jones, Scott T. "Multiple Scenario Planning Atlantic Richfield's Experience." *Journal of Business Forecasting,* Fall 1985, pp. 19-23.

439. Snyder, Neil H. "Validating Measures of Environmental Change." *Journal of Business Research,* Feb. 1987, pp. 31-43.

440. Snyder, Neil H., and Glueck, William. "Can Environmental Volatility Be Measured Objectively?" *Academy of Management Journal,* Mar. 1982, pp. 185-192.

441. Spekman, Robert E. "A Strategic Approach to Procurement Planning." *Journal of Purchasing and Materials Management,* Winter 1981, pp. 2-8.

442. Spencer, M.; Clark, C.; and Hoguet, P. *Business and Economic Forecasting.* New York: McGraw-Hill, 1961.

443. Stanat, Ruth. "Field Sales Intelligence Systems." *Information Management Review,* Winter 1989, pp. 17-23.

444. Starbuck, W.H. "Organizations and Their Environments." in *Handbook of Industrial and Organizational Psychology,* Edited by Marvin D. Dunnette. New York: Wiley Interscience, 1983.

445. Stearns, Timothy M.; Hoffman, Alan N.; and Heide, Jan B. "Performance of Commercial Television Stations as an Outcome of Interorganizational Linkages and Environmental Conditions." *Academy of Management Journal,* Mar. 1987, pp. 71-90.

446. Stein, Jane. "Managing for the Future." *Business & Health,* July/Aug. 1986, pp. 45-47.

447. Steiner, George A. *Strategic Planning: What Every Manager Must Know.* New York: Free Press, 1979.

448. Steiner, George A. *The New CEO.* New York: Free Press, 1983.

449. Steiner, George A.; Kuhn, Harry; and Kunin, Elsa. "The New Class of Chief Executive Officer." *Long Range Planning* (UK), Aug. 1981, pp. 10-20.

450. Stiles, Curt. "The Advent of Strategic Information Systems." *Managerial Planning,* Sept./Oct. 1980, pp. 23-27.

451. Stoffels, John D. "Environmental Scanning for Future Success." *Managerial Planning,* Nov./Dec. 1982, pp. 4-12.

452. Strebel, Paul J. "The Stock Market and Competitive Analysis." *Strategic Management Journal* (UK), July/Sept. 1983, pp. 279-291.

453. Stroup, Margaret A. "Environmental Scanning," in Visionary Leadership: Implementing Tomorrow's Strategy. *Conference Proceedings.* Oxford, Ohio: The Planning Forum, 1987.

454. Stroup, Margaret A. "Environmental Scanning at Monsanto." *Planning Review,* July/Aug. 1988, pp. 24-27.

455. Stubbart, Charles. "Are Environmental Scanning Units Effective?" *Long Range Planning* (UK), Jun. 1982, pp. 139-145.

456. Sutton, Howard. "Keeping Tabs on the Competition." *Marketing Communications,* Jan. 1989, pp. 42-45.

457. Svatko, James E. "Analyzing the Competition." *Small Business Reports,* Jan. 1989, pp. 21-28.

458. Synnott, W.R. "Information Weapons." *Information Strategy: The Executive's Journal,* Fall 1987, pp. 12-17.

459. *System W.* IBM Edition. Ann Arbor, Michigan: Comshare Inc., 1987.

460. Taeuber, Conrad, "America in the Seventies: Some Social Indicators." *The Annals of The American Academy of Political and Social Science,* Jan. 1978.

461. Talbert, L.R. "External Forces Shape Tomorrow's Offices." *Modern Office Procedures,* June 1980, pp. 39-40.

462. Tandon, Rajiv. "Strategic Planning In An Era of Uncertainty." *Journal of Business Strategy,* Winter 1985, pp. 94-97.

463. Taylor, Bernard. "Strategic Planning for Social and Political Change." *Long Range Planning* (UK), Feb. 1974, pp. 33-39.

464. Taylor, Stephen J. *Modelling Financial Time Series.* New York: Wiley, 1986.

465. Terreberry, Shirley. "The Evolution of Organizational Environments." *Administrative Science Quarterly,* Mar. 1968, pp. 590-613.

466. Terry, P.T. "Mechanisms for Environmental Scanning." *Long Range Planning* (UK), June 1977, pp. 2-9.

467. "Textile World Special Report: The Look of 1976." *Textile World,* Jan. 1976, pp. 38-50.

468. Thaler, Robert L. and Koehn, Hank E. "The Future Can Be Researched." *Financier,* Aug. 1980, pp. 41-44.

469. *The Future: A Guide to Information Sources.* 2nd Edition. Washington, D.C.: World Future Society, 1977.

470. "The Never-Marrieds Have Doubled Since '70," *Milwaukee Journal,* 10 September 1987, p. 3A.

471. Thomas, Howard. "Mapping Strategic Management Research." *Journal of General Management* (UK), Summer 1984, pp. 55-72.

472. Thomas, Philip S. "Environmental Scanning — The State of the Art." *Long Range Planning* (UK), Feb. 1980, pp. 20-28.

473. Thomas, Philip S. "Scanning Strategy: Formulation and Implementation." *Managerial Planning,* July/Aug. 1984, pp. 14-20.

474. Thompson, J.D. *Organizations in Action.* New York: McGraw-Hill, 1967.

475. Thompson, Thomas W. "Scanning Tomorrow's Banking Environment." *United States Banker,* Nov. 1987, pp. 79-80.

476. Tichy, Noel M. and Ulrich, David. "The Challenge of Revitalization." *New Management,* Winter 1985, pp. 53-59.

477. Toffler, Alvin. *Future Shock.* New York: Random House, 1970.

478. Toffler, Alvin. *The Adaptive Corporation.* New York: McGraw-Hill, 1985.

479. Toffler, Alvin. *The Third Wave.* New York: Wm. Morrow & Co., 1980.

480. Tosi, H.; Aldag, R.; and Storey, R. "On the Measurement of the Environment: An Assessment of the Lawrence and Lorsch Environmental Uncertainty Questionnaire." *Administrative Science Quarterly,* Mar. 1973, pp. 27-36.

481. Tucker, Kerry, and McNerney, Sharon Long. "How to Establish an Issues-Tracking System." *Public Relations Journal,* Jan. 1988, pp. 33-34.

482. Tuggle, Francis D., and Gerwin, Donald. "An Information Processing Model of Organizational Perception, Strategy and Choice." *Management Science,* June 198 pp. 575-592.

483. Tukey, John W. *Exploratory Data Analysis.* Reading, Massachusetts: Addison-Wesley, 1977.

484. Tushman, Michael L., and Anderson, Philip. "Technological Discontinuities and Organizational Environments." *Administrative Science Quarterly,* Sept. 1986, pp. 439-465.

485. Tyson, Kirk W.M. "Using Databases Versus Clipping Services in Competitor Intelligence Gathering." *Online,* Mar. 1988, pp. 85-87.

486. Uhl, Norman P. "Using Research For Strategic Planning," in *New Directions for Institutional Research #37,* Edited by Norman P. Uhl. San Francisco: Jossey-Bass, 1983.

487. Ullmann, Arieh A. "Issues Management: Integrating Value Audits in Strategy Formulation." *Journal of General Management* (UK), Summer 1986, pp. 35-54.

488. Ulrich, Dave; Geller, Andrew; and DeSouza, Glenn. "A Strategy, Structure, Human Resource Database: OASIS." *Human Resource Management,* Spring 1984, pp. 77-90.

489. Urban, Glen L., and Hauser, John R. *Design and Marketing of New Products.* Englewood Cliffs, New Jersey: Prentice-Hall, 1980.

490. Utterback, James. "Environmental Analysis and Forecasting." *Strategic Management: A New View of Business Policy & Planning.* Edited by Charles Hofer and Dan Schendel. St. Paul: West Publishing, 1979.

491. U.S. Bureau of the Census. *Statistical Abstract of the United States* (Various Years). Washington, D.C.: Government Printing Office.

492. U.S. Congress, House of Representatives. *Congressional Foresight: History, Recent Experience and Implementation Strategies.* Report for the Committee on Energy and Commerce. Washington, D.C.: Government Printing Office, Dec. 1982.

493. U.S. Congress, House of Representatives. *Foresight in the Private Sector: How Can Government Use It?* Report for the Committee on Energy and Commerce. Washington, D.C.: Government Printing Office. n.d.

494. U.S. Congress, House of Representatives. *Strategic Issues: Historical Experience, Institutional Structure and Conceptual Framework.* Report for the Committee on Energy and Commerce. Washington, D.C.: Government Printing Office, July 1982.

495. U.S. Department of Commerce. *Social Indicators,* 1976. Washington, D.C.: Government Printing Office, 1977.

496. Valigra, Lori, "Software for Smart Executives," *Digital Review,* 18 May 1987, pp. 67-69.

497. Van Wyk, Rias J. "Panoramic Scanning and The Technological Environment." *Technovation* (Netherlands), May 1984, pp. 101-120.

498. Van Doren, Doris, and Spielman, Alan. "Hospital Marketing: Strategy Reassessment in a Declining Market." *Journal of Health Care Marketing,* Mar. 1989, pp. 15-24.

499. Vella, Carolyn, and McGonagle, John J., Jr. "Shadowing Markets: A New Competitive Intelligence Technique." *Planning Review,* Sept./Oct. 1987, pp. 36-38.

500. Vinso, Joseph. "Financial Planning for the Multinational Corporation with Multiple Goals." *Journal of International Business Studies,* Winter 1982, pp. 43-58.

501. Volkema, Roger J. "Problem Formulation in Planning and Design." *Management Science,* June 1983, pp. 639-652.

502. Voos, Paula B. "Environmental Factors in the Labor-Management Relationship." *Monthly Labor Review,* Apr. 1986, pp. 47-48.

503. Waddell, William C. *The Outline of Strategy.* Oxford, Ohio: The Planning Forum, 1986.

504. Waddell, William C. "Strategic Decision Making Tools." *Business Forum,* Summer 1982, p. 32.

505. Wagner, G.R. "Strategic Thinking Supported by Risk Analysis." *Long Range Planning* (UK), June 1980, pp. 61-68.

506. Waller, R.A. "Assessing the Impact of Technology on the Environment." *Long Range Planning* (UK), Aug. 1977, pp. 8-12.

507. *Ward's Automotive Yearbook* (Various Years). Detroit: Ward's Communications Inc., Annual.

508. Wartick, Steven L. "How Issues Management Contributes to Corporate Performance." *Business Forum,* Spring 1988, pp. 16-22.

509. Wartick, Steven L. "The Major Business and Society Journals." *Business Forum,* Summer 1984, pp. 24-27.

510. Wartick, Steven L., and Cochran, Philip L. "The Evolution of the Corporate Social Performance Model." *Academy of Management Review,* Oct. 1985, pp. 758-769.

511. Weigelt, Keith, and MacMillan, Ian. "An Interactive Strategic Analysis Framework." *Strategic Management Journal* (UK), Summer 1988, pp. 27-40.

512. Weiner, Edith. "Future Scanning for Trade Groups and Companies." *Harvard Business Review,* Sept./Oct. 1976, p. 14.

513. Weiner, Edith, and Brown, Arnold. "Stakeholder Analysis for Effective Issues Management." *Planning Review,* May 1986, pp. 27-31.

514. Weitzel, John R. "Strategic Information Management: Targeting Information for Organizational Performance." *Information Management Review,* Summer 1987, pp. 9-19.

515. Wessel, David, and Bulkeley, William M. "Lotus Maps a Strategy to Sustain Growth." *The Wall Street Journal,* 8 July 1976, p. 6.

516. "What's Happening with DSS?" *EDP Analyzer,* July 1984, pp. 3-16.

517. Wheelwright, Steven C. "Management by Model During Inflation." *Business Horizons,* June 1975, pp. 33-42.

518. Wheelwright, Steven C. and Makridakis, Spyros. *Forecasting Methods for Management.* 2nd Edition. New York: Wiley, 1977.

519. "Where the Big Econometric Models Go Wrong." *Business Week,* 30 March 1981, pp. 70-73.

520. Willard, Timothy, and Fields, Daniel M. "Helping Congress Look Ahead." *Futurist,* May-June 1989, pp. 23-27.

521. Williams, Martha. "The State of Databases Today: 1990." *Computer-Readable Databases,* 6th Ed.. Edited by Kathleen Young Marcaccio. Detroit: Gale Research, Inc., 1990.

522. Willis, Gordon. "Forecasting Technological Innovation." *Corporate Strategy and Planning,* Edited by Bernard Taylor and John Sparks. New York: Wiley, 1977.

523. Wilson, Ian. "Forecasting Social and Political Trends." *Corporate Strategy and Planning,* Edited by Bernard Taylor and John Sparks. New York: Wiley, 1977.

524. Wiseman, Charles. "Attack & Counterattack: The New Game in Information Technology." *Planning Review,* Sept./Oct. 1988, pp. 6-12.

525. Wissema, Johan G. "Morphological Analysis." *Futures,* Apr. 1976, pp. 146-154.

526. *World Energy Outlook Through 2000.* Wilmington, Delaware: Conoco Inc., 1985.

527. Wright, Norman B. "Today's Corporate Apocalypse — A Strategic Response." *Business Quarterly* (Canada), Autumn 1988, pp. 21-26.

528. Wright, Peter. "Strategic Management Within A World Parameter." *Managerial Planning,* Jan./Feb. 1985, pp. 33-46.

529. Wriston, Walter B. *Risk & Other Four-Letter Words.* New York: Harper & Row, 1986.

530. Yoder, Stephen Kreider. "U.S. Software Firms Set Sights on Japan." *The Wall Street Journal,* 30 May 1986, p. 24.

531. Zeithaml, Carl P. "Critical Issues in Management Development Programs for the 1980's." *Texas Business Executive,* Summer 1980, pp. 34-37.

532. Zeitz, Gerald, "Interorganizational Dialectics." *Administrative Science Quarterly,* Vol. 25, 1980, pp. 72-88.

533. Zentner, Rene. "Scenarios: Past, Present and Future." *Long Range Planning* (UK), Feb. 1982, pp. 12-20.

534. Zinkhan, George, and Gelb, Betsy. "Competitive Intelligence Practices of Industrial Marketers." *Industrial Marketing Management,* Nov. 1985, pp. 269-275.

535. Zuckerman, Howard S. "Redefining the Role of the CEO: Challenges and Conflicts." *Hospital & Health Services Administration,* Spring 1989, pp. 25-38.

536. Zweig, Phillip. "Straws in the Wind." *Financial World,* Nov. 3, 1987, pp. 126- 128.

537. Zwicky, Fritz. *Morphology of Propulsive Power.* Pasadena, California: Society for Morphological Research, 1962.

538. Zwicky, Fritz, and Wilson, A.G. *New Methods of Thought and Procedure.* New York: Springer-Verlag, 1967.

INDEX